WITHDRAWN

Putting Faith in Partnerships

CONTEMPORARY POLITICAL AND SOCIAL ISSUES
Alan Wolfe, Series Editor

Contemporary Political and Social Issues provides a forum in which social scientists and seasoned observers of the political scene use their expertise to comment on issues of contemporary importance in American politics, including immigration, affirmative action, religious conflict, gay rights, welfare reform, and globalization.

Putting Faith in Partnerships: Welfare-to-Work in Four Cities,
  by Stephen V. Monsma

Putting Faith in Partnerships
Welfare-to-Work in Four Cities

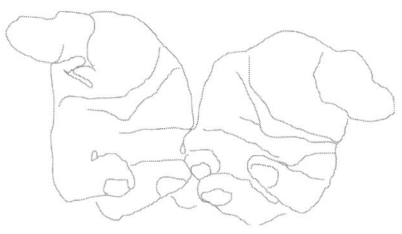

Stephen V. Monsma

With a Foreword by John J. DiIulio Jr.

The University of Michigan Press
Ann Arbor

Copyright © by the University of Michigan 2004
All rights reserved
Published in the United States of America by
The University of Michigan Press
Manufactured in the United States of America
♾ Printed on acid-free paper

2007　2006　2005　2004　　4　3　2　1

No part of this publication may be reproduced, stored in a retrieval system, or transmitted in any form or by any means, electronic, mechanical, or otherwise, without the written permission of the publisher.

A CIP catalog record for this book is available from the British Library.

Library of Congress Cataloging-in-Publication Data

Monsma, Stephen V., 1936–
Putting faith in partnerships : welfare-to-work in four cities / Stephen V. Monsma ; with a foreword by John J. DiIulio, Jr.
　　p.　cm. — (Contemporary political and social issues)
Includes bibliographical references and index.
ISBN 0-472-11393-3 (cloth : alk. paper)
1. Welfare recipients—Employment—United States.　2. Public-private sector cooperation—United States.　3. Church charities—United States.
I. Title.　II. Series.

HV95.M65　2004
362.5'84'0973—dc22　　　　　　　　　　　　　　　　2003027591

To Hester M. Monsma, sister and friend

Foreword

This extraordinary book by an extraordinary scholar may succeed in taming one of the most contentious public policy debates of our time; namely, the battle over whether government ought to partner with religious organizations that supply social services, and, if so, how.

Stephen V. Monsma's *Putting Faith in Partnerships* is a remarkable, in-depth, four-city study of public-private welfare-to-work partnerships. Monsma, a Pepperdine University political scientist, not only challenges much conventional wisdom on church-state issues, but also offers specific, policy-relevant advice about how government might in the future foster faith-based approaches to supplying social services and ameliorating social ills without violating well-established constitutional norms or courting myriad practical problems. The literature on the subject has been exploding, but if policymakers, activists, researchers, journalists, and average citizens were to carefully read just one academic book about faith-based issues, I would pray it be this one.

As Monsma writes, "there clearly is a centuries-old tradition in the United States of government helping to provide certain public services by funding the social services rendered by nonprofit organizations, including faith-based nonprofit organizations." Years before anyone had heard the term *faith-based,* Monsma was producing path-breaking historical, empirical, and cross-national research on how diverse, "religiously based" organizations (as he would prefer to call them) serve secular and civic purposes. For example, his 1996 classic, *When Sacred and Secular Mix,* documents that faith-based family and child care agencies, international aid and relief organizations, and colleges and universities are often deeply religious in their programming, even when they function as legally separate nonprofits apart from any parent congregations or denominations.

Now, in *Putting Faith in Partnerships,* Monsma once again greatly advances our knowledge about the actual cast and characters, the real strengths and limits, of public-private social service delivery partnerships involving community-serving faith-based organizations. Neither orthodox secularists who demand strict church-state separation nor orthodox sectarians who insist that religious groups be permitted to proselytize with public funds; neither right-wing ideologues who are allergic to government nor left-wing ideologues who are addicted to it; neither theorists who romanticize civil society nor theorists who deny that families, churches, and other civil institutions matter greatly to social welfare will find comfort in these data-rich pages and the pluralistic perspective that emerges from Monsma's scrupulously fair-minded approach to the subject.

In the mid-1990s, when I began promoting "faith factor" research, arguing that most social capital in America (volunteers, charitable contributions, civic good works) is religious or "spiritual capital," and advancing policy-relevant ideas about how "faith-based organizations" matter to social welfare, some ostensible experts insisted that social services provided by local congregations and other religious nonprofits, however laudable, were few, short term, and largely confined to food, clothing, and temporary shelter. But, thanks to major studies by Monsma, Ram A. Cnaan of the University of Pennsylvania, Stephanie Boddie of the University of Washington at St. Louis, Nisha Botchwey of the University of Virginia, and other good social scientists, it is now obvious to almost everyone that faith-based organizations figure prominently in delivering literally hundreds of different types of social services. Monsma aptly cites Cnaan as concluding that the "role of the religious community in the provision of social services is enormous and secondary only to that of government."

Putting Faith in Partnerships shows that welfare-to-work programs are no exception. As Monsma reports, Chicago, Dallas, Philadelphia, and Los Angeles together harbor some 1,600 welfare-to-work programs. He studied about 500 of these programs, finding them to be variously administered by government agencies; for-profit organizations; large, secular nonprofit organizations that depend on paid, professional staff; small, community-anchored secular nonprofit organizations that rely heavily on volunteers; faith-based organizations that keep their religious elements largely separate from the social services they provide (faith-segmented); and faith-based organizations that tend to integrate religious elements into the social services they supply (faith-integrated). Combined, the two types of faith-based organizations figure prominently in welfare-to-work programs in each city, from 14.1 percent of all such programs in Los Angeles to 40.6 percent of all such programs in Philadelphia.

But how, if at all, can and should government support faith-based welfare-to-work and other social service programs? The first major federal statutes prohibiting government from discriminating against religious organizations seeking public funds available to groups that deliver social services were passed with bipartisan support and signed into law by President Bill Clinton in 1996. Under these "charitable choice" provisions, faith-based organizations can now compete for selected federal public funds on the same basis as all other nonprofits, provided that they honor relevant federal civil rights laws, do not discriminate against any client on the basis of religion, and do not use the funds to proselytize, lead worship services, or support sectarian activities. Neither federal nor state government can require an otherwise qualified faith-based organization to remove religious art, icons, scripture, or other symbols as a condition for applying for or receiving public funds or technical assistance.

During the 2000 presidential campaign, I met with both major candidates and advised both campaigns on various domestic issues. When George W. Bush became president, he asked me to join his senior staff as the first director of the new White House Office of Faith-Based and Community Initiatives. As I told the president and stated publicly at the time, for health and professional reasons, I would serve for only six months, or just long enough to complete and publish the charitable choice implementation study expressly mandated by the executive orders that established the new office. I served about eight months, announcing my resignation on August 20, 2001, the morning after we released *Unlevel Playing Field,* a report detailing grant making patterns in five federal departments (Justice, Education, Labor, Housing and Urban Development, and Health and Human Services).

As that review found, faith-based organizations that provide social services receive very little public money, even when they strictly follow all charitable choice rules. For instance, from south-central Los Angeles to north-central Philadelphia, many local religious groups run exemplary after-school education and literacy programs. But, in 2000, these organizations received less than 2 percent of Department of Education discretionary grants across 11 different funding programs. Likewise, thousands of community-serving ministries sponsor anti-delinquency programs, help adult parolees get a fresh start, and more. But, in 2001, the Justice Department awarded a mere .03 percent of its discretionary grants to faith-based organizations.

Among its many other special strengths, *Putting Faith in Partnerships* contains reliable data and analyses that should help to discipline debates concerning what is behind this gap in faith-based government funding and what might work best to help close it. For example, according to *Protecting the Civil Rights and Religious Liberty of Faith-Based Organizations,* a report released by my former White House office in June 2003, faith-based organizations are "reluctant to administer federally funded programs" because they "could be subject to different" intergovernmental "rules and regulations" governing whether they can "hire according to [their] religious beliefs." Others have asserted that most faith-based groups either fear that government partnerships beget program secularization or have no desire to expand services with or without public funds, or both.

Monsma's findings pour cold empirical water on such claims. For starters, faith-based welfare-to-work programs, like most faith-based programs, rely greatly on volunteers, not paid, full-time staff. In Monsma's huge sample of faith-based welfare-to-work programs, 60 percent are faith-segmented, not faith-integrated. Of the former, just 2.8 percent hire only co-religionists, and only another 6.9 percent give preferences in hiring to co-religionists. Among those receiving government contracts, nearly 40 percent complain about paperwork demands, but none reports that partnering with government makes them "less efficient" or reduces volunteer manpower in favor of paid, full-time personnel.

Rather, two-thirds say that getting government dollars has permitted them to expand their services to more people in need, and only 8 percent feel that the partnership with government has caused them to "cut down" on their religious emphases and practices. Even 4 in 10 of the faith-integrated programs have no religiously based hiring restrictions, and none reports being dissatisfied with how government has managed its end of the service delivery contracts.

Instead, over 90 percent of all those who lead faith-based welfare-to-work programs want to expand their programs "greatly" or "somewhat." Over half receive no public funds, but 6 in 10 want to apply. While public-private partnerships involving faith-based programs have been increasing, faith-based organizations are still rejected for funding at about three times the rate of secular nonprofits, even though there is no "firm evidence" that they perform any less well.

Monsma observes that faith-based welfare-to-work programs are more of a piece with their small, secular community-based counterparts than the latter are vis-à-vis the big three—the government agencies, the large secular nonprofits, and the increasingly ubiquitous for-profit government grantees—that still dominate this service delivery sector. But he is also careful to note that many of the faith-based organizations' "staff and clients" are "overwhelmingly African American," such that, barring policy efforts "to emphasize faith-based programs," most "of the overwhelmingly African American programs will be missed."

In my view, therein lies one real reason for the gap in faith-based government funding: even perfectly well qualified local minority-led faith-based groups, both congregations and legally independent nonprofits, are not given equal treatment in the government contracting process and receive little, if any, cognate technical assistance or support from government.

Indeed, in 2001, five years after charitable choice became federal law, Philadelphia, where, as Monsma calculates, 4 in 10 welfare-to-work programs are faith-based, only one faith-based welfare-to-work program, an African American–led, faith-segmented 501(c)(3) program founded by a local black church, has received one penny of federal funding for a year or more. Monsma estimates that small, faith-segmented welfare-to-work programs serve, on average, 200 clients a year on $90,000 annual budgets that include very little, if any, public funding, while large, professional secular nonprofits serve, on average, 400 clients a year on amply tax-supported budgets nearing $900,000 a year—ten times the funding for only two times the clients.

Thus, if, as Monsma observes, the faith-based programs' "potential capacity . . . is greater than their current capacity," it is, in my view, largely because their present public support is so paltry, both in absolute terms and relative to what secular nonprofit and for-profit organizations receive from government coffers and in the form of technical assistance from government agencies. And, because inner-city community-serving ministries are disproportionately minority-led and serve predominantly low-income people of color, the failure to implement and expand charitable choice laws has a disproportionately adverse impact on urban African American and Latino children, youth, families, and communities. The First Amendment (church-state) issues at stake here are real and important, but so, alas, are the Fourteenth Amendment ("equal protection of the laws") issues.

Monsma highlights the growing "role of conservative Protestants" in social service delivery, noting that over 4 in 10 of the welfare-to-work programs led by orthodox Protestant believers are nonetheless faith-segmented, not faith-integrated. Thus, it is unjustifiably prejudicial to assume, as so many in the mainstream media do, that just because a faith-based program is founded, organized, or staffed mainly or even entirely by evangelical Christians, it is bound to involve proselytizing or religious discrimination against prospective clients.

Monsma pierces another prevalent assumption by showing that faith-based welfare-to-work programs that "integrate religious elements into their programming" are less, not more, likely to be run by a congregation than by a legally independent nonprofit group. The "programs sponsored by faith-based nonprofit entities" are generally as religious as "those sponsored directly by religious congregations themselves." He also finds that "less than 30 percent of the welfare-to-work programs" are "run directly by congregations."

In light of these facts, and to "make public-private partnerships less controversial," Monsma recommends that henceforth "government partnerships" with faith-based organizations exclude "the social service programs of churches or other religious congregations." Otherwise, he reasons, we come "too close to unnecessarily mixing church and state"; besides, "the symbolism of the government writing checks directly to churches is all wrong."

To fully appreciate the evidence and reasoning behind this recommendation, one must treat oneself to the complete intellectual feast in the pages of this book. As for me, I would be sympathetic to Monsma's provocative policy proposal—essentially, as I would characterize it, excluding churches, synagogues, mosques, and other congregations, but including integrally religious and other faith-based nonprofits, under charitable choice protections and related statutory rules and administrative protocols—under one hitherto unmet condition; namely, that faith-based organizations be assured governmental technical assistance and capacity-building help with respect to everything from notifications of funding availability to grant-writing procedures, from volunteer mobilization to financial management.

Recent history makes me skeptical that, without congregations in the eligibility pool, there can be any reasonable political hope of this happening anytime soon, or anytime at all. Recall that on January 29, 2001, the day President Bush launched his new Office of Faith-Based and Community Initiatives, I was rightly the second, not the first, person he introduced. The first was former Indianapolis mayor Stephen Goldsmith, whom the president praised as a government reform visionary and nominated to head the Corporation for National Service (CNS). The president explicitly directed the new faith-based initiatives office and affiliated centers in cabinet departments, working with CNS's to-be-revitalized AmeriCorps and other programs, to focus, laser-like, on implementing existing charitable choice laws while identifying and recommending ways to overcome nongovernmental barriers to increasing faith-based organizations' capacity to serve the nation's needy and neglected citizens.

But, before it officially opened on February 20, 2001, the new office was engulfed by conflicting demands, most notably demands by some religious conservatives who insisted that the administration abandon charitable choice in favor of new "beliefs and tenets" and related provisions that would permit religious groups to proselytize with public funds, discriminate freely on religious grounds in hiring, and accept generous service-delivery vouchers. Meanwhile, Goldsmith did eventually become CNS chairman, but House Republicans nonetheless zeroed out the agency's budget and, on-the-record Republican presidential preferences to the contrary notwithstanding, continued to bash the agency and its "paid volunteers."

Despite Goldsmith's gallant public and behind-the-scenes efforts, CNS never even began to play the technical-assistance, capacity-building, or other roles promised by the White House in 2001, and reiterated by it after 9/11 and during 2002 as the president launched the new USA Freedom Corps office. By mid-2003, as a result of unrelated controversies, the agency that was supposed to help drive the administration's faith-based and community efforts was fighting for its own fiscal and political life.

Monsma extrapolates that at least 35,000 congregations function directly as faith-based social service providers. Arguably, in addition to respecting their civil rights and valuing how their civic results might expand with due government funding and technical assistance, there is a political reason for keeping these community-serving congregations in the charitable choice pools. Today, as in 2001, such pressure as exists for implementing and expanding charitable choice, for real, in ways that benefit America's most truly disadvantaged citizens, often comes from congregations and their leadership.

To cite just one example, in 2001, the Church of God in Christ (COGIC), a Pentecostal Christian denomination that is the country's second largest, and fastest growing, African American church community, was the first publicly to proclaim support for implementing the charitable choice laws touted by President Clinton and targeted for expansion by President Bush. COGIC has spawned many legally independent faith-based programs, most notably the Ella J. Baker House and National Ten-Point Leadership Foundation ministries led by Boston's Reverend Eugene F. Rivers III. But COGIC also has numerous congregation-based programs that are worthwhile, and its leaders' hopes for receiving equal treatment in the government grant-making process, as well as technical assistance from CNS and other agencies, for *both* types of programs led them to support the bipartisan plans first articulated by the president.

So, even while I am not sure that I can yet adopt Monsma's chief policy prescription as my own, I am sure that *Putting Faith in Partnerships* is the finest empirical study of its kind yet published and that, whatever one's specific policy preferences or general point of view, this book will enlighten, enliven, and elevate understanding.

John J. DiIulio Jr.
Philadelphia, Pennsylvania
July 2, 2003

Contents

List of Tables	xvii
Acknowledgments	xix
I. Public-Private Partnerships: Trends and Issues	1
II. The Providers of Welfare-to-Work Services	40
III. The Services Provided	84
IV. The Government-Provider Relationship	125
V. Public-Private Partnerships: Public Policy Issues	172
Appendix A. The Questionnaire Survey	215
Appendix B. Two Key Distinctions	222
Appendix C. The Questionnaire	227
Notes	237
Bibliography	259
Index	265

List of Tables

1.	Types of Welfare-to-Work Programs	59
2.	Nonprofit/Secular versus Community-Based Programs	60
3.	Educational Levels, Nonprofit/Secular versus Community-Based Programs	61
4.	Religiously Based Practices, Faith-Based/Segmented versus Faith-Based/Integrated Programs	62
5.	Employees, by Program Type	63
6.	Employee Educational Levels, by Program Type	64
7.	Percentage of Programs from a Minority Community	65
8.	Faith-Based Programs, by Faith Tradition	66
9.	Sponsoring Entities of Faith-Based Programs	68
10.	Year Programs Began, by Program Type	70
11.	Types of Welfare-to-Work Programs, by City	70
12.	Number of Programs versus Number of Full-Time Employees, by Program Type	72
13.	Median Number of Part-Time Employees and Volunteers, by Program Type	73
14.	Median Budget and Number of Clients Served, by Program Type	75
15.	Growth in Clients Served, 1996–2001, by Program Type	76
16.	Expansion Plans, by Program Type	76
17.	Expansion Desires, by Program Type	77
18.	Types of Homeless Services and Sponsoring Organizations	86

19. Faith-Based and Secular Nonprofits' Meeting of Major Needs of the Homeless, On-Site versus Off-Site — 89
20. Services Provided, by Program Type — 98
21. Services Provided Divided by Intensity of Interactions, by Program Type — 100
22. Services Provided Divided by Intensity of Interactions, by Sponsoring Entity of Faith-Based Programs — 102
23. Mean Number of Job-Oriented and Life-Oriented Services Provided, by Program Type — 103
24. Mean Percentage of Life-Oriented Services Offered out of All Services Offered, by Program Type — 104
25. Percentage of Funding from Government, Faith-Based and Secular Homeless Programs — 128
26. Percentage of Funding from Government, Faith-Based and Secular Child and Family Agencies — 128
27. Percentage of Funding from Government, Faith-Based Programs Funded under Charitable Choice — 129
28. Assessments of Relationship with Government by Faith-based Organizations with Government Contracts under Charitable Choice — 130
29. Types of Programs Receiving No Government Funds — 138
30. Percentage of Programs Receiving No Government Funds, by City and Program Type — 138
31. Mean Percentage of Budgets from Government Funds, by Program Type — 140
32. Percentage of Budgets from Government Funds — 143
33. Reasons for No Government Funds, by Program Type — 144
34. Types of Contact with Government, by Program Type — 148
35. Number of Types of Contact with Government, by Program Type — 149
36. Satisfaction with Government Contacts, by Program Type — 151
37. Results of Receiving Government Funds — 154
38. Positive versus Negative Results of Government Funds, by Program Type — 155
39. Results of Government Funding, by Program Type — 156
40. Response Rates, by City — 217

Acknowledgments

One acquires many debts while engaging in a major research project such as the one on which I report here. In this case, four debts in particular stand out. First, I am indebted to the hundreds of busy administrators of welfare-to-work programs who took time to fill out a questionnaire they no doubt felt was overly long and sometimes ineptly worded. Many of them and their staffs also welcomed my associate researcher or me into their agencies, spent hours discussing their programs and their perspectives on them, and allowed us to observe much of what was going on. Without their wonderful and gracious cooperation, this research could never have been accomplished.

Second, I wish to acknowledge the dedication and abilities of my associate researcher, Carolyn M. Mounts. She worked full-time for fourteen months on this project. Her tireless efforts in identifying welfare-to-work programs in four different cities, her work with the student assistants, and her traveling about the country to interview persons at various welfare-to-work programs were indispensable to the success of this project. She did all this with competence, efficiency, constant goodwill, and unfailing optimism during the inevitable ups and downs of the research.

Third, the Smith Richardson Foundation's funding for this research project was indispensable. Without the foundation's support, neither the study nor this book could have been accomplished. I especially want to thank Dr. Phoebe Cottingham, former senior program officer at the foundation. She saw me through several drafts of my initial research proposal, and her interest in and commitment to this project were a major source of encouragement for me. This book and the study on which it is based are better for her efforts.

Fourth, I desire to acknowledge the role played by my home institution, Pepperdine University, in the achievement of this project. Its president, Andrew Benton; the dean of the liberal arts college, David Baird; Geraldine Kennedy, formerly of the Office of Corporate and Foundation Relations; and many of my colleagues were important in my being able to conduct this research and write this book. They gave me emotional support and encouragement, assisted in rearranging teaching schedules, and helped in the formulation of my thoughts and ideas. One of my colleagues, Khanh-Van T. Bui, deserves special mention because of her help with many of the statistical analyses in this book.

There are many others whom I also need to thank. I think of Ann Annis of the Social Research Center at Calvin College, which handled the mailing of the questionnaires and the tabulating of the responses. Several Pepperdine students—Louis Dezseran, Emilie Wolff, Renee Brooks, and Larry Ballard—handled much of the tedious work of typing lists, checking information, and making calls to verify information. Jill Witmer Sinha, a University of Pennsylvania graduate student, helped to identify the Philadelphia welfare-to-work programs. To some degree, this has been a family project. My son, Martin Monsma, and my son-in-law, Patrick Flanagan, read the entire manuscript and suggested many useful improvements in the wording and flow of ideas. I also want to thank my wife, Mary C. Monsma, who—as she has done over the years on many different projects—supported me in my work. Finally, I desire to acknowledge my sister, Hester M. Monsma, who through the years has been a "best friend" and has encouraged me in this and many other projects that I—sometimes wisely and sometimes foolishly—have taken on. I dedicate this book to her.

1 Public-Private Partnerships
Trends and Issues

Polls regularly show that Americans believe government should play an active, positive role in helping the sick, the old, the very young, and others who are experiencing severe needs; the same polls show Americans are deeply distrustful of government. For example, a recent national poll showed that a surprising 81 percent favored "guaranteeing every American adequate medical care, whether or not they can pay for it," and only 31 percent favored "reducing welfare payments to persons living in poverty." Meanwhile, the same poll found that only 4 percent of the respondents reported they had "a lot of confidence in government," while 60 percent reported they had only "a little confidence" or "no confidence."[1] Lester M. Salamon has referred to "the conflict that has long existed in American political thinking between the desire for public services and hostility to the governmental apparatus that provides them."[2] Similarly, Peter Berger and Richard John Neuhaus began their watershed 1977 book, *To Empower People,* with this observation: "Two seemingly contradictory tendencies are evident in current thinking about public policy in America. First, there is a continuing desire for the services provided by the modern welfare state. . . . The second tendency is one of strong animus against government, bureaucracy, and bigness as such."[3]

Berger and Neuhaus continued: "The contradiction between wanting more government services and less government may be only apparent. More precisely, we suggest that the modern welfare state is here to stay, indeed that it ought to expand the benefits it provides—

but that alternative mechanisms are possible to provide welfare-state services."[4] The alternative mechanisms they had in mind were nongovernmental organizations. They termed them *intermediate structures*—those organizations and institutions that lie between individuals in their private lives and large public institutions. They focused on neighborhoods, families, religious congregations, and voluntary associations as key examples of intermediate structures.

In the 27 years since the Berger and Neuhaus book came out, there has been a rising chorus of voices suggesting that many public services can best be delivered not by government agencies themselves, and not only by the mediating structures Berger and Neuhaus highlighted, but by for-profit companies and a wide range of nonprofit agencies, including religious congregations and other faith-based organizations.[5] As David Osborne and Ted Gaebler wrote in their best-selling book, *Reinventing Government,* "It makes sense to put the delivery of many public services in private hands (whether for-profit or nonprofit), if by doing so a government can get more effectiveness, efficiency, equity, or accountability."[6] Some students of public policy and public administration have emphasized that for-profit companies and the competition they engender are a particularly effective means of delivering public services.[7]

Most recently, many voices are arguing for the ability of religiously rooted organizations to deal effectively with such seemingly intractable social ills as drug abuse, homelessness, recidivism among ex-offenders, and welfare dependency. Ram Cnaan is one such voice. He has called for "a coherent public policy that brings together what practice, wisdom, and emerging research has taught us: that the religious-based social service system can be nothing less than an important partner in a complex system of services at the local level."[8] The late 1990s saw a flood of news stories highlighting the potential of faith-based organizations to perform miracles of healing in the broken worlds of poverty, crime, and drug abuse.[9] *Washington Post* columnist E. J. Dionne was not exaggerating when he wrote: "All of God's children are talking about faith-based organizations these days and what these groups are doing to lift up the poor, reduce teen pregnancy, fight crime and rebuild urban neighborhoods."[10]

The 2000 presidential campaign added impetus to the use of faith-based organizations in partnership with government to solve persistent social ills. George W. Bush made this a centerpiece of his campaign for the presidency. He declared, "In every instance where my administration sees a responsibility to help people, we will look first to faith-based organizations, charities and community groups that have shown their ability to save and change lives."[11] Not to be outdone, the Democratic candidate, Al Gore, declared: "I have seen the difference faith-based organizations make. The men and women who work in faith- and values-based organizations are driven by their spiritual commitment. . . . And good programs and practices seem to follow, borne out of that compassionate care."[12]

On assuming the presidency, one of the first actions taken by George W. Bush was the creation of the White House Office of Faith-Based and Community Initiatives. He declared, "We must heed the growing consensus across America that successful government social programs work in fruitful partnership with community-serving and faith-based organizations—whether run by Methodists, Muslims, Mormons, or good people of no faith at all."[13]

Present in the title of the White House office that the Bush administration created and in George W. Bush's comments just quoted is a dual emphasis on faith-based and community-based organizations. In chapter 2, I will explore in greater detail the distinction between organizations of these types, as well as other distinctions. Here, it is important only to clear away some of the terminological underbrush, by noting that nonprofit social service organizations are often divided into three categories: faith-based organizations (nonprofits with a religious base or orientation); community-based organizations (nonprofits that are small, nonprofessionalized, and neighborhood oriented); and large, professionalized, areawide nonprofit organizations. The distinctions between these categories will be made sharper as this study proceeds.

At one time, President Bush's reference to a "growing consensus across America" on the wisdom of using private, nongovernmental entities to deliver essential social services was not simply wishful thinking or political hyperbole. Osborne and Gaebler's *Reinventing Government,* cited earlier, was endorsed by President Bill Clinton; its title was used by a task force headed by Vice President Al Gore; and Republicans, such as Mayor Stephen Goldsmith of Indianapolis, also spoke highly of it.[14] What has come to be termed *charitable choice* was included in the Personal Responsibility and Work Opportunity Act (1996), the Welfare-to-Work Act (1997), the Community Services Block Grant program (1998), and the Substance Abuse and Mental Health Services Administration's drug treatment program (2000). Charitable choice consists of legal provisions designed to allow faith-based organizations to compete for government contracts on an equal basis with secular nonprofits, to protect the religious autonomy of faith-based organizations that contract with government, and to protect the religious freedom rights of recipients of government-funded services from faith-based groups. These legal provisions were passed four separate times, with the approval of the Clinton administration and by overwhelming bipartisan majorities in Congress.

Since 2001, however, this consensus has evaporated. Conflict has replaced consensus. The criticisms and attacks started once President Bush created the White House Office of Faith-Based and Community Initiatives and took other steps to strengthen governmental partnerships with faith-based and other community nonprofit groups.[15] Some argued that charitable choice violates the First Amendment and inadequately protects the religious rights of persons receiving services from religious providers.[16] Others attacked as blatant discrimination the charitable choice provision that faith-based groups could favor persons of like-minded faith in their hiring decisions. Yet others claimed that faith-based groups had neither the desire nor the capacity to take on major new tasks. Some voices added that many faith-based groups were already receiving government funds and that the Bush initiative was a solution in search of a problem. Many claimed there was no evidence that faith-based groups are more effective in delivering social services than are government agencies or secular groups. Some saw the initiative as no more than a thinly disguised Republican attempt to curry favor with inner-city African American churches. Various church leaders feared the loss of their independence if they accepted government funds for their social service programs. John DiIulio—who left the ivy-covered halls of the University of Pennsylvania to take the position as the Bush administration's first head of the Office of Faith-Based and Community Initiatives—must have felt as though he had walked into the middle of a back-alley brawl between rival street gangs. He escaped back to the more peaceful precincts of the University of Pennsylvania after only eight months.

Meanwhile, the use of for-profit firms to provide social services—while attracting less national attention—has also proven controversial. Government workers and their unions, who stand to lose jobs, have opposed such efforts.[17] Some advocates for the poor have feared that the drive for profits will overwhelm the desire to serve those in need. Others argue that the greater flexibility and effectiveness of for-profit companies remain to be proven.[18]

There is, however, one thing on which the proponents and opponents of greater use of nongovernmental entities to provide social services agree: that we simply do not know very much about for-profit, faith-based, and other nonprofit providers of social services and their relationships with government. An article in the *Chronicle of Higher Education* stated: "The field [of social science] is only beginning to seek answers to the questions now crowding its agenda: What are religious groups doing to reduce poverty, substance abuse, teenage pregnancy, juvenile delinquency, and other social ills? Are they more effective than their secular counterparts? Can they take on more responsibility? And is religious faith itself indispensable to their results?"[19] A report from a respected group of diverse policymakers and advocates headed by former Senator Harris Wofford wrote, "More sophisticated understandings of what it means to be faith-based and community-based needs to be developed."[20] In discussing faith-based community development efforts, Avis Vidal wrote that "they are among the least well researched aspects of the community development field."[21] Similarly, Ana Greenberg has written, "Yet as commentators champion the efforts of religious communities, little is known about the scale of faith-based public/private partnerships underlying the social safety net."[22]

The formation of effective, appropriate public policies regarding governmental partnerships with private entities has been hampered by an absence of information and a lack of well-developed concepts with which to frame the questions at issue. Misrepresentations, inaccurate beliefs, and a simple vacuum of information abound. In political debate, persons with self-interests to promote or preconceived biases to defend rush in when appropriately framed issues and carefully researched information are not available. This has been the case when it comes to public-private partnerships.

This book seeks to contribute to filling this void. It focuses on service programs seeking to assist welfare recipients in obtaining gainful, self-supporting employment. In other words, it focuses on welfare-to-work services. This book seeks to set the background and context for the issues in the area, to frame these issues in a proper manner, to synthesize the findings of previous research in this area and integrate them with the findings of a study of welfare-to-work programs in four major cities, and to consider the public policy implications that flow from these findings. This book seeks, in short, to fill some of the gap that currently exists in our knowledge of nongovernmental social service entities and their current and potential role as partners with government in meeting pressing social needs.

The first of the following sections of this chapter puts today's issues into a proper historical and theoretical context, by noting briefly both the long-standing and the increasing use of governmental partnerships with a wide variety of private entities in the social services field. The second section considers arguments both for and against such partnerships. The third section presents a theoretical framework with which to organize and view the issues that arise in conjunction with public-private partnerships. The fourth section then briefly outlines the key First Amendment, church-state issues raised when government partners with faith-based organizations. The fifth section considers and seeks to frame appropriately the major issues and questions that are at the forefront of public policy debate today regarding government partnering with private providers of social services. Finally, the chapter closes with an introduction to the study that is the basis for much of this book, a study of welfare-to-work programs in four cities.

Two final, clarifying observations need to be included in this introductory section of the chapter. Each deals with my choice of terminology throughout this book. First, when I write of "public-private partnerships," I am referring to collaborative arrangements between one or more government agencies and nongovernmental organizations that are providing a service that public policy has judged as contributing to the public good. I have chosen to use the term *public-private partnerships* because of its felicitousness and because it communicates what I have in mind, despite the possibility of its carrying with it some inaccurate implications. One ought not to equate the notions of "public" and "governmental." They are not the same. Nongovernmental organizations can be public organizations offering public services, fully as much as governmental organizations are public organizations offering public services. Our language sometimes reflects this. "Public restrooms," for example, are not government-operated restrooms but restroom facilities that are open to the public. Luis Lugo makes the following necessary point.

> We now commonly use the designation "public school," for example, to refer exclusively to government-run schools. Yet independent, non-government schools are engaged in the same public educational enterprise as are the government schools. The difference lies in the way these schools are owned and operated, not in their basic educational function. If we apply the same reasoning to churches and other faith-based charities, we would see that, though not government-owned, they certainly fulfill an essentially public function.[23]

Secular nonprofit, faith-based, and for-profit welfare-to-work programs would normally be considered part of the private, not the public, sector. Yet each of these program types provides a public service in that it provides to the general public (not just to its own members or to some other exclusive, highly limited group) a service that society has judged to be in support of the public good. Each provides a public benefit to the general public. In that sense, each is public in nature, even though privately owned and operated. As Lugo goes on to express, "In short, the state has no monopoly over the public square; it shares that space with other institutions which have equally valid claims."[24] This is a basic, underlying contention of this book. Thus, the terms *government-nongovernmental partnerships* or *government partnerships with nongovernmental entities* are more accurate than the term *public-private partnerships*. But, bowing to common usage and to the virtue of conciseness over cumbersomeness, I will here use the term *public-*

private partnerships to refer to government-nongovernmental partnerships, even while insisting that it is less than accurate to assume equations between the notions of "public" and "government" and the notions of "nongovernmental" and "private."

A second clarifying observation is that I use the terms *government* or *governmental* to refer indiscriminately to governmental officials and offices on the federal, state, and local levels. In the welfare-to-work field in particular, federal, state, and local governments are all involved in an often confusing manner. Much of the money and often regulations and standards originate at the federal level, but state and sometimes local money is commingled with money from Washington, and the implementation of welfare-to-work programs are, with some exceptions, carried out on the state or local levels. Happily, for the purposes of this study, it is generally not necessary to disentangle the respective roles played by federal, state, and local agencies and officials. Thus, throughout this book, I use the terms *government* or *governmental* without attempting to specify whether it is the federal, state, or local level of government that is involved. In most instances, all three are involved.

Historical Background: What Is and Is Not New

In what may be the first instance in American history of a public-private partnership supplying social services, the town records of Fairfield, Connecticut, dated April 16, 1673, read, "The town desires and orders Seriant Squire and Sam Moorhouse to take care of Roger Knaps's family in this time of their great weakness: and to procure for them such necessary comforts . . . as they stand in need of, and it shall be satisfied out of the town treasury."[25] Walter Trattner reports, "The most common seventeenth-century practice . . . was to place the poor in private homes at public expense."[26] He goes on to summarize the use of public-private partnerships to deal with poverty in colonial America.

> Clearly then, at this time, social welfare was a partnership. Private philanthropy complemented public aid; both were part of the American response to poverty. While, from the outset, the

public was responsible for providing aid to the needy who, in turn, had a right to such assistance, as soon as they could afford to do so, private citizens and a host of voluntary associations also gave generously to those in distress. . . . [T]his cooperative approach to the problem is one of the more noteworthy aspects of American colonial history.[27]

This pattern of public-private partnerships continued throughout the nineteenth century. In 1806, the New York Orphan Asylum Society opened, and within a few years, it was providing a home for 200 orphans—with the help of a state subsidy.[28] A particularly striking example of government's use of faith-based organizations to deliver public services during the nineteenth century was the use of various church agencies to educate, train, and work with Native Americans. J. Bruce Nicholas has described this long-lasting program.

The government's use of church workers to help build diplomatic, cultural, and religious ties with the Indian Nations continued unbroken from before the Revolution at least through 1912. . . . Baptists, Jesuits, Presbyterians, Moravians, Congregationalists, and others combined their private resources with resources of the [government's] Civilization Fund. By 1826 there were thirty-eight such government-subsidized schools.[29]

One can question the wisdom and justice of a policy that worked to undermine Native American cultures; no one can question the existence of a long-standing practice of government subsidizing nonprofit, faith-based organizations to provide educational and social services.

An 1889 survey of 17 major private hospitals found that 13 percent of their collective income came from government sources.[30] As of 1892, about one-half of the funds expended on the poor in the District of Columbia went to private charities.[31] In 1901, a Cornell University professor concluded, after extensive research, that "except [for] possibly two territories and four western states, there is probably not a state in the union where some aid [to private charities] is not given either by the state or by counties and cities."[32]

This is not to say that government provided the majority of funding—or even was always a major source of funding—for most health and social service organizations in the nineteenth and early twentieth centuries. Government funding was greatest in the cities of the Northeast and Midwest and was less in other areas of the country, and even where government funding was the greatest, a majority of the funds for health and social services typically came from fees and private contributions, not from government tax dollars.[33] Nevertheless, there clearly is a centuries-old tradition in the United States of government helping to provide certain public services by funding the social services rendered by nonprofit organizations, including faith-based nonprofit organizations.

Although government funding of health, educational, and social services provided by private, nonprofit organizations was common throughout American history, it rapidly expanded during the last half of the twentieth century, as Dennis Young has explained.

> Governmental involvement and financial support of private, nonprofit organizations providing higher education, hospital care, and social services, began in the early republic, continued unabated through the nineteenth and twentieth centuries. . . . Observers seem to agree, however, that governmental support of nonprofit organizations did not become extensive until the mid-twentieth century.[34]

In the 1960s—with President Lyndon Johnson's War on Poverty and its various programs to combat a variety of social ills—the practice of government funding of nonprofit organizations increased rapidly. Steven Rathgeb Smith and Michael Lipsky report that "government contracting of nonprofit agencies rose sharply in services previously limited to a relatively small number of agencies, dependent on private funds, including daycare, homeless shelters, child protection, counseling, home health, legal aid, family planning, respite care, and community living."[35] Ironically, President Ronald Reagan's attempts in the 1980s to reduce the size of government also led to more government funding of nonprofit organizations, as Smith reports: "The result [of Reagan's cutbacks] was a marked increase, albeit quite variable depending upon the state, in government funding of nonprofit agencies."[36] Both the liberal War on Poverty in the 1960s and the conservative reduction of government in the 1980s resulted in more governmental partnerships with nonprofit organizations. As a result, Mark Rom was not exaggerating when he wrote, "In virtually every area of social welfare policy, the United States is considering, or experimenting with, public-private partnerships to deliver services."[37] Rom has also documented the increasing reliance on for-profit firms to help deliver welfare-related services. Such firms as Lockheed, Maximus, Curtis and Associates, TTI America, and EDSI (Engineering Design Systems, Inc.) are providing extensive services in case management, training, and job placement.[38]

The resulting widespread existence of government partnerships with for-profit, faith-based, and other nonprofit organizations has frequently been documented by scholars. Lester Salamon, for example, has noted that "a widespread partnership has developed between the [government and nonprofit] . . . sectors, and with for-profit businesses as well, creating a 'mixed economy' of welfare in which public and private, nonprofit and for-profit action are mixed in often complex and confusing ways."[39] Salamon reports that in the social services field, 37 percent of the nonprofits' income comes from the government (with another 20 percent from private giving and 43 percent from fees the organizations charge).[40] He also documents that for-profit firms play a large role in the provision of social services. According to Salamon, for-profit firms account for 28 percent of the revenues in the social services field (compared to 61 percent for the nonprofits and 11 percent for government) and for 22 percent of the employment (compared to 55 percent for the nonprofits and 23 percent for the government).[41] A study of private colleges and universities, child and family service agencies, and international aid and relief agencies found that 98 percent of the colleges and universities, 90 percent of the child service agencies, and 67 percent of the international aid agencies received government funding.[42] Eighty-seven percent of the secular nonprofit welfare-to-work programs included in the study I discuss later in this book reported receiving government funds, with an average of 73 percent of their budgets coming from government sources; of the faith-based welfare-to-work programs, about one-half received government funding, with an average of 42 percent of their budgets coming from government sources. One can debate the wisdom and the consequences of government working in collaboration with for-profit, faith-based, community-based, and large, secular nonprofit organizations to provide public social services that American society has deemed vital; no one can debate the existence of these collaborative relationships.

Public-Private Partnerships: The Rationale

Examining the case that has been made for and against government forming partnerships with private, public-serving entities is the first step toward properly framing the issues surrounding such partnerships. As one gains a greater understanding of the rationales proffered by those favoring and those opposing these partnerships and of the assumptions and beliefs underlying those rationales, one is in a better position to pose the questions that need to be answered if the reasonableness and effectiveness of these partnerships are to be assessed. Since the cases being made for these partnerships vary—depending on whether the partnership is with a large, secular nonprofit; a community-based nonprofit; a faith-based nonprofit; or a for-profit organization—describing the case being made and the assumptions underlying that case is a complex task.[43] In this section, I first suggest a rationale that is frequently used in support of government partnerships with nongovernmental entities generally, then I explore three rationales often given for partnerships with secular nonprofits and two additional rationales often given for partnerships with faith-based nonprofits specifically. Next, I consider the basic argument frequently made on behalf of government partnerships with for-profit firms. Then, I consider certain frequently alleged dangers or pitfalls of government partnerships with nongovernmental entities.

First, a key argument made generally in support of government funding and working in partnership with a wide variety of nongovernmental agencies is that doing so will lead to an ability to experiment with new approaches and to a welcome flexibility, both of which are missing when programs are carried out by established government bureaucracies. It is argued that government bureaucracies by their very nature—especially with the advent of civil service rules and government employee unions—tend to become locked into certain approaches and to change only slowly. As a result, it is alleged, they will continue to pursue less than optimal strategies even when those strategies are not working or are working poorly. An often-cited example of an unchanging, unresponsive bureaucracy is the Immigration and Naturalization Service (INS). In 2002, it mailed out routine visa extensions to two of the September 11 hijackers six months after their suicidal hijackings. It is argued that nongovernmental entities are more nimble in responding to changing circumstances and more able to take risks with new approaches. This is so for several reasons. A government agency is more risk adverse and therefore less likely to experiment with new approaches, because failure can bring down heavy criticism from the media and elected officials. Nongovernmental agencies, in contrast, may be less risk adverse, since any failure will not bring the same public criticism and condemnation. Also, efforts to change government programs—whether doing so involves growth, downsizing, or merely shifting responsibilities around—may conflict with civil service regulations, union objections, or squeals of protest from politically connected interest groups. It is easier for private organizations to make changes and risk new endeavors. Moreover, flexibility is gained by government's ability to cancel or not renew a contract with one organization and give it to another. All this is theory, and whether or not this is the way the real world in fact works is an unresolved question, but this first rationale—as well as each of those to follow—at least points toward the important questions that need to be asked and answered.

A basic argument often advanced for the position that it makes particularly good sense for government to fund and in other ways collaborate with nonprofit organizations rests on the belief that nonprofit employees tend to have a very strong sense of dedication or commitment to the work of the nonprofit. Government employees, so it is alleged, tend to see their jobs as "just a job," as a means to earn a paycheck and provide for themselves and their families. Nonprofit employees are more likely to be motivated by a sense of vocation or calling, seeing their work as a means to fulfill a desire to be of service to others and their community.

Two additional, often-voiced arguments especially apply to community-based nonprofit organizations. One is that community-based organizations are one of the few stable institutions left in economically deteriorating neighborhoods. As a neighborhood deteriorates, retail stores and factories depart, leaving community-based organizations as one of the few positive features left in the neighborhood. Thus, it is reasoned, when government decides to revitalize a neighborhood, it only makes good sense to make use of and build on one of the few remaining community assets, instead of seeking to build positive structures from scratch. A second argument that applies with special force to community-based nonprofits is that they are rooted in and are an integral part of the neighborhoods in which they are located—in a way that government agencies, composed of civil servants, most of whom live miles away, can never be. Community-based nonprofits are marked by their staffs living in the same neighborhoods as the people they serve. Thus, they can relate to the people they serve, and the people they serve will have a higher level of trust in them than could be the case for more distant, professionalized structures.

These arguments made on behalf of either nonprofit organizations generally or small community-based nonprofit organizations also apply to faith-based nonprofit organizations. In fact, many argue that they apply with particular force in the case of faith-based organizations, since churches and other faith-based organizations are likely to have especially dedicated staff who see their work as a calling from God; are especially prevalent in poor, minority neighborhoods; and are especially likely to be deeply rooted in and a part of the social structure of those neighborhoods.

There are two additional reasons why many persons today argue that faith-based groups offer the best hope for a renewed attack on persistent, seemingly intractable social ills. One reason holds that individual faith comprises an important element encouraging persons to overcome such challenges as drug and alcohol abuse, spouse abuse, or the feelings of hopelessness that often accompany poverty and joblessness. Positively, religion can help build attitudes conducive to finding and keeping employment, resisting drugs and alcohol, and overcoming other challenges of life. Ana Greenberg has pointed out that policymakers and religious leaders are increasingly arguing that "the effectiveness of faith-based social services delivery is linked to the individual experience of faith."[44] This argument is based on mounting evidence that religious faith is positively correlated with a host of desirable social attributes, such as lower crime rates, fewer out-of-wedlock births, less drug and alcohol abuse, better health, higher self-esteem, and less suicide.[45] Since religion is positively related to such attributes as these, the logical conclusion holds that programs incorporating a faith element into them may be more successful in helping persons overcome social ills than may be programs that do not. Thus, many argue that religious programs have at their disposal an extra tool that nonreligious programs do not have.

There also exists a fairness or equity argument that is less often made but is nonetheless viable: if government is going to fund a wide variety of secular nonprofit programs, it should also fund faith-based programs on the same basis. This position argues that government ought not to favor religious providers over secular ones or vice versa. Such factors as a proven track record, a proposal's quality, and the needs that will be met should be weighed as the government decides with which agencies it will partner; whether or not they are faith-based in itself should not. To do otherwise would be to discriminate against faith-based organizations, and that would be a violation of the norm of governmental religious neutrality.

The basic argument made in favor of government collaborations with for-profit firms to provide public social services rests on the idea that the profit motive and competition lead to higher-quality services at lower costs. This is the free market argument. The profit motive will help assure high-quality services, innovation, and flexibility. In the for-profit world, performance and economic rewards are closely correlated. Everyone realizes this, thereby creating a mind-set among the leaders and employees of for-profit companies that emphasizes constant innovation and change aimed at improving the services being provided. In contrast, the assumption is that both monopolies and assured government contracts lead to higher costs and lower quality, since there is no incentive to hold costs down or to achieve greater quality. Performance and costs are disconnected from continued employment and organizational growth. By putting for-profit firms in direct competition with government agencies and traditional non-profit contractors, costs will be held down, and the quality of services delivered will go up. The recipients of the government services will be the ultimate winners.

There are arguments against government partnerships with all four types of nongovernmental entities. Four arguments are frequently made. One applies to all four types of nongovernmental entities. This argument holds that working with nongovernmental entities—whether they are for-profit, community-based, faith-based, or large nonprofit organizations—can in actual practice lead to new inefficiencies. Grants and contracts may be awarded because of political influence and long-term, overly cozy relationships, not on rational, effectiveness-oriented criteria. Particularly in the social services field, it is difficult to construct firm, easily measurable standards of service delivery and effectiveness. In the absence of such standards, inertia, long-standing and comfortable networks, and political favoritism may play major roles. Inefficiencies and lower service quality may be the end results, rather than the hoped-for opposites.

Some also claim that nonprofit organizations receiving large amounts of government money will themselves quickly begin to look very much like large government agencies, regardless of whether the nonprofits are secular or faith-based, large or small. With money comes strict standards, voluminous record keeping, and complex regulations. This will, in turn, lead to increased bureaucratization and a loss in creativity and flexibility. In fact, some have argued for a dilemma that is hard to escape. If the nonprofits are very large and are heavily financed by government, they will be able to meet the needs of many of those whom they are seeking to serve, but they are likely to begin to look almost exactly like government agencies. If the nonprofits are small, community-based, and not funded by government, they will be able to maintain independence from government—with the presumed advantages that go with that independence—but they will tend to remain small and therefore able to serve only a very limited number of persons in need.

When the nonprofit that is acting as a partner with government in meeting human needs is a religious nonprofit, the added allegation is sometimes made of a violation of the religious freedom rights of either the taxpayer whose money is going to the faith-based program or the service recipients who may object to or be made uncomfortable by the religious elements in the program. The taxpayer's right may be violated if his or her tax money is going to fund a religious program that is not of his or her faith. A Jewish taxpayer's money may end up going to a Christian program; a Christian taxpayer's money may end up going to a Muslim program. Some believe this is a violation of the First Amendment and of basic religious freedom. Even more often mentioned is the potential violation of the religious freedom rights of recipients of services from a faith-based organization whose religious beliefs are at variance with those of some of the recipients.

Finally, the argument is made that for-profit companies will naturally face pressures to increase the profit margin by reducing the level of services given. Every dollar spent on recipient services means one dollar less in profit. Under such circumstances, there will be very real pressure to cut services to the bone. After all, as it is sometimes put, the goal is to make money, not to serve those in need. A controversy erupted in Los Angeles County in 2000 over contracting out welfare-to-work services to a for-profit firm.[46] This controversy illustrates the questions that are often raised when it is proposed that government partner with for-profit firms in delivering social services. Some questioned the propriety of for-profit companies making money, as it were, from some of the poorest and most needy in society. One opponent of contracting with a for-profit firm to provide welfare-to-work services stated: "This is the kind of work that should never be contracted out. This money that is meant to make people self-sufficient should not be going to stockholders."[47] Another opponent declared, "There is no place for private profit in the public welfare system."[48] A county supervisor claimed that the for-profit firm would not deliver the same quality services as would the county workers. The major opponent of contracting with the for-profit firm was the union representing county workers, and the two persons just quoted were both union officials. This indicates that the protection of public jobs may also be a factor in the questions that are raised over using for-profit firms to deliver social services.

It is instructive to note that all seven arguments that have been advanced in support of public-private partnerships in providing social services rest on the assumption that the nongovernmental entities will be able to collaborate and receive funding from government and yet maintain a large measure of autonomy. The second argument advanced against such collaborations rests on the belief that the nongovernmental providers will in fact not be able to maintain their autonomy but will shortly start to look very much like their parallel government providers. If, in fact, nongovernmental providers that receive government funding and in other ways partner with government end up losing an ability to innovate and experiment with new programs and approaches, a major claimed advantage would be lost. If they would professionalize and bureaucratize like their government counterparts, they would lose their staff members' sense of vocation or calling and separate themselves from the neighborhoods they serve. If faith-based organizations would end up secularizing, any advantages that religion gives them would be lost. In short, if partnerships between government and nongovernmental providers result in those nongovernmental providers becoming much like their governmental counterparts, it is hard to articulate a rationale for moving down this road. Thus, any schemes aimed at expanding public-private ventures simply must contain, both in their conceptualization and in their execution, means to protect the autonomy or independence of the nongovernmental entities. The public good, of course, demands that they must be held accountable for the funds they receive and the public trust they have been given; the public good equally demands that a certain autonomy and freedom of action be safeguarded. Both are important. A balance must be sought.

Later chapters of this book explore whether or not and by what means this balance is being maintained in the welfare-to-work field. The next section of this chapter puts forward a conceptual framework that seeks to create a theoretical basis for understanding the responsibilities of government to assure accountability, while also respecting the autonomy of for-profit, secular nonprofit, and faith-based organizations.

A Theoretical Framework for Analyzing the Questions at Issue

Throughout the history of the United States, beginning with the earliest days of the republic, there have been passionate debates over the proper extent of government's role in society. One side focuses on the rational, systematic approach that government can utilize to meet the challenges of the day, whether challenges of terrorism, economic dislocations, environmental degradation, a faltering health care system, or widespread poverty in the midst of a wealthy society. Those holding this position argue that only government has the power required to raise the funds, coordinate the action, and enforce the national norms of equality needed to deal adequately with contemporary needs. Those on the other side of this debate fear the consequences of an overly powerful government, one that confiscates one's wealth through ever higher taxes, interferes with one's use of one's land, tells business owners how to run their businesses, and seeks to make all equal regardless of effort or merit. They fear what has been called the "nanny state."

The opening paragraphs of this chapter spoke of Americans' desire for many social, health, and educational services but of their continuing distrust of government as the source of those services. As a way out of that dilemma, it pointed to governmental use of private agencies to deliver the services. But this really does not resolve the dilemma; it only pushes it one step back. It still leaves the question of what role government is to play in the lives and programs of those private organizations that provide the desired public services. Is government simply to give them money and then turn them loose to accomplish the magic that it is often claimed they can accomplish? Or is government to use its authority and its money to set the goals that the nongovernmental entities are to reach and then to mandate the means by which they are to reach those goals? If we adopt the former tactic, how can we prevent outright fraud, as well as a hit-and-miss approach to dire social needs—an approach that leaves some persons or areas overserved and others underserved? If we adopt the latter tactic, will not government turn the nongovernmental providers into clones of itself, losing the hoped-for benefits of reliance on them to deliver essential services?

E. J. Dionne and Ming Hsu Chen ask, in the context of faith-based providers, how can "sacred places serve civic purposes."[49] The question is not only how sacred places can serve civic purposes but also how nongovernmental entities generally—whether faith-based or secular—can serve civic, or public, purposes. The goal of this section is to offer some theoretical insights into how to explore and perhaps even to answer that question.

In very rough terms, there are three basic approaches to the question of the proper involvement of government in dealing with societal needs and problems: the libertarian, the statist, and the pluralist. Each approach has a corresponding answer to the question of government's proper relationship with nongovernmental entities that are providing public social services. First, there is the libertarian approach. The old saying that the government that governs least governs best is the watchword of the libertarian approach. Its spirit is captured in a saying that Ronald Reagan sometimes invoked: "Government isn't the answer to our problems, government *is* the problem." The libertarian response to almost every societal need or problem it identifies is lower taxes and less government. It believes that a free market and free individuals, released from the constraints of governmental regulation and direction, will prosper and, in time, overcome existing problems.[50]

A libertarian perspective takes what Dennis Young has termed a "supplementary" approach to government's relationship with private providers: "In the supplementary model, nonprofits are seen as fulfilling demand for public goods left unsatisfied by government."[51] As government's provision of services increases, the role played by nonprofits decreases, and vice versa. The two sectors do not pursue a coordinated strategy; each has its separate responsibilities and fields of activities.

Some of the recent calls for greater reliance on faith-based and other nongovernmental entities have had aspects of this libertarian approach. Marvin Olasky, in his book *The Tragedy of American Compassion,* essentially called for government to withdraw from social welfare programs, in the belief that faith-based and other charities would step in and do a better job than government was doing.[52] This is the libertarian approach. Those, such as Olasky, who take this approach favor minimal government control over any funding of nonprofits whenever government enters into a collaborative agreement with them.

A second perspective on the role of government in modern society is the statist approach. The statist approach sees government as the necessary and appropriate source of programs and initiatives to deal with the problems and needs of modern society. It sees the problems and the interdependence of modern society as so overwhelming that only a rational, planned, coordinated, national attack on them will do. Thus, government is the focus, the center point, of society's efforts to deal with poverty, environmental degradation, terrorism, and a host of other modern ills. Any other approach appears to be too limited, too localized, too uncoordinated.

This perspective often will approve or even advocate joint public-private efforts to deal with persistent societal needs. But it leaves no doubt that the government is in the driver's seat. In fact, it tends to see private organizations delivering public services as virtual extensions of government, as delivering government services. Sheila Kennedy has written, "Whether government delivers drug counseling, job placement, or any other service through a state agency or a faith-based organization, the program is state action."[53] Smith and Lipsky have declared, "Workers in nonprofit agencies receiving government contracts are now agents of government."[54] One commentator in a *New York Times* opinion column opposing the original charitable choice addition to the 1996 act restructuring the Aid to Families with Dependent Children (AFDC) welfare program was clearly operating out of this mind-set. He wrote that the charitable choice proposal "would permit states to give tax dollars to religious organizations that display religious messages in areas where people receive *Government services.*"[55] The writer assumed that if independent faith-based organizations would receive government funding to help provide welfare services, those services would be transformed into government services. The independent faith-based group would, in effect, be transformed into a government agency. Stephen Macedo revealed a similar mind-set when he wrote: "we should not aim to immunize faith-based institutions receiving public funds from all pressures toward openness and inclusion. If religious believers sometimes feel they are being asked to 'tone down' their religiosity, that will often be the price of agreeing to serve as a provider of public services."[56] This position is sometimes expressed in the saying that public values must follow public dollars.

There are profound problems with the libertarian and statist perspectives on government's role in society and on the relationship between government and private providers. The libertarian perspective underestimates the intractableness of today's societal problems and the difficulty in rooting out underlying causes of homelessness, drug addiction, poverty, and other ills. History is not a good witness to the ability of American society to overcome deep-seated ills—such as racism, unemployment, poverty, environmental degradation, spouse abuse, and more—without government playing a prominent role. Recent history has also taught us the limitations of a statist approach. The renewed emphasis on more localized nonprofit, faith-based, and for-profit efforts to deal with basic social problems has grown out of the conclusion that we as a society are not doing very well with inner-city education, overcoming drug abuse, preventing violent gang behavior, discouraging teenage pregnancies, preventing criminal recidivism, decreasing generational poverty, and more. The emerging consensus from many voices on both the Left and the Right is that the large government bureaucracies created by the New Deal and the Great Society initiatives—as well-meaning as they were—are just not well suited for dealing with many social problems that continue to bedevil American society.

Ultimately, the statist approach to working with and utilizing nongovernmental entities to address social needs is not a new approach at all. After one turn around the statist track, we will have expended a lot of energy but will end up exactly where we have started. If nongovernmental entities are seen as no more than the conduits through which governmental programs and services are to be delivered, those nongovernmental entities and the programs they deliver will be constricted by carefully prescribed programs and the standards, rules, and regulations that accompany them. One ends up with programs that in a technical sense may be nongovernmental in nature but that for most intents and purposes look very much like the government programs and bureaucracies they were supposed to be replacing.

What is needed is a perspective that respects and affirms a positive role for government in society but that also respects and affirms a positive role for nongovernmental entities as independent actors, not simply extensions of the state. Though nongovernmental actors should not be totally free to operate as they see fit, neither should they lose a strong measure of independence. Thus, a means to sort out the appropriate roles of government and of the nongovernmental providers of public services needs to be articulated.

Peter Frumkin was correct when he observed, "I believe that a new, more detached perspective on public-nonprofit relations is needed—one that preserves some of the boundaries between sectors, that gives nonprofits as much freedom as possible, and that makes broad, multidimensional appraisals of their performance possible."[57] Similarly, Fred Glennon has written, "Implicit in this notion of partnership and cooperation is a mutual relationship where the autonomy and the integrity of each partner is affirmed and respected."[58] Frumkin and Glennon are right. If there are to be true public-private partnerships, it is crucial to have an appropriate framework of concepts that supports neither government simply abdicating its responsibilities to private entities nor government dominating and taking over the private entities.

This leads to pluralist theory, the third approach to the role of government in society. It is the third basis on which to view the government-private relationship in providing essential public services. Pluralism—sometimes referred to as structural or principled pluralism—has its roots in Catholic social teaching and in some strains of Protestant thinking, especially in the neo-Calvinist thinking most fully developed and articulated in the Netherlands.[59] I am convinced that it is the most appropriate theoretical framework to apply to the understanding and evaluation of government's relationship with faith-based and other nongovernmental entities. It accurately depicts the way society is in fact structured. Also, it posits a normative basis for a robust role in society for both government and nongovernmental entities.

Pluralism begins by recognizing that society is composed of more than simply autonomous individuals and the government. There exists a host of social structures—from families and informal circles of friends to more formal associations, such as religious congregations, neighborhood associations, recreation and sports clubs, societies for the arts, charitable organizations, advocacy groups, and many, many more. These structures are not accidental or peculiar to the United States or any other society. Although their form and nature will vary from one society to another, they are an inherent and necessary aspect of every society. Their existence is a matter of empirical observation, not theoretical projection. Every society—even every so-called primitive society—has family or kinship groupings (however defined), cooperative work groups, and social interaction or friendship groups. Modernized societies have many more formally organized groups that come together for certain specialized tasks—worship, recreation, advocacy, and so forth. The very universality of social structures within the larger society witnesses to their inherent, innate nature. To be human is to form social structures; to do so is not a choice that human beings make or one that they could equally easily choose not to make.

Two additional observations stem from the innate character of social structures: a set of healthy social structures is essential for a healthy society, and social structures themselves possess certain inherent rights or protections. First, given human beings' social nature, they need other human beings to develop fully as human beings, that is, to realize fully their intellectual, moral, and emotional capacities. It is in families, work groups, peer groups, groups of friends, religious groups, and advocacy groups that we learn values and morals, develop trust, learn a healthy sense of self-worth, and accomplish chosen goals. In short, healthy individuals live their lives as members of countless groupings, not as isolated individuals. The official platform of the communitarian journal *The Responsive Community* makes the needed point in clear terms.

> American men, women, and children are members of many communities—families; neighborhoods; innumerable social, religious, ethnic, workplace, and professional associations; and the body politic itself. Neither human existence nor individual liberty can be sustained for long outside the interdependent and overlapping communities to which all of us belong.[60]

The second observation that flows from the innate character of social structures is also crucial. Enlightenment liberalism emphasized the importance of individual rights. It was not wrong in doing so. Certainly individual rights are crucial to a free society respectful of human beings as free moral agents. But the tradition of Enlightenment liberalism tends to ignore or overlook the role and importance of social structures and associations, and in doing so, it ends up limiting the very individual rights it is committed to protecting at all costs. To put it differently, the integrity of social structures and associations must be safeguarded in order to protect fully the rights of individuals. A basic fact is that individuals find fulfillment, purpose, and meaning in the context of their involvement in associations and groups. Thus, if the integrity of these social structures is not safeguarded, individuals will be limited in their pursuit of meaning and fulfillment. R. E. M. Irving, in describing the political theory of the Christian Democratic parties of Western Europe, wrote that "the 'natural social structures,' such as trade unions, family associations and regional bodies, must be given full rein to play their part in this new-style democracy, because they are the vehicle through which the individual can develop his full personality."[61]

To take an example, if a society guarantees individuals the complete freedom of religious faith but then does not protect the integrity of religious associations, the religious freedom guaranteed to individuals would for most be illusory. Most persons desire and believe it vital to exercise their religious belief in community, in conjunction with other fellow believers, but would in this case be limited in their ability to do so.

For a healthy, vibrant society to exist—one in which all persons are able to develop their human capacities as fully as possible in keeping with their inclinations or the dictates of their consciences—it is essential for one to think in terms of social structures possessing certain rights that should be protected. Closely related to this concept of rights is that of autonomy. Both concepts refer to the freedom of a social structure to define its membership and to select and pursue its goals. This means that the government must not—totalitarian-like—seek to dictate to and control the membership, goals, and direction of a social structure, whether it be nuclear families, the Sierra Club, or the Roman Catholic Church. This does not mean that social structures possess an absolute autonomy. To protect the basic rights of other groups and individuals and to promote the welfare of society as a whole, limits must be set by government on social structures. Nuclear families may lose custody of their children if they neglect and abuse them, the Sierra Club may not use violent means to protest environmental degradation, and the Roman Catholic Church may not protect pedophile priests from the legal consequences of their acts. Social structures possess more of a quasi autonomy than an absolute autonomy. But that does not lessen the basic point: an open, free, democratic society simply must make room for and protect the immense range of social structures found in society.

This will lead to a pervasive, persistent pluralism of associations, groups, and structures. These associations, groups, and structures will differ greatly from one another. But that is all right and to be expected. A genuine pluralism does not fear this. Here, it is important to make a distinction between pluralism within a group and pluralism among groups. Sometimes, the tendency of American society is to support efforts to assure that all social structures will be similar in that they will contain the same pluralistic mix of religion, ethnicity, gender, belief, and other key characteristics. Periodically, for example, colleges or schools that seek to be composed of one gender, predominantly of one racial group, or of one religious perspective are subjected to criticism. Sometimes, under some circumstances, that criticism may be appropriate. However, there is another type of pluralism, namely, that of pluralism *among* social structures. This position says it is all right if certain social structures are largely uniform in terms of certain characteristics. This does not destroy and may even strengthen the diversity and pluralism of society, since persons can choose from a variety of different structures with which to align themselves. If all or most structures were similar in terms of the same mix of characteristics, one would no longer have any real choice.

Many of these theoretical perspectives of structural pluralism are bound up in the concept of subsidiarity, which has been a prominent part of Catholic social teaching.[62] It recognizes a hierarchy of social structures, from small local groups, to broader structures, to local or regional governments, to the national government. It then says that social tasks should be performed on the lowest level consistent with good order and the public good. While not denying—but, rather, asserting—a robust role for national governments, it insists that local structures should not do what the family can do, regional structures should not do what local structures can do, and national structures should not do what regional structures can do. Local, regional, and national structures include both governments and other social structures, such as voluntary associations and social service agencies. When this principle is followed, the integrity and autonomy of the various social structures are protected, since the principle seeks to preserve "a sphere of free activity in the social-economic order."[63]

Similarly, pluralist thought focuses on the importance of a zone of autonomy or freedom that inheres in or surrounds social structures. Luis Lugo has written: "Thus while the political community geographically may be the most encompassing, it is not exhaustive in the sense that it is capable of meeting all human needs. The temptation to make it so has been the misguided, and ultimately self-defeating, goal of all forms of collectivism of the right and the left."[64] He went on succinctly to summarize much of pluralist thought: "One way to express the complex and multi-faceted reality of life in society is to say that the political community is a community of communities."[65] To elaborate a bit, one of the clearest summaries of pluralist thought is found in the following words.

> The heart of the pluralistic thesis is the conviction that government must recognize that it is not the sole possessor of sovereignty, and that private groups within the community are entitled to lead their own free lives and exercise within the area of their competence an authority so effective as to justify labeling it a sovereign authority. To make this assertion is to suggest that private groups have liberties similar to those of individuals and that those liberties, as such, are to be secured by law from governmental infringements.[66]

According to this summary, and as Lugo also pointed out, the role of government is extensive in the pluralist vision. It has an active, society-wide role to play in coordinating societal efforts to achieve the public good that touches on every other societal structure. As the Catholic thinker J. Bryan Hehir has written, "The specific and essential role given the state in the protection and promotion of the common good guarantees it a significant social role in response to human needs."[67] But government is not intensive. It ought to seek to coordinate, help, and empower the other societal structures, never to supplant and replace them.

Frumkin has criticized Lester Salamon's use of partnership language to describe the public-private relationship. The former claims that in fact government has so come to dominate the relationship that it no longer is a true partnership.[68] He calls for "pluralist autonomy" to mark the public-private relationship and for a downplaying of partnership language. Pluralist autonomy would lead to giving "nonprofit organizations as much independence as possible while meeting the accountability needs of the public sector."[69] One can disagree about the use of partnership language. I personally like it and use it in this book, because there is nothing inherent in the language to imply that one party in a partnership is dominant over the other. In fact, the opposite is true. The term *partnership* implies that both parties work together to achieve a common goal. Lugo made this implication explicit when he titled his essay on pluralist theory and antipoverty efforts *Equal Partners,* with the equal partners being government, on the one hand, and faith-based and other nonprofit organizations, on the other.

This is the vision to which pluralist theory leads; it is a vision of pluralist autonomy. It accords government policy a vital coordinating, agenda-setting role. It is not libertarian. But neither is it statist. Pluralist theory accords nongovernmental entities a robust, independent role in meeting public needs, and government is to respect that role and seek to empower these entities to be all that they aspire to be. Government is not to subvert and undermine nongovernmental entities (as long, of course, as they are acting within the norms of an ordered, democratic society and are respectful of the rights of other groups and individuals). Nongovernmental entities do not fulfill a robust, independent role because they have been assigned it by the government and hold it at its sufferance. They have as much right to fulfill their role as the government has to fulfill its role. They are equal partners with government; the partners have different, but complementary, roles to play. Neither partner should attempt to trespass on the role of the other.

Much of the debate and controversy swirling around President

Bush's faith-based and community initiative and other efforts to increase the role of nongovernmental organizations in providing needed social services can be explained by the different perspectives from which different persons are operating. Libertarians tend to assume that as more reliance is placed on nongovernmental entities, money will be saved, the role of government will be reduced, and taxes will be cut. When this does not occur, their enthusiasm for the various proposals diminishes. Meanwhile, some of those working out of statist assumptions see the various proposals as no more than a libertarian plot to get government out of the business of caring for the most needy in society. Other followers of the statist approach embrace the various proposals, but with the explicit or hidden assumption that nonprofits—whether faith-based or secular—will largely act as agents of the government. When they find out that the advocates of public-private partnerships insist that those nongovernmental providers be able to maintain their independence from government and thereby to maintain their distinctive character and vision, they see discrimination and favoritism. The differing libertarian, statist, or pluralist perspectives that persons hold go a long way toward explaining current controversies surrounding proposed governmental collaborations with nongovernmental—and especially faith-based—providers. Realizing this will in itself help to clarify the issues and analyses to be presented in this book

Church-State Issues and Public-Private Partnerships

Earlier in this chapter, I noted that many faith-based organizations receive government funds for the social service programs they provide to the public. Given the ringing words the Supreme Court has sometimes used to outlaw government funding of religion, some may find this surprising. In one seminal case, for example, the Court expressly declared:

> No tax in any amount, large or small, can be levied to support any religious activities or institutions, whatever they may be called, or whatever form they may adopt to teach or practice religion. . . . In the words of Thomas Jefferson, the clause against

establishment of religion by law was intended to erect "a wall of separation between church and state." . . . That wall must be kept high and impregnable.[70]

Note the near absolute language used by the Court: "*No* tax in *any* amount, large or small" may go to support "*any* religious activities or institutions" (emphasis added). The language would seem to preclude any government funding of faith-based social service agencies or programs. But this is hardly the case. Many studies have documented that each year, literally billions of taxpayer dollars flow to religiously based colleges and universities, family and child care agencies, international aid and relief agencies, drug rehabilitation programs, hospitals, community development corporations, and more.[71]

How can this be? How can near absolute language forbidding government funding of faith-based activities and institutions exist alongside billions of government dollars flowing to faith-based educational, health, and social service programs? The answer lies in two different lines of reasoning used by the Supreme Court to justify such funding. It is important to understand both lines of reasoning, since which one is utilized has huge consequences for the assumptions, and therefore for the terms and conditions, under which faith-based social service programs receive government funding.

One line of reasoning attempts to maintain the strict separation principle of no aid to religion, as articulated in the *Everson* decision, but it makes a distinction between the secular services and the religious activities of a faith-based organization and argues that government may fund the former but not the latter. This can be accomplished, so the reasoning goes, as long as an organization is not "pervasively sectarian" in nature; that is, the organization must not, to quote one Supreme Court decision, be one "in which religion is so pervasive that a substantial portion of its functions are subsumed in the religious mission."[72] This principle assumes that faith-based social service programs now receiving government funds are not pervasively religious, that they are able to separate the religious elements of their programs from the secular elements, and that the government money is only going to fund the organizations' secular services. These assumptions open the way for government funding agencies to examine the nature of faith-based organizations to make certain they are not "too religious"—that is, are not "pervasively sectarian"—and to make certain that tax dollars are only funding activities that are wholly secular in nature.

A second line of reasoning is based on the *equal treatment or neutrality principle,* also sometimes called *positive neutrality.* It has come to prominence in the past 10 to 20 years, and one observer has written, "Scholars generally agree that the Court has gradually moved in the direction of a neutrality position."[73] Jeffrey Rosen has written, "The Supreme Court is on the verge of replacing the principle of strict separation with a very different constitutional principle that demands equal treatment for religion."[74] The equal treatment or neutrality principle says that government may fund the educational or social services being provided by religiously based organizations as long as it is doing so on an equal basis with similar or parallel services provided by secular organizations—that is, so long as it is doing so neutrally. The idea is that government does not favor or advantage religious over secular worldviews as long as it is treating faith-based groups no better than, but also no worse than, their secular counterparts. Justice Clarence Thomas wrote in a Supreme Court opinion for a plurality of four justices: "if the government, seeking to further some legitimate secular purpose, offers aid on the same terms, without regard to religion, to all who adequately further that purpose, . . . then it is fair to say that any aid going to a religious recipient only has the effect of furthering that secular purpose."[75] The nature of the faith-based organization receiving the funds—whether or not it is "pervasively sectarian"—is not the issue. The issues, rather, are twofold: the nature of the services being rendered and the conditions under which the government funds are made available. Thus, one needs to answer two key questions under the equal treatment or neutrality standard: (1) whether the government funds are going to support a secular or temporal public policy goal and not an otherworldly, religious goal; and (2) whether government distributes the funds to organizations of all faiths and of a purely nonreligious, secular nature without regard to their religious or secular nature. If the answer is yes to both questions, there is no constitutional problem. Thus, whether or not a faith-based organization is "pervasively sectarian" is not the key question; the key questions are the nature of the services being funded and the terms under which they are funded.

Although the Supreme Court may, as Rosen claims, be on the verge of adopting the equal treatment or neutrality principle, it has not yet done so. One cannot be sure whether, in the future, the Supreme Court will fully embrace it; will retreat from it and reassert the strict separation principle of no aid to religion; or will settle on some compromise accommodating the two principles. Although partisans on both sides often state with confidence the exact state of First Amendment interpretations as they apply to government funding of faith-based organizations, the truth is that this area of law is highly uncertain and in flux. No one can predict with any real confidence where the Court will end up.

Adding to the uncertainty is the fact that almost no cases dealing directly with government funding of health or social services provided by faith-based organizations have been litigated before the Supreme Court. There was one case in 1899 about government funding for a Catholic hospital and one case in 1988 about government funding for programs dealing with adolescent sexual activity and pregnancies (both decisions held that the funding was constitutional).[76] That has been it. Almost all that has been written about First Amendment interpretations as they relate to government funding of faith-based public services is based on Supreme Court decisions made in other settings—especially in the educational field—which are then extrapolated to faith-based health and social services. As a result, it is hard to overstate the degree of constitutional uncertainty regarding government partnerships with faith-based social service providers.

This book and the study reported herein do not have as their focus the thorny issue of First Amendment interpretation as it applies to public-private partnerships; neither can it totally avoid this issue. As I report the findings of the study in later chapters, I will relate them to the constitutional church-state issues that were introduced in this section.

Public Policy Issues

Five key sets of public policy questions emerge from the ongoing debates over public-private partnerships. The remainder of this book seeks to throw additional light on many of these questions, based on the findings of the study reported herein.

Public Policy Issue Area 1: What is the capacity of nongovernmental entities? This question seeks to determine whether or not there are community-based, faith-based, and other nonprofit programs, as well as for-profit programs, that are ready and able to take on added responsibilities. What is the number, size, and nature of those programs that already actively provide welfare-to-work services? What is their current capacity? Are they able and willing to expand to assume greater responsibilities? Is their level of sophistication such that they are potentially able to collaborate with government agencies' inevitable and necessary standards of accountability and rules for the delivery of services?

More precisely, capacity needs to be conceptualized in two ways. One is that of current and potential size. If nongovernmental agencies are to provide a significant portion of welfare-to-work or other social services, they need to exist in sufficient number and size to take on this task. Alternatively—if they are now very small—they need to be willing to expand to take on added responsibilities. Capacity should also be conceptualized in terms of the level of sophistication or of basic organizational experience and skills. To partner with government is to drive a Formula One race car—it can be great fun, but one needs a certain level of skill and ability if one is not to end up in a flaming wreck. Especially to engage in a financial partnership in which government is supplying funds for the services rendered, an organization needs a not-so-minimal level of organizational and managerial experience and skills.

This may pose a challenge for faith-based and small community-based providers that many hope can play a larger role in meeting vital public service needs in distressed, inner-city communities. Their small size and nonprofessional, street-level contacts with those in need may make them especially effective in relating to and helping those in severe need. But these very same qualities raise questions about their ability to work in partnership with government. In addition, faith-based organizations need to navigate some tricky church-state issues in addition to all the other requirements inherent in public-private partnerships. In short, do the nongovernmental entities expected to play a greater role in the provision of social services possess the capacity needed for successful partnerships with government?

This question is crucial, because if for-profit, community-based, and faith-based entities are present in such few numbers and possess such low levels of experience and skills that they simply cannot be more than marginal players in the provision of welfare-to-work or other social services, the movement to devolve the delivery of more services to them is a nonstarter from the outset. If, however, there are presently many such entities providing services, if many are already partnering with government, if many are large enough or are willing and able to expand their services, and if many have the sophistication to partner with government, then—from a public policy point of view—the option of looking to them for the delivery of more services to those in need is a viable option. Chapter 2 considers who the nongovernmental providers of welfare-to-work services are in the four cities under study and seeks to make some judgments in terms of their capacity to provide such services.

Public Policy Issue Area 2: Do for-profit, large nonprofit, community-based, and faith-based providers deliver social services any differently than do government providers? The heart of the case for creating more public-private partnerships rests in the assumption that the nongovernmental providers deliver services differently than do traditional government agencies. If the nongovernmental providers are clones of government providers, essentially doing the same thing in the same way, it is hard to make a case in favor of a major effort to move the delivery of more services to the nongovernmental providers. If, however, they provide services in a distinctive manner—one that distinguishes them from the way services are being delivered by government agencies—there is at least a basis for building a case to shift public policy toward greater utilization of public-private partnerships. Today, claims are made that community-based and faith-based programs in particular are distinctive in the way they deliver services to those in need. Such claims need to be tested. Chapter 3 considers the nature of the welfare-to-work services being delivered by the various program types and whether or not government-run programs differ from the other program types.

Public Policy Issue Area 3: What are the extent and nature of public-pri-

vate partnerships that already exist, and are there currently barriers to community-based and faith-based organizations partnering with government? These two questions are related. Together, they ask whether or not community-based and faith-based programs are being shut out of partnerships with government due to biases against them. Is the current partnering system tilted in favor of for-profit and large, secular nonprofits at the expense of the faith-based and the smaller community-based programs? One needs to ask whether or not and to what extent government already partners with community-based and faith-based welfare-to-work programs. To the extent that government does not do so, is it due to discriminatory practices that tilt the playing field against such programs, or can it be explained either by the desires of the community-based and faith-based groups themselves or by appropriate, necessary government standards that tend to exclude them? Chapter 4 considers the entire topic of current government partnerships with nongovernmental entities in the four cities under study. It seeks to demonstrate the extent and nature of those partnerships, both financial and nonfinancial, and to marshal evidence relating to whether or not discriminatory practices against community-based and faith-based providers exist.

Public Policy Issue Area 4: Is it possible to construct public-private partnerships without the private entities losing their autonomy? Just as there would be little reason to develop more public-private partnerships if the nongovernmental providers deliver the same services in the same way as are government providers, there would be little reason to do so if government would force all of its partners into the same mold. Again, one would end up with the same services being provided in the same way. As I pointed out earlier, all of the arguments that have been advanced in favor of public-private partnerships rest on the assumption that the nongovernmental entities partnering with government will be able to maintain a measure of autonomy that will result in their preserving distinctive programs. Many fear that with government funding will come a loss of control of the recipient agencies' own programs. Such popular sayings as "He who pays the piper calls the tune" and "With government shekels come government shackles" attest to the existence of such fears. Thus, a crucial issue is whether or not we can construct public-private partnerships that do not result in government dominating the relationships to the extent that the nongovernmental providers lose almost all freedom to construct and run their own programs.

This task is made more difficult by the fact that government has legitimate responsibilities of financial accountability for the money it spends. It also has responsibilities to protect as well as serve those in desperate need of services. How does it—and how can it—meet those responsibilities and yet protect the autonomy of for-profit, nonprofit, community-based, and faith-based providers of welfare-to-work and other social services? A subset of questions comes into play when the nonprofit organizations with which government is entering into a financial partnership are faith-based in nature. Then, one must also consider questions of church-state relations. Added to the government responsibilities just mentioned is the responsibility to make sure that the religious freedom rights of the faith-based providers, the general taxpayer, and the recipient of services—all three—are being respected. Chapter 4 considers—in addition to the issue of the extent and nature of government-private partnerships—the issue of what is being done to protect the autonomy rights of private entities entering into partnerships with government, as well as what government policies are at the same time doing to meet government's public interest responsibilities.

Public Policy Issue Area 5: Are nongovernmental entities more effective in delivering social services? It is often claimed that for-profit, faith-based, and community-based social service programs have higher success rates than do government programs and large, professionalized nonprofit programs. This study, however, does not seek to address the question of whether or not this is in fact the case. Doing so would raise an entire set of methodological issues and concerns that the current study was not designed to meet. Exploration of this issue area must await future studies.

The Study

This book reports a study of welfare-to-work programs in four major American cities: Los Angeles, Chicago, Philadelphia, and Dallas. The study was conducted between March 2001 and early 2002. It utilized a written questionnaire that broadly surveyed welfare-to-work programs in these four cities, as well as in-depth, on-site visits to 51 of the programs. (For more details on the study and how it was conducted see app. A; for a copy of the questionnaire that was used see app. C.) I chose these four cities because of their geographic distribution, large size, and strategic importance. In the case of all four cities, I included welfare-to-work programs in the core city and in the immediate, urban metropolitan area. By including these four cities, I included three of the four cities with the largest TANF (Temporary Assistance for Needy Families) caseloads in the nation (Los Angeles, Chicago, and Philadelphia). Only Dallas is not in the top four.

In this study, I defined the term *welfare-to-work* very broadly to refer to all programs that seek to enable persons to move from welfare dependency to economic self-sufficiency. I am not referring only to the federal Department of Labor's welfare-to-work program, and although TANF recipients made up a large proportion of the welfare recipients receiving services from the programs studied, I made it clear to the participating providers that the study included "programs to assist persons towards economic self-sufficiency" (to quote from the title of the questionnaire used). Health care, transportation, and child care programs were excluded unless they were incorporated into other services aimed directly at assisting persons receiving welfare assistance to acquire the needed education, skills, or attitudes to assist them toward economic self-sufficiency. More specifically, the first question of the questionnaire asked each responding program if it provided any of the following services: job search, education/literacy, education/English as a second language, education/GED preparation, education/vocational training or work skills, work preparedness (job interviewing skills, relating to coworkers, appropriate dress, etc.), life skills training (self-esteem, budgeting, etc.), job placement, job internships/apprenticeships, client assessment, and mentoring. Only programs that offered one or more of these services were included in the study.

The research was conducted in three stages. First, my associate researcher and I compiled lists of all of the welfare-to-work programs in the four target cities. We ended up with a total of 1,559 programs on the list. In the second stage, we mailed out the questionnaires to each of these programs. The questionnaire inquired concerning such information as size, age, expansion plans and desires, sponsoring entity, religious nature and sponsorship (if a faith-based program), government funding, contacts with government, and evaluation of government contacts.

For the questionnaire survey by mail, we followed the total design method described by Don Dillman.[77] This involved an introductory letter, the questionnaire mailing, and two follow-up mailings for those who did not respond initially. Of the 1,559 questionnaires sent out, a total of 582 completed questionnaires were returned (a return rate of 37.3 percent). Of the responding programs, 73 (or 4.7 percent of the total) stated that they in fact were not providing any of the listed welfare-to-work services at that time. This resulted in 509 usable questionnaires. The return rate varied somewhat by city, with Los Angeles and Dallas having the highest return rates, each at 41 percent, followed by Chicago at 36 percent and Philadelphia at 30 percent. This resulted in 200 of the 509 completed questionnaires being from Los Angeles, 133 from Chicago, 94 from Dallas, and 82 from Philadelphia. These return rates, while not outstanding, were at acceptable levels for research of this sort. In addition, as I explain in appendix A, there is strong evidence indicating that the initial list of welfare-to-work programs was in fact a highly accurate list of all welfare-to-work programs in the four cities. Also, based on area or neighborhood, there is evidence that the responding programs did not differ greatly from those not responding (again, see app. A).

The third stage of the research involved on-site visits to 51 of the welfare-to-work programs that responded to the questionnaire. These visits were conducted by either the associate researcher or me. We visited 10 programs in each of the cities of Chicago, Philadelphia, and Dallas and 21 in Los Angeles. Most of the visits lasted for two days, but a few were for only one day, due either to scheduling difficulties or to the programs being so small that one day was sufficient. The associate researcher and I selected the programs for the intensive site visits by first categorizing all of the responding programs in a city according to type—government-run, for-profit, secular nonprofit, faith-based/segmented, and faith-based/integrated programs (for the segmented-integrated distinction see chap. 2). Next, we divided these five program types into large, more professionalized programs and small, less professionalized programs. This yielded ten different program types for each city, and one program was selected from each category, based on several key criteria that indicated they were typical of the programs in each category. More programs were selected for on-site visits from among the Los Angeles providers due to the ease of conducting these visits (we are located in the Los Angeles area) and because of the extremely large, diverse nature of Los Angeles.

During these on-site visits, we interviewed each program's director and other members of the management team, as well as frontline staff members who work directly with the welfare clients.[78] We observed class sessions and other activities that were going on, and when possible, we interviewed some of the clients who were receiving services. We also often obtained written materials such as program descriptions, class handouts, and newsletters. A nonstructured set of issues or questions to be covered served as a guide for these visits, but a maximum amount of flexibility was encouraged in order to take advantage of the specific programs being observed and to allow the visits to flow naturally. We tape-recorded almost all of the interviews, transcribed some, and kept copious notes of all. In addition, we kept a written record of our observations and reactions to what we observed. The goal of these on-site visits was to supplement the information revealed in the completed questionnaires by determining the underlying reasons for the key patterns revealed by the questionnaires and by gaining an in-depth feel for and insight into the nature of the programs. The findings I present in this book make use of both the data garnered by the questionnaire and the insights made possible by the on-site visits. I also quote from the interviews and written materials in order to give greater insight into my conclusions and to illustrate them. In doing so I preserve the anonymity of the programs and the persons quoted due to issues of political sensitivity and client confidentiality.

11 The Providers of Welfare-to-Work Services

Perhaps the most basic unanswered questions plaguing discussions of increasing the use of public-private partnerships to deliver social services involves the number and characteristics of the private entities that are expected to be government's partners. If for-profit and various types of nonprofit organizations are to play new, major roles in the delivery of social services in partnership with government, there must exist nonprofit and for-profit entities able and willing to play the roles projected for them. Yet little is known about the existence, number, variety, capacity, and intent of nongovernmental social service agencies. This chapter seeks to cast new light on these very basic questions.

More specifically, this chapter first presents a categorization of welfare-to-work and other social service programs that appears helpful in light of current calls for greater reliance on public-private partnerships for the delivery of social services. In the next three sections, I consider what existing studies and commentators have found regarding nonprofit social or human service organizations generally, faith-based social service organizations specifically, and, more briefly, for-profit and small, community-based social service agencies. The next four sections of the chapter then present data and insights dealing with the types, numbers, and characteristics of welfare-to-work programs in the four major cities included in my study. In the final section of the chapter, I discuss the public policy implications of the chapter's findings.

A Classification of Social Service Providers

This study is based on a sixfold classification of welfare-to-work programs: (1) government-run programs; (2) for-profit programs; (3) secular nonprofit programs that are large and professionalized; (4) small, secular nonprofit programs that are grassroots or community-based in nature; (5) faith-based programs that keep their religious elements largely separate from the social services they provide; and (6) faith-based programs that tend to integrate religious elements into the social services they provide. I chose these six categories because they reflect many of the distinctions being made in current public policy debates over utilizing public-private partnerships for the delivery of social services. Also, as will be shortly seen, previous research either assumes some of these distinctions or argues for their helpfulness in understanding the world of nongovernmental social service providers. The remainder of this section details these six categories of programs and the rationale for their selection.

Government programs. There are many claims that government programs do not provide social services very well and that nongovernmental entities provide them more efficiently and effectively. Implicit in these claims is the assumption that government agencies and nongovernmental entities provide social services in quite different ways. To explore this claim and others, it is important, for the purposes of analysis and understanding, to keep welfare-to-work programs that are located in and run by government agencies as a separate category from the other program types.

For-profit programs. Given both the claims being made on behalf of for-profit social service programs and the tendency of many analysts to make a basic distinction between the for-profit and nonprofit sectors, it is necessary to keep the for-profit welfare-to-work programs in their own, separate category. To mix for-profit programs in with nonprofit programs on the mere basis that both program types are private, or nongovernmental, in nature would destroy any ability to make comparisons between them. It is often assumed that the profit motive leads for-profit firms to have a different ethos and different patterns of organization and behavior than those of nonprofit agencies, even though observers often vary in the negative or positive evaluations they attach to these differences. By exploring for-profit programs separately, we can explore these assumptions.

Nonprofit, secular, professionalized programs. Once for-profit programs have been established as a separate category for analysis, it logically follows that nonprofit programs would constitute the opposing category. Lester M. Salamon has identified the nonprofit sector as comprised of "organizations that are private, self-governing, non-profit-distributing, voluntary, and of public benefit."[1]

Including all nonprofit welfare-to-work programs in one category, however, would constitute such a large, comprehensive category that comparisons and analyses would be difficult. Also, current public policy debates frequently make claims based on two further distinctions. One of these is the distinction between secular and faith-based organizations. As I noted in the previous chapter, many public policy observers and advocates are calling for greater use of faith-based entities to deliver vital social services. Many claims are being made for the efficacy of faith-based organizations' delivery of social services. The very existence of the White House Office of Faith-Based and Community Initiatives bears witness to the relevance of this distinction. By separating secular and faith-based programs, this study will be able to compare these two program types.

A second distinction often made among nonprofit organizations is between large, highly professionalized nonprofits and small, grassroots nonprofits run by a handful of paid staff and heavily dependent on volunteers and part-time workers. Lester Salamon has taken note of the increasing professionalization of many nonprofit organizations.

> Along with increased visibility and growing demand for their services, nonprofit organizations have become increasingly professionalized. . . . Indeed, between the late 1970s and the mid-1990s, the paid staff of nonprofit organizations has grown at an annual rate that is more than 60 percent higher than that of all nonagricultural employment. . . . In the process, many of these organizations have become quite complex institutions. . . . Not surprisingly, to cope with this increased complexity, nonprofit management has had to become increasingly professional.[2]

A professionalized nonprofit organization is one that employs a full-time, fully credentialed staff, rather then relying heavily on volunteers and on a part-time staff with limited education. Staff members are well-educated professionals providing services in keeping with the latest norms of national credentialing agencies, such as the National Association of Social Workers. Size and professionalization tend to go together, since large size and the increased budgets that go with large size are needed to support full-time, highly trained staffs. Thus, the third category of welfare-to-work programs established for the purposes of this study is that of large nonprofit, secular, professionalized programs. I will refer to them as *nonprofit/secular programs*.

Nonprofit, secular, community-based programs. In contrast to the large, professionalized nonprofit welfare-to-work programs are the small, grassroots or community-based nonprofit programs. Elizabeth Boris has stated that most nonprofit organizations are of this type: "The nonprofit sector, however, is composed overwhelmingly of small, community-based entities with meager resources. . . . [M]ost have modest budgets, use only volunteer labor, and operate locally."[3] While Salamon noted the increasing professionalization of nonprofit organizations, he also noted a reinvigoration of grassroots groups: "While the nonprofit sector has grown increasingly professional, there is also evidence of continued vitality in the grass-roots base of the sector throughout the country."[4] Community-based programs have more volunteers and fewer full-time, paid staff than the large, professionalized nonprofits. The paid staff they have often has a limited education and does not possess professional credentials to the same degree as does the staff of professionalized nonprofits.

The importance of making this distinction between large, professionalized and small, community-based nonprofits lies in the public policy claim that the large, professionalized nonprofits suffer many of the same problems that large government agencies experience: inflexibility, a lack of creativity and innovation, and attempts to apply theoretical approaches that are out of touch with street-level realities.[5] In contrast, it is often argued that the small, community-based nonprofits tend to possess attributes that make them more effective: flexibility, caring attitudes, and a closeness to the people being served. President George W. Bush's creation of a White House Office of

Faith-Based *and Community* Initiatives (emphasis added) stands as witness to the importance, in public policy thinking, of the distinction between large, professionalized nonprofits and small, community-based nonprofits. It is important that this study reflects this general distinction and seeks to test some of the claims and more specific distinctions being made. Thus, the fourth category of welfare-to-work programs established for the purposes of this study consists of small, grassroots, community-based, secular nonprofit programs. I will refer to them as *community-based programs*.[6]

Faith-based, segmented programs. The welfare-to-work programs included in this category are those with a religious orientation, character, or background. In that sense, this category includes programs that are a mirror opposite of the two previous categories, which include only nonprofit programs without a religious component or orientation. It is important to separate out secular and faith-based programs, due to the current public policy debates over the present and potential role faith-based social service providers can and ought to play in meeting the public's social service needs.

An additional distinction—one between two different types of faith-based welfare-to-work programs—is also crucial. This distinction is based on whether the religious elements present in the program are explicit and interwoven, or integrated, into the services being provided or are largely implicit (i.e., in the background and unarticulated) and clearly separate from the services being provided. If the religious elements are implicit and clearly separate from the welfare-to-work services, the faith-based program should be considered segmented. I will refer to this fifth category of programs as *faith-based/segmented programs*.

Faith-based, integrated programs. Distinct from faith-based programs in which the religious elements are implicit and separate from the welfare-to-work services offered are faith-based programs in which the religious elements are explicit and integrated into the services provided. I am here referring to programs that have also sometimes been called *holistic programs*. Ronald Sider and Heidi Unruh have defined *holistic providers* as those "who combine techniques from the medical and social sciences with inherently religious components such as prayer, worship, and the study of sacred texts."[7] Such programs constitute what I call *faith-based/integrated programs*.[8] They form the sixth and final category of welfare-to-work programs.

The distinction between faith-based/segmented and faith-based/integrated programs is important, since much of the current debate surrounding the use of faith-based organizations to deliver public social services revolves, first, around questions of the relative effectiveness of the these two different types of faith-based programs and, second, around questions of the appropriateness and value of government partnering with these two different program types. There are two issues here. One is the claim that faith-based social service programs are more successful precisely because of an explicit religious or faith element. If this is the case, it is important to look separately at faith-based programs that integrate religion into the services they provide, as opposed to faith-based programs that keep faith elements in the background and separate from their social services. The other issue is one of religious freedom and First Amendment requirements. Some persons have claimed—and some past Supreme Court decisions seem to support—that government funds may not go to support programs with a pervasively religious character. Thus, faith-based/integrated programs and faith-based/segmented programs raise different questions regarding religious freedom and the First Amendment.

Current Research Findings: The Nonprofit Sector

This section and the two that immediately follow briefly survey current research findings regarding, first, the nonprofit sector generally; second, the faith-based nonprofit sector; and finally, community-based and for-profit social services entities. As will shortly be seen, research in some of these areas is spotty and incomplete. There is, however, a plethora of persuasive evidence documenting a large and growing nonprofit sector in the social services field—this much is clear. Lester Salamon has estimated that as of the mid-1990s, there were 66,000 nonprofit social service agencies in the United States.[9] In addition, he estimated that there were 1.2 million persons employed by nonprofit social service agencies. This constituted 55 percent of all social service employees, compared to 22 percent employed by for-profit firms and 23 percent by government agencies.[10]

Many additional studies could be cited to illustrate the large size of the nonprofit social service sector. For example, a national study of assistance programs for the homeless found that 79 percent of the 40,000 programs studied were run by nonprofits, with only 13 percent run by government agencies and with a miniscule 0.6 percent run by for-profit firms.[11] To take another example, in New York City, 70 percent of the children in foster care are served by nonprofit agencies.[12] Wisconsin nonprofits have successfully competed for contracts to provide welfare caseload services under that state's rigorous performance-based rules. Seventy percent of Wisconsin's TANF caseload services is being provided by either nonprofit or for-profit entities.[13] No one can doubt the size and importance of the nonprofit sector in the social services field.

It is also clear that the nonprofit sector is growing, and it is growing especially rapidly in the social services area. Eric Twombly of the Urban Institute has documented that the "nonprofit sector grew dramatically from 1992 to 1996" and that "growth among nonprofit human service providers outpaced growth in the remainder of the nonprofit sector, particularly in urban areas."[14] He charted 53 major metropolitan areas and found that the number of nonprofit human service agencies increased by an average of 41 percent from 1992 to 1996, from an average of 220 to an average of 310.[15] Among the four cities that were studied in the research reported in the present book, Twombly reported that Los Angeles experienced a 58 percent increase, from 855 to 1,353; Dallas a 43 percent increase, from 263 to 375; and Chicago a 39 percent increase, from 810 to 1,124 (Philadelphia was not included in Twombly's study).[16] In short, a key segment of the nonprofit sector included in Twombly's study—nonprofit social service agencies in large metropolitan areas—was experiencing rapid growth just prior to the study on which I report in this book.

Another noteworthy aspect of the nonprofit sector as it relates to the social services field is the extent to which there already are government partnerships with nonprofit organizations. As Peter Frumkin has stressed, "the nonprofit sector had become by the late 1970s the principal vehicle for the delivery of government financed human services."[17] Mark Carl Rom cites a General Accounting Office study to conclude, "Federal, state, and local governments are all creating public-private partnerships . . . to operate social welfare functions; as measured by the numbers of partnerships, services, and dollars, these efforts are growing."[18] In the area of research reported in the present book, Rom reports: "federal government has sponsored many employment and training programs, and most of these programs have used private agencies to deliver services. In fact, since the 1960s, more federally funded employment and training services have been contracted out than not. . . . Most of the contractors for these programs have been nonprofit or public organizations."[19] Although systematically gathered statistics are often lacking, enough is known to conclude that the field explored in this book is rich in government partnerships with nonprofit agencies.

All of the studies just cited help to demonstrate that nonprofit social service organizations have the capacity to take on the provision of a large amount of the nation's social services. Here, capacity is conceptualized as the size needed to handle large numbers of persons in need of services, as well as the skills and experience needed to compete for and manage government contracts and grants. The evidence indicates that the nonprofit sector possesses the necessary capacity in both senses.

All that has been said so far refers to nonprofit social service programs as a whole, however. I have not taken into account distinctions between faith-based and secular nonprofits and large, professionalized and community-based nonprofits. The next two sections consider these distinctions.

Current Research Findings: Faith-Based Organizations

Up until about ten years ago, little attention was paid to the fact that much of the nonprofit sector consisted of organizations with a religious affiliation or orientation. Thomas Jeavons wrote in 1994, "It is important to note, however, that as interest in the independent sector and nonprofit organizations has been increasing, attention on the part of scholars to the religious roots of the sector and to religious organizations has been almost nonexistent."[20] In 1990, Peter Dobkin Hall commented, "Quite clearly, the scholarship of philanthropy has given religion remarkably short shrift."[21] All that is changing, however.

Researcher after researcher is now discussing the presence and implications of large numbers of faith-based organizations within the non-profit sector. Much of the new interest in faith-based organizations—and especially religious congregations—in their role as providers of social services was stimulated by an early study by Virginia Hodgkinson and her colleagues.[22] This study showed that a large majority of religious congregations had human service or welfare programs; made their facilities available to community groups; provided in-kind assistance, such as food and clothing, to the needy; and donated money to charitable organizations. Salamon's analysis shows that 61 percent of all individual charitable contributions go to religious organizations, as do 43 percent of all volunteer hours.[23]

Many different studies have gathered evidence of faith-based groups' active involvement in the provision of social services. For example, in a study of programs assisting the homeless, Laudan Aron and Patrick Sharkey found that as of 1996, faith-based organizations ran 32 percent of all the homeless programs and 41 percent of the non-profit homeless programs.[24] Ram Cnaan, after an extensive review of existing studies, concluded, "The role of the religious community in the provision of social services is enormous and secondary only to that of government."[25] His own survey of religious congregations in Philadelphia demonstrated the following:

> . . . religious organizations represent a major part of the American welfare system. Tens of thousands of people in the Philadelphia area are being helped by all kinds of programs, from soup kitchens to housing services, from job training to educational enhancement classes. One can only imagine what would happen to the collective quality of life if these religious organizations would cease to exist. . . . It is obvious that our public system depends on the complementary existence of a religious-based welfare system that enables the public sector to provide limited assistance without public outcry.[26]

Peter Dobkin Hall has found that "the fastest growing segment of charitable tax-exempt organizations in the past half-century are religious congregations (usually theologically conservative, non-denominational bodies) and religiously-tied human service providers."[27] Salamon summarizes: "Indeed, religious institutions are near the epicenter of American philanthropy. . . . [N]o account of the U.S. nonprofit sector would therefore be complete without some attention to the religious institutions the sector also contains."[28]

Two important questions remain unanswered, however. One of these questions is rooted in a distinction often not made: that between religious congregations and faith-based organizations legally separate from any congregation or association of congregations. Much of the research on faith-based groups has focused on religious congregations—not on nonprofit organizations legally independent from religious congregations but affiliated with or closely tied to a particular congregation, group of congregations, or faith tradition.[29] Such organizations are usually organized as 501(c)(3) nonprofit entities.

There are numerous, sophisticated, well-researched studies of religious congregations but very few sophisticated studies that focus on nonprofit faith-based organizations that are legally incorporated separately from congregations. Thus, there is much that we simply do not know about the latter. Even worse, some of the research and public policy discussions surrounding faith-based organizations as deliverers of social services fail to make this crucial distinction. At times, some researchers compound the confusion by not clearly distinguishing between religious congregations and religiously based groups that are legally separate and distinct from a congregation. Two observers, for example, seem to be using the terms *religious group* and *congregation* interchangeably in the following quotation: "The intrusion of government auditors into a religious group's financial affairs also poses concerns. If a congregation commingles its funds with government funds, the government would have the right to review all financial records."[30]

There are many faith-based social service programs run not by congregations or associations of congregations but by legally independent, separately organized entities. For example, based on a study of community development corporations, Avis Vidal reported that "the most common way for congregations to enter community development on their own is to establish and spin off an affiliated nonprofit organization—typically a CDC."[31] If only congregation-run services would be studied, major groups, such as Catholic Charities, would be left out, as would large faith-based organizations that are well known in their communities, such as the West Angeles Community Development Corporation in Los Angeles, Central Dallas Ministries in Dallas, Bethel True Life in Chicago, and Nueva Esperanza in Philadelphia. The latter four organizations are large, well-established, multiservice faith-based organizations that I encountered in my study of welfare-to-work programs in these four cities; yet none would be included in studies focusing on actual congregations and excluding independent faith-based social service organizations. Persuasive evidence points to the fact that the latter indeed play a significant role in certain social service areas. One analysis of parachurch organizations—that is, religiously based organizations that are legally separate from any denomination or local church—has pointed out, "Studies now suggest that almost half of the giving to religion is going to parachurch organizations, not to the traditional local churches or denominations."[32] John Green and Amy Sherman studied 389 faith-based programs (in 15 states) that had received government funding under one or more of the programs to which charitable choice provisions apply. They found that only 22 percent of the programs receiving government dollars were religious congregations, while 78 percent were faith-based, nonprofit organizations.[33] Ram Cnaan lists and describes 33 noncongregational faith-based organizations active in providing social services in Philadelphia.[34] Salamon cites a study that puts the number of faith-based charities registered with the Internal Revenue Service at 10,000 and that further estimates there may very well be an additional 2,500 that are not registered with the IRS.[35]

The distinction between social service programs run directly by religious congregations themselves and those run by religiously based or affiliated organizations legally independent from religious congregations is important. It is often assumed that the former are more likely to have religious elements integrated into them than are the latter. This, in turn, has implications for government funding of these programs. The observation Senator Joe Lieberman made in a 2001 speech is typical: "Traditionally, faith-based charities that receive federal funds to provide social services have had to set up separate nonprofits that were free of any religious involvement."[36] But this observation can be questioned. A previous study of mine demonstrated that many faith-based family and child care agencies, international aid and relief organizations, and colleges and universities were deeply religious in their programming even when taking the form of legally separate nonprofit entities. Many of these received government funds. I found, for example, that of the faith-based child service agencies that were most integrally religious, 67 percent received government funding.[37] In their study, Green and Sherman found that of the faith-based programs organizationally independent of a congregation, 40 percent in some way explicitly brought religion into their programming.[38] Thus, a key question to be explored is whether or not welfare-to-work programs run directly by religious congregations differ from those run by legally separate nonprofit entities and, in particular, whether or not the former are more integrally religious than the latter.

A second unanswered question relates to the capacity of faith-based programs. Some researchers have questioned the capacity of faith-based social service providers to meet a significant portion of society's social service needs. A number of studies of congregations' social service ministries have noted their very small size and limited nature. They reported that most congregation-based social service ministries are limited to short-term services, such as emergency clothing or food, and are very small in size. As Carol De Vita has noted, several studies have found that congregations with social service programs often have no paid staff or an average of only one paid staff member and a median budget in the $5,000 to $15,000 range.[39] Mark Chaves, based on a national study of congregations, has reached similar conclusions, namely, that most congregations involved in social services provide fairly limited services, such as food pantries or clothing closets, and that even those programs are small in nature. He found that 11 percent of a national sample of congregations "have clothing projects, 18 percent have housing/shelter projects and 33 percent have food-related projects." But he went on to point out that fewer than 10 percent of the congregations had programs that involved longer-term, more intensive contacts with recipients: "Programs that appear to involve only short-term or fleeting kinds of contacts with the needy are far more common among congregations than programs that involve more intensive or long-term, face-to-face interactions."[40] Concerning community development corporations, another researcher found, "On average, the faith-based groups are younger and smaller than their secular counterparts, appear to have significantly smaller full-time staffs, and are more than twice as likely to have annual operating budgets of less than $500,000."[41] De Vita, after surveying a number of studies of religious congregations in several different areas of the country, concluded, "Nearly all of the congregations in these studies offer some type of community outreach program or social ministry." But then she went on to point out, "Most of these community programs relied on volunteers and operated on very small budgets."[42]

As I noted earlier, in addition to size, capacity includes whether or not a provider has the level of sophistication, experience, and skills needed to partner successfully with government. Concerning the ability of faith-based groups to compete for government funds, two researchers have commented:

> Many religious leaders worry that the majority of faith-based groups lack adequate infrastructure and experience to meet government funding requirements. . . . In many instances, these organizations do not have the capacity to identify funding opportunities, write proposals, manage multiple funding streams, report their activities to funders, and deliver their social service programs. Capacity issues can be particularly acute in lower-income neighborhoods.[43]

Arthur Farnsley offers some empirical evidence on the capacity of churches and other faith-based groups to compete for government contracts. In a study of grant applications for a summer employment program in Indianapolis, he found that 11 percent of the applications from faith-based groups fell into the categories of poor quality or very poor quality and that 69 percent fell into the high-quality category. Among the secular organizations, none of their applications fell into one of the poor-quality categories, while 86 percent fell into the high-quality category.[44] This study shows that although the large majority of the faith-based applicants were able to put together strong, high-quality applications, an even higher percentage of the secular applicants were able to do so. In brief, the capacity of faith-based organizations, defined in terms of both size and needed skills and experience, remains an open question in need of further exploration.

But this is not the entire story. Most of the research cited in discussions of faith-based organizations' capacity studied only religious congregations, not faith-based organizations that operate separately from religious congregations. As seen earlier, the latter are numerous and need to be taken into account to have a complete picture. This conclusion is reinforced by studies that have found that social programs run by faith-based organizations independent of congregations differ markedly from those run directly by religious congregations. Green and Sherman, in their study cited earlier, found that the programs run by faith-based organizations were larger, with 73 percent of them having more than 100 clients, compared to only 31 percent for the congregation-run programs. Faith-based organizations also ran programs that involved more extensive contacts with clients than did congregations (57 percent of the faith-based organizations had programs involving extensive contacts with clients, compared to only 32 percent of the congregation-run programs). Green and Sherman also found that the faith-based organizations were more broadly involved in antipoverty efforts, with 65 percent of the faith-based organizations involved in at least five of six listed antipoverty activities, compared to 48 percent of the congregation-run programs.[45] In judging capacity, faith-based organizations that are organizationally separate from religious congregations clearly need to be distinguished from religious congregations and the programs they run directly.

Even when programs run by religious congregations are being considered, one must be careful not to assume that because only a small percentage of congregations offer a certain service, their cumulative impact is equally small. As Chaves has written, "A small percentage of active congregations does not imply trivial absolute levels of contribution."[46] Given the extremely large number of religious congregations in the United States, even when only a small percentage of congregations is providing a certain service, this can still add up to tens of thousands of congregations. For example, Chaves reported that less than 10 percent of the religious congregations in his national study reported engaging in intensive social services, such as substance abuse, mentoring, or job training. But if one would extrapolate that to the estimated 350,000 congregations in the United States,[47] one ends up with an impressive number of congregations—some 35,000—sponsoring such services. De Vita cites a study in which "only" 12 percent of Michigan United Methodist churches was interested in expanding services to welfare recipients.[48] Yet if one projects this onto all congregations in the United States, there would be 42,000 congregations interested in expanding services to welfare recipients. Similarly, Cnaan reports that "only" 29 percent of the 24 churches he studied in Philadelphia had programs for single parents.[49] Extrapolate that onto the 350,000 religious congregations in the nation, and one finds 101,500 congregations interested in providing services to single parents. My point is not that one can confidently extrapolate percentages from such small samples onto the nation as a whole. Rather, it is that even when only a minority of congregations is providing a certain social service, one cannot safely assume that the potential collective impact of congregations providing that service is inconsequential.

Nevertheless, when all is said and done, one cannot disagree with De Vita when she writes, "Whether local congregations have the capacity or desire to increase their level of involvement, however, is still largely untested."[50] Even when studies include faith-based organizations legally separate from religious congregations, many questions remain.

Current Research Findings: For-Profit and Community-Based Providers

There are a large number of studies dealing with both the nonprofit sector generally and faith-based organizations more specifically. But there is an almost total lack of studies to call on in the case of for-profit and small, community-based providers of social services. This section reports on what is known, but the findings and conclusions that previous research presents are thin.

First, in regard to for-profit providers, though for-profit firms have been active in providing social services for some time, it appears that they have only begun to do so in any real numbers in recent years. Even this conclusion, however, is based more on case studies and general impressions than on any systematic studies. For example, Rom pointed out that since the passage of the Personal Responsibility and Work Opportunity Reconciliation Act (PRWORA) in 1996, states have been allowed and even encouraged to contract out virtually their entire welfare programs. He concluded, "As a result, large for-profit companies (such as Ross Perot's former company, EDS; Lockheed Martin; and IBM) have entered the welfare market with a marked enthusiasm for helping the poor."[51] He went on to point out that Curtis and Associates had a contract worth $9 million in one Wisconsin city alone and that in late 1998, another for-profit firm providing welfare services, Maximus, had 3,000 employees and $140 million in revenues.[52] Kirsten Grønbjerg argues that there has been a revolution in the human services field since the early 1960s and that a part of this revolution is the "broad array of service provider types—public, nonprofit, for-profit, and individual providers—[that] have emerged."[53] Yet she is forced to concede: "The overall financial profile of the for-profit human service sector is not known. . . . Most likely, their access to government funding has increased over the past decade or so."[54] Salamon has reported that as of the early 1990s, 30 percent of the private job training organizations were for-profit in nature.[55] For-profit firms are apparently playing an increasingly important role in the human services field, including, since the 1996 passage of PRWORA, in the welfare field. As Grønbjerg writes, "Human services are now increasingly characterized by tri-sector relationships that include for-profit providers."[56] But there is insufficient research of a systematic nature to say much more than this. There is enough research to conclude that any study of the welfare-to-work field needs to include for-profit firms if it is to be complete.

There is a similar lack of good, systematic research in the case of small, community-based human service providers. David Horton Smith has pointed out: "[the] relative research inattention by scholars makes grassroots associations the main dark matter of the NPS [nonprofit sector]. Many researchers in our field cannot seem to see them, to note their existence, numbers, and effects."[57] Part of the problem is that nonprofit associations with incomes of less than $25,000 a year do not need to register with the Internal Revenue Service, yet many studies of nonprofits use IRS figures to estimate the number and types of nonprofits in the United States. By this methodology, these studies miss most of the grassroots, community-based nonprofit organizations. Smith goes on to estimate, based on a number of previous studies, that there are "many millions" of small, grassroots nonprofits in the United States. His specific estimates of the number of nonprofit organizations range from 7.5 to 9.5 million total nonprofits, with about 1.4 million being larger, IRS-registered profits. This leaves 6 to 8 million grassroots, community-based nonprofits.[58] Whatever the actual number, clearly it is extremely large—reaching into the millions. How many of these are social service nonprofits and how many of the social service nonprofits are engaged in welfare-to-work activities are, to my knowledge, questions that have not been researched. However, based on the large number of community-based nonprofits active in communities across the nation, one must assume there are a goodly number.

A number of writers have looked to community-based programs as providers of flexible, innovative, empathetic services. Robert Woodson, for example, has contrasted "conventional professional programs with those of grass-roots initiatives" and believes the latter to be more effective.[59] The expectation is that those programs that are truly grassroots in nature will, first, lack the bureaucratic regulations that inhibit creativity and change and, second, have close ties to the communities in which they are located. These close ties will result in staff members "who live within the same zip codes as the people they serve,"[60] in a large number of part-time and volunteer staff members, and in some staff members who at one time were recipients of the services being offered.

The question of how many nonprofit social service agencies fit this sort of a profile of community-based providers remains unanswered. I know of no systematic study that has even attempted to operationalize this concept or that has gone into the field to find out the numbers, capacity, and nature of community-based nonprofit organizations. Certainly there is room to raise capacity questions, as there is in the case of faith-based providers. Community-based organizations may be close to the people they serve, and they may have an empathy that larger organizations lack. But do they exist in sufficient numbers and size that, collectively, they can make a notable impact on persistent social ills with which public policy is seeking to deal? Moreover, do they have the experience, skill, and resources needed to play in the arena of government contracts and grants? Current research casts almost no light on these questions, but they will be explored in the study reported in this book.

The Six Program Types

This section begins the reporting of the findings of the study of welfare-to-work programs in four cities. Here, I focus on dividing the 509 welfare-to-work providers included in the study into the six basic categories outlined earlier in this chapter. The questionnaire used in the study asked each of the responding programs to indicate whether it was a public, government program; a private, for-profit program; a private, nonprofit program with no religious base or history; a private, nonprofit program that "at one time had a religious orientation, but today has evolved into a program that is largely secular in nature"; or a private, nonprofit program "that continues to have a clear religious base and orientation" (see app. C, Q9). I chose to rely on the organizations' self-identification for this basic categorization, because other studies have demonstrated the reliability of self-identification and the difficulties and uncertainties inherent in trying to categorize organizations based on factors such as organizational structure, sources of funding, and mission statements.[61] In response to this question, 125 of the welfare-to-work programs identified themselves as government programs, 26 as for-profit programs, 173 as nonprofit programs with no religious base or history, 53 as nonprofit programs that once had been religious but now are secular, and 123 as religious or faith-based nonprofit programs. Nine programs did not identify themselves as falling into one of these five categories. It is important to note that, here and elsewhere, the study asked for information about the welfare-to-work *programs,* not the entire organizations running the programs, some of which sponsored additional, non–welfare-to-work programs.

For purposes of analysis, I began by combining the nonprofit programs that indicated they had never been religious with those that said they once had been religious but now were "largely secular in nature." I did so on the basis that all share the common characteristics of being nonprofit entities and being largely or completely nonreligious or secular in nature. The reason I included on the questionnaire the option for a program to identify itself as once religious but now secular was to discourage organizations that were now secular, but had been religious in the past, from selecting the religious option. Clearly, they belong in the secular camp, even though they had a religious orientation earlier in their history. This resulted in a total of 226 secular nonprofit welfare-to-work programs in the four cities.

As I noted earlier in this chapter, it was important to divide the secular, nonprofit programs into small, community-based programs and large, more professionalized programs. I did so on the basis of the total number of full-time employees, the percentage of full-time workers out of the total workforce (i.e., the percentage of full-time employees out of all full- and part-time employees and volunteers), and the educational levels of the employees. To qualify as community-based, a program had to be marked by two of the following three criteria: there had to be six or fewer full-time employees,[62] full-time employees had to make up less than one-half the program's total workforce, and the average employee education level had to be lower than having had some college classes. (See app. B for an exact account of how the distinction between community-based and nonprofit/secular programs was made.) Based on these criteria, I found that 139 of the programs fell into the nonprofit/secular category and 83 into the community-based category.

Next, I subdivided the faith-based programs into those that integrate certain religious elements into the welfare-related services they provide and those that largely keep any religious elements separate from their welfare-related services. This was done based on the number and types of religiously inspired practices in which the faith-based programs indicated they engaged, in response to a laundry list of religiously inspired practices that was included in the questionnaire (app. C, Q11; see table 4 later in this chapter). Practices that implied a more integrative commitment, such as "using religious values or motivations to encourage clients to change attitudes or values" and "giving preference in hiring staff to persons in agreement with your religious orientation," were weighted more heavily than less integrative practices, such as "using religious values as a guiding motivation for staff in delivering services" and "placing religious symbols or pictures in the facility where your program is held." (See app. B for an exact account of how the distinction between segmented and integrated programs was made.) Seventy-two programs fell into the faith-based/segmented category and 48 into the faith-based/integrated category.

The number of programs that fell into each of the six categories of programs is given in table 1.[63] Two patterns are immediately clear from this table. First, the number of nonprofit welfare-to-work programs in the four cities that responded to the questionnaire by far outnumber the government programs (342—when one combines the two secular and two faith-based categories—to 125) and the for-profit programs (342 to 26).[64] Any understanding of the welfare-to-work efforts in all four of the cities needs to take into account the huge contribution being made by nonprofit agencies and their programs.

Second, among the nonprofit programs, the larger, more professionalized programs outnumber the community-based programs—139 to 83. However, many community-based programs were distinguishable from the larger, more professionalized nonprofit welfare-to-work programs. In fact, 16.8 percent of all welfare-to-work programs studied were secular and community-based in nature. Table 2 demonstrates that the measure I used to distinguish between the larger, more professionalized and the smaller, less professionalized programs was successful in making this distinction.[65] As measured by the number of full-time employees, the nonprofit/secular programs were much larger, with a median of 15 full-time employees versus only 3. Also, they were marked by sharp differences in the median percentage of full-time workers that make up their entire workforce. The median

TABLE 1. Types of Welfare-to-Work Programs

Program Type	N	Percentage of Total
Government	125	25.4
For-profit	26	5.3
Nonprofit/secular	139	28.2
Community-based	83	16.8
Faith-based/segmented	72	14.6
Faith-based/integrated	48	9.7
Total	493	100.0

workforce of the nonprofit/secular programs was made up of nearly 75 percent full-time workers, while the median workforce of the community-based programs was made up of only 17.4 percent full-time workers. In other words, the community-based programs relied much more heavily on part-time and volunteer workers than did the nonprofit/secular programs. This indicates that the latter tended toward greater professionalization.

Somewhat surprisingly, there were almost no differences in the median and mean educational levels of the employees of the two program types. The median educational level of the nonprofit/secular programs was only slightly higher than that of the community-based programs (see table 2), and the mean educational levels of the community-based and nonprofit/secular programs was an identical 3.4 (with 3 representing the "some college" level and 4 the "college graduate" level). Table 3, however, demonstrates that when considering all of the individual employees of the two different types of providers, not the mean educational levels of the providers, there were significant differences in educational levels between the two groups. In other words, the educational levels in table 2 are based on the median of the programs' mean educational levels (thus, all the *programs* are weighted equally); table 3 is based on the educational levels of all of the individual employees of the two different program types (thus, all of the *employees* are weighted equally). A majority of the nonprofit/secular employees had at least a college degree, while this was true of only a little more than one-third of the employees of the community-based providers.

TABLE 2. Nonprofit/Secular versus Community-Based Programs

Program Type	Median Number of Full-Time Employees	N	Median Percentage of Full-Time Employees in Workforce[a]	N	Median Educational Level[b]	N
Nonprofit/secular	15.0	135	74.8	128	3.4	131
Community-based	3.0	83	17.4	82	3.2	73

[a]Median percentage of full-time employees out of all workers (full-time, part-time, and volunteer).

[b]To find these figures, I first found the mean educational level for each program's full- and part-time employees and then found the median of the educational means for all of the nonprofit/secular programs and all of the community-based programs, using the following scale: 1 = less than high school, 2 = high school graduate, 3 = some college, 4 = college graduate, and 5 = a graduate degree.

The differences between the educational findings reported in tables 2 and 3 can be explained by the fact that among the community-based programs were a number of very small agencies with only one or two employees, often highly educated, thereby raising the median and mean educational levels of the community-based providers. There were seven community-based programs with only one employee, and five of these employees had at least a college degree (one had a graduate degree). Such programs tended to raise the median and mean educational levels of the community-based programs, even while the overall educational level of workers in the community-based programs was lower than that of workers in the larger nonprofit/secular programs.

The bottom line is that the measure I developed to distinguish between nonprofit/secular and community-based programs was successful in identifying programs with clear differences between them. Compared to the nonprofit/secular programs, the community-based programs were indeed much smaller. They were also less professionalized, as measured both by the percentage of their full-time employees out of their total program staffs and by their employees' educational attainment. At least in the welfare-to-work area, the emphasis of the Bush administration and Congress on including community-based groups in governmental funding schemes is targeting an identifiable subset of programs that are providing services in their communities.

Of all the welfare-to-work programs, 24 percent were faith-based in nature. This means there were indeed many faith-based welfare-to-work programs; in fact, almost as many faith-based programs as government-run programs responded to the questionnaire. As with community-based programs, in the welfare-to-work field in the four major

TABLE 3. Educational Levels, Nonprofit/Secular versus Community-Based Programs

Program Type	High School or Less (%)	Some College (%)	College Graduate (%)	Graduate Degree (%)	Total N^a	%
Nonprofit/secular	26.1	17.2	43.5	13.2	4,980	100
Community-based	41.2	24.1	24.9	9.8	884	100

[a]Total number of full- and part-time workers employed by all of the nonprofit/secular or community-based programs.

$\chi^2 (3) = 149.97, p < .001$.

metropolitan areas studied, the Bush administration's efforts to include faith-based groups in governmental funding schemes is focusing on an identifiable group of programs that are actively providing services in their communities.

It is also important to note that of the faith-based programs, 40 percent fell into the "integrated" category—that is, programs that take a holistic approach that integrates explicit religious elements and values into the services provided. That the segmented and integrated faith-based programs truly differ in the degree to which religious elements were integrated into their programming can be seen from table 4,[66] where the questionnaire's laundry list of 10 possible faith-based practices, plus an eleventh, "other" category, is given along with the percentages of the two types of faith-based providers that indicated they engage in each of these practices. Religious art, prayer, voluntary religious exercises, use of religious values to influence clients, and urging clients to make religious commitments were all common among the faith-based/integrated programs, but not among the faith-based/segmented programs. In addition, in response to questions of whether they either gave preference in hiring staff or only hired staff in religious agreement with the organization, a sizable 56.3 percent of the faith-based/integrated programs stated they did one or the other, com-

TABLE 4. Religiously Based Practices, Faith-Based/Segmented versus Faith-Based/Integrated Programs (in percentages)

Religiously Based Practice	Faith-Based/ Segmented ($N = 72$)	Faith-Based/ Integrated ($N = 48$)
Religious symbols or pictures in facility	29.2	50.0
Opening or closing sessions with prayer	16.7	79.2
Using religious values in motivating staff	66.7	87.5
Voluntary religious exercises, such as worship or Bible studies	25.0	60.4
Required religious exercises, such as worship or Bible studies	0.0	25.0
Using religious values to encourage clients to change attitudes	37.5	95.8
Encouraging clients to make personal religious commitments	5.6	64.6
Giving preference in hiring staff to persons in religious agreement[a]	6.9	33.3
Only hiring staff in religious agreement[a]	2.8	29.2
Giving preference to clients in religious agreement	1.4	2.1
Other religiously based practices	16.7	14.6

[a]If one takes the percentage of programs that either give preference in hiring or only hire persons in religious agreement, 56.3% of the faith-based/segmented programs and 9.7% of the faith-based/integrated programs indicated they do one or the other.

pared to only 9.7 percent of the faith-based/segmented programs. There currently is debate on whether or not holistic programs should qualify for government funding. Whatever position one takes on this issue, these data show it is not a trivial question, since many of the faith-based welfare-to-work programs fall into this holistic, or "integrated," category. They truly seek to integrate religious aspects into the services they provide. Someone attending a faith-based/integrated welfare-to-work program will know he or she is in a faith-based program.

Tables 5 and 6 expand on tables 2 and 3 to include all six program types, instead of including only the nonprofit/secular and community-based programs. They reveal a clear division in terms of size and professionalism (as operationalized in this study). Table 5 dramatically shows that there is a very basic divide in terms of the programs' number of full-time employees and the percentage of the programs' workforces that were made up of full-time employees. The government, for-profit, and nonprofit/secular programs were much larger and had much higher percentages of their workforces composed of full-time employees than was the case with the community-based, faith-based/segmented, and faith-based/integrated programs. In terms of educational levels of the employees, the picture is much more mixed. Table 5 shows there were no clear differences in the median education

TABLE 5. Employees, by Program Type

Program Type	Median Number of Full-Time Employees	N	Median Percentage of Full-Time Employees in Workforce[a]	N	Median Educational Level[b]	N
Government	10.5	112	64.1	103	3.4	104
For-profit	15.0	25	75.6	22	3.3	22
Nonprofit/secular	15.0	135	74.8	128	3.4	131
Community-based	3.0	83	17.4	82	3.2	73
Faith-based/segmented	3.0	67	15.6	65	3.5	47
Faith-based/integrated	3.5	48	13.4	47	3.3	39

[a]Median percentage of full-time employees out of all workers (full-time, part-time, and volunteer).
[b]To find these figures, I first found the mean educational level for each program's full- and part-time employees and then found the median of the educational means for all of the programs in each of the six program types, using the following scale: 1 = less than high school, 2 = high school graduate, 3 = some college, 4 = college graduate, and 5 = a graduate degree.

levels of the programs' paid staffs. Table 6, however, shows that the employees of the two types of faith-based programs and the community-based programs had similar, relatively low educational levels. The for-profit programs' employees, though, were very close to the community-based and faith-based programs in educational levels. The government and nonprofit/secular programs were the highest in terms of their employees' education. This is somewhat surprising, since by many other measures, the for-profit programs were similar to the government and the nonprofit-secular programs and dissimilar from the community-based programs and the two types of faith-based programs. Perhaps for-profit programs attempt to save on costs by hiring less highly educated staff than do government and nonprofit/secular programs. Also, for-profits tend to hire previous clients of their programs to work on their staffs. They reported that 20 percent of their current full-time and part-time employees were previous clients of their programs, a higher percentage than that of any other type of program. There may be both programmatic and cost-savings motivations for this latter tendency.

The key conclusion to reach from these comparisons is that by a number of measures, the six program types fell into two camps, with the government, for-profit, and nonprofit/secular programs in one camp and the community-based, faith-based/segmented, and faith-based/integrated in another. This conclusion adds support to the claim by the Bush administration that it makes sense to have a White House office that pays special attention to the needs of both faith-based and community-based social service groups. In a number of basic charac-

TABLE 6. Employee Educational Levels, by Program Type

Program Type	High School or Less (%)	Some College (%)	College Graduate (%)	Graduate Degree (%)	Total N[a]	%
Government[b]	30.8	22.3	38.9	8.1	6,221	100.1
For-profit	40.8	21.9	28.6	8.8	868	100.1
Nonprofit/secular	26.1	17.2	43.5	13.2	4,980	100.0
Community-based	41.2	24.1	24.9	9.8	884	100.0
Faith-based/segmented	45.0	18.0	25.2	11.8	846	100.0
Faith-based/integrated	37.4	22.9	29.4	10.2	489	99.9

[a]Total number of full- and part-time workers employed by the programs.
[b]One extreme outlier that apparently misinterpreted the educational level question was eliminated from these calculations.

teristics, these groups are very similar and thus could be presumed to face similar problems in efforts to win government grants or to compete for government contracts.

Additional Program Characteristics

Several additional characteristics are helpful in promoting an understanding of the differing natures of the six program types. One is the differing percentages of the programs that are anchored in either the African American or the Latino communities. Table 7 shows the percentages of the programs reporting that at least 90 percent of both their clients and their paid staff were either African American or Latino. Clearly, the faith-based programs had a higher percentage of programs rooted in the African American community, with almost one-fourth of them reporting that both their staffs and their clients were at least 90 percent African American. That the break came between the two types of faith-based programs and the community-based programs indicates that, as others have observed,[67] African American churches and their related agencies are often strong institutions in Black neighborhoods of urban central cities, active in providing social services to their neighborhoods. Although the numbers are extremely small, the highest proportion of Latino programs is found among the faith-based/segmented and community-based programs, not the faith-based/integrated or other programs. The two programs that fell into the faith-based/segmented category were both sponsored by mainline Protestant denominations, one Methodist and the other

TABLE 7. Percentage of Programs from a Minority Community

Program Type	African American (%)	Latino (%)	African American and Latino Combined (%)	N
Government	5.7	1.9	7.6	105
For-profit	15.0	0.0	15.0	20
Nonprofit/secular	14.6	1.5	16.1	130
Community-based	13.3	4.0	17.3	75
Faith-based/segmented	24.1	3.7	27.8	54
Faith-based/integrated	22.5	0.0	22.5	40

Note: This table is based on the percentage of programs in which 90% or more of both the staff and the clients are African American or Latino.

Presbyterian. Three of the nine overwhelmingly Latino programs were community-based.

Table 8 shows the faith traditions of the organizations sponsoring the faith-based welfare-to-work programs, which are further divided into segmented versus integrated programs. One observation based on this table is the small number of Jewish organizations included in the survey. In part, this is no doubt caused by the fact that among the faith-based welfare-to-work programs, Christian groups indeed far outnumber Jewish groups. A further explanation may lie in the fact that a number of the organizations whose names indicated Jewish roots stated in their questionnaires that they are now secular in nature. The 3 percent of Jewish programs found in this study is in line with the 2 percent of Jewish programs found by Green and Sherman in their 15-state study of organizations contracting to provide services under charitable choice legal provisions.[68]

For many who are accustomed to thinking of the mainline Protestant tradition as being more socially active than the conservative, or evangelical, Protestant tradition,[69] the most surprising finding in table 8 may be that a majority of all of the faith-based programs and some 75 percent of the faith-based/integrated programs were spon-

TABLE 8. Faith-Based Programs, by Faith Tradition

Faith Tradition	Faith-Based/ Segmented		Faith-Based/ Integrated		All Faith-Based	
	%	N	%	N	%	N
Jewish	2.8	2	2.1	1	2.6	3
Roman Catholic	15.7	11	4.3	2	11.1	13
Protestant, mainline[a]	38.6	27	14.9	7	29.1	34
Protestant, conservative[a]	38.6	27	74.5	35	53.0	62
Other	4.3	3	4.3	2	4.2	5
Total	100.0	70	100.0	47	100.0	117

[a]The distinction between mainline and conservative Protestant traditions was made by including in the mainline Protestant category all programs that identified their tradition as "Protestant interdenominational, mainline or liberal," plus those that indicated they were "Protestant denominational" and further gave as their denomination Methodist, Presbyterian, Lutheran, United Church of Christ, Episcopal, American Baptist, or Disciples of Christ. Included in the conservative Protestant category were those programs that identified themselves as "interdenominational, evangelical" or "interdenominational, pentecostal," plus those that indicated they were "Protestant denominational" and further reported that they were nondenominational or gave as their denomination Baptist (other than American Baptist), Assembly of God, Christian Reformed, Salvation Army, Pentecostal, or Seventh- Day Adventist.

sored by groups in the conservative Protestant tradition. One well-known scholar has confidently asserted:

> Theologically conservative, "gathered" congregations are unlikely to support programs intended to reach those who have not already professed belief and adhered to behavioral restrictions required for membership in these groups. . . . Theologically liberal congregations and denominations and Roman Catholics, on the other hand, tend to direct their service provision efforts towards broader client populations, making them available on the basis of need rather than membership.[70]

Similarly, another scholar has written, "Evangelical Christians may be building new communities of love—but mainly congregation by congregation, without strong ties that include, bridge, and reach out."[71] My study shows that in the case of welfare-to-work programs in the four target cities, this conclusion is less than accurate. The explanation may lie in part in the fact that mainline Protestant denominations have been losing membership for some time and may be retrenching in actual social service programs, instead opting to lobby government for programs they see as promoting greater social justice. Robert Putnam has written: "While mainline Protestantism still is a significant part of the religious landscape, these congregations are dwindling, aging, and less involved in religious activities."[72] Meanwhile, conservative Protestant denominations and parachurch organizations are growing, exhibiting a renewed vitality, and starting to emphasize direct social involvement. Based on a national survey, sociologist Christian Smith has noted: "If ever liberal [mainline] Protestantism was distinguished by its social-Gospel activism, it appears to be so no more. The evidence suggests, however, that evangelicals may be the most committed carriers of a new social Gospel."[73] In addition, when one keeps in mind that most inner-city, predominantly African American congregations—many of which are sponsoring various social service activities—fall into the conservative Protestant camp, the large number of conservative Protestant welfare-to-work programs in large urban centers becomes more understandable. Green and Sherman also found that "just over 40 percent of the nonprofits [they] surveyed were associated with evangelical Protestantism."[74] The findings reported here are also in line with a national study of religious congregations that found white evangelical congregations offering almost as many "outreach ministries" as moderate Protestant, Catholic, and Orthodox congregations.[75]

The Catholic and mainline Protestant programs are notable for largely falling into the segmented category (11 out of the 13 Catholic programs and 27 out of the 34 mainline Protestant programs did so). It is also worth noting that 27 out of 62, or 44 percent, of the conservative Protestant programs fell into the faith-based/segmented category. This indicates that in the welfare-to-work field, one cannot simply equate conservative Protestantism with faith-based/integrated programs.

Another observation dealing with the faith-based welfare-to-work programs relates to the entities sponsoring and running them. Much of the current debate concerning government funding of faith-based social service programs revolves around the question of the constitutionality and appropriateness of government funding the social service activities of religious congregations. As I noted earlier in this chapter, it is widely assumed that social service activities run directly by religious congregations are more likely to integrate religious elements into their programming than are social service activities sponsored by entities—such as 501(c)(3) nonprofit entities—that are legally separate from actual congregations. This study reveals a quite different picture (see table 9). If anything, the faith-based/integrated programs—when compared to the faith-based/segmented programs—

TABLE 9. Sponsoring Entities of Faith-Based Programs

Sponsoring Entity	Faith-Based/ Segmented (%)[a]	Faith-Based/ Integrated (%)[a]	Faith-Based Total (%)[a]
Sponsored and run by religious congregation	32.4	23.4	28.8
Sponsored and run by a national denomination or regional network of congregations	4.2	4.3	4.2
Run by a separate entity such as a 501(c)(3)[b]	59.2	80.9	67.8
Other	11.3	8.5	10.2
Number of responding faith-based programs	71	47	118

[a]The percentages total to more than 100% because a number of programs checked more than one option.

[b]And sponsored by a religious congregation, several congregations, a national denomination or regional network, or individuals.

were less likely to be run by a congregation and more likely to be run by a legally separate entity. When the questionnaire asked faith-based welfare-to-work programs about their sponsoring entities, 32.4 percent of the faith-based/segmented programs and only 23.4 percent of the faith-based/integrated programs reported they were sponsored and run by a religious congregation. Over 80 percent of the faith-based/integrated programs and less than 60 percent of the faith-based/segmented programs reported they were run by a legally separate entity—such as a 501(c)(3) nonprofit organization. In short, the providers that integrate religious elements into their programming were actually less likely to be run directly by a congregation itself than were the providers that do not integrate religious elements into their services—the exact opposite of conventional wisdom.

The importance of these findings is strengthened by noting from table 4 the many religiously based practices in which the faith-based/integrated programs reported engaging and then by realizing that 80 percent of these programs are run not directly by congregations but by entities legally separate from any congregation or network of congregations. This was also confirmed by the site visits made by my associate researcher and me. An executive of a Dallas faith-based/integrated provider that is an independent 501(c)(3) nonprofit entity sponsored by several local churches described her agency's philosophy in these words: "We are faith-based—we strive to be the hands of Christ for the homeless. Our desire is to touch them as if they are Christ Himself. We don't preach to them; we don't require them to attend any church services. But everything comes from a biblical perspective." This faith-based organization and many others that we visited or that responded to the questionnaire demonstrate that—at least in the welfare-to-work field—the often-made assumption that congregation-run programs are more integrally religious than programs run by separate entities is not accurate.

Table 10 shows that there are no significant differences between the various program types in respect to the time periods when they started. The 1981–96 period when the era of welfare cutbacks, added work requirements, and public-private partnerships received a renewed emphasis—is the period when the largest percentages of the programs came into existence. But this is true of the government-run programs

TABLE 10. Year Programs Began, by Program Type

Program Type	1959 or Before (%)	1960–80 (%)	1981–96 (%)	1997–2001 (%)	N	Total (%)
Government	7.0	15.8	43.0	34.2	114	100.0
For-profit	4.0	16.0	32.0	48.0	25	100.0
Nonprofit/secular	5.2	20.1	36.6	38.1	134	100.0
Community-based	2.4	13.4	47.6	36.6	82	100.0
Faith-based/segmented	4.4	11.8	51.5	32.4	22	100.1
Faith-based/integrated	4.3	14.9	51.1	29.8	14	100.1

$\chi^2(15) = 11.00, p = .75$.

as well as the nongovernmental programs. This trend continued into the 1997–2001 period, which saw the implementation of the 1996 PRWORA, but it clearly anteceded the passage of this act. It is especially interesting to note that the big surge in faith-based welfare-to-work programs was also in the 1981–96 time period—not since 1997, when charitable choice was first included in the federal welfare act. Almost one-half of the for-profit programs have come into existence since 1997, indicating that the use of for-profit firms to deliver welfare-to-work services may be a more recent phenomenon than is the reliance on either faith-based or secular nonprofit providers.

Geographic Differences in the Distribution of Program Types

Table 11 shows the six types of welfare-to-work programs divided by the four cities included in the study. Several interesting patterns

TABLE 11. Types of Welfare-to-Work Programs, by City

	Chicago		Dallas		Los Angeles		Philadelphia	
Program Type	N	%	N	%	N	%	N	%
Government	13	10.2	16	17.0	86	44.8	10	12.7
For-profit	8	6.3	10	10.6	4	2.1	4	5.1
Nonprofit/secular	50	39.1	15	16.0	51	26.6	23	29.1
Community-based	30	23.4	19	20.2	24	12.5	10	12.7
Faith-based/segmented	17	13.3	22	23.4	17	8.9	16	20.3
Faith-based/integrated	10	7.8	12	12.8	10	5.2	16	20.3
Total	128	100.1	94	100.0	192	100.1	79	100.2

$\chi^2(15) = 100.01, p < .001$.

emerge. Chicago is distinguished by having the largest number of secular, nonprofit programs—62.5 percent of the total, when one combines the nonprofit/secular and community-based programs. Its nonprofit/secular programs outnumbered the community-based programs 50 to 30 (or 39.1 percent of the total number of Chicago programs), yet there were also a large number of community-based programs (23.4 percent of all Chicago programs). Philadelphia and Dallas are notable for their large proportions of welfare-to-work programs provided by faith-based agencies (40.6 percent and 36.2 percent, respectively, when one combines the integrated and the segmented faith-based programs). These proportions, higher than those in the other two cities, may reflect the emphasis that Texas's former governor George W. Bush and Mayor John Street of Philadelphia have placed on faith-based approaches in meeting social needs.[76] Dallas's proportion of for-profit providers (nearly 11 percent) exceeds the proportions in the other cities, but it still is a small proportion of all of Dallas's providers. Dallas is also notable for having more community-based than nonprofit/secular providers, while the other three cities have more nonprofit/secular than community-based providers. Los Angeles is marked by a stronger reliance on governmental programs (almost 45 percent of all providers) than is evidenced in the other three cities, although Los Angeles also relied heavily on nonprofit/secular providers. Of the four cities studied, it has the smallest proportion of community-based and faith-based providers.

Program Size

It is also important to explore the relative size of the six program types. As I noted earlier, a number of writers have questioned the capacity of the community-based and faith-based programs to meet more than a minimal amount of the society's social service needs. My data show that their questions are at least partially well founded. Table 12 compares the total number of government, for-profit, nonprofit/secular, community-based, faith-based/segmented, and faith-based/integrated programs with the total number of full-time staff employed by the six program types. I use the number of full-time, paid employees as the most reliable measure of program size. Using the number of clients is problematic, since a wide variety of welfare-to-work programs were included in the survey. Some of the programs had very intensive programs, involving long-term contacts with the clients; others had shorter-term, less intensive contacts with clients. Thus, comparing the number of clients served could be highly misleading. A review of the completed questionnaires and the many site visits indicated that the annual budget figures given in the completed questionnaires may not be fully reliable. One-fourth of the programs did not supply budget figures, and of those that did, some appear to have given the budget figure for the entire organization, others for the specific welfare-to-work program under study (the latter response was intended). Thus, although I shortly report the figures for the number of clients and annual budgets, I have more confidence in the figures for the number of full-time employees as an accurate measure of program size.

Table 12 dramatically shows that as one moves from simply the number of welfare-to-work programs to an estimate of the size of those programs based on the number of full-time employees, the government programs assume a much larger role, nonprofit/secular programs assume a somewhat larger role, the for-profit programs maintain about the same role, and the community-based and both types of faith-based programs assume much smaller roles. Although only 25.2 percent of the programs were government programs, those programs employed

TABLE 12. Number of Programs versus Number of Full-Time Employees, by Program Type

Program Type	Number of Programs	Percentage of Programs out of Total	Total Number of Full-Time Employees	Percentage of Full-Time Employees out of Total
Government[a]	124	25.2	5,116	47.2
For-profit	26	5.3	629	5.6
Nonprofit/secular	139	28.3	3,980	35.5
Community-based	83	16.9	435	3.9
Faith-based/segmented	72	14.6	608	5.4
Faith-based/integrated	48	9.8	272	2.4
Total	492	100.1	11,040	100.0

[a]One extreme outlier that apparently misunderstood the question was eliminated from these calculations. It reported almost as many full-time employees as did all the other government programs combined.

almost one-half of the full-time staff employed by all of the programs in the study. Meanwhile, even though community-based programs are almost 17 percent of the total number of programs, they employ less than 4 percent of the full-time employees. Similarly, while the faith-based programs constituted 24.4 percent of all the programs studied, they employ only 7.8 percent of the full-time staff. In fact, the community-based, faith-based/segmented, and faith-based/integrated programs combined employ only 11.7 percent of the full-time workers employed by all of the welfare-to-work programs. The nonprofit/secular and government programs together employ over 80 percent of all of the full-time employees. These are the programs the study found to be dominating the welfare-to-work field in the four cities studied.

It could, however, be argued that the community-based and faith-based programs are actually larger than is indicated by their number of full-time employees, since, as I reported earlier, they rely more heavily on part-time employees and volunteers than do the government and nonprofit/secular programs. Table 13 shows the median number of part-time employees and volunteers that the various types of organizations reported.[77] The various program types did not significantly vary in the number of part-time employees used, although the small number of part-time employees will of course loom larger in the small community-based and faith-based programs than in the other, larger programs. The different types of providers did dif-

TABLE 13. Median Number of Part-Time Employees and Volunteers, by Program Type

Program Type	Median Number of Part-Time Employees*	Programs Reporting Number of Part-Time Employees	Median Number of Volunteers in a Month**	Programs Reporting Number of Volunteers in a Month
Government	3.0	110	0.0	112
For-profit	2.0	23	0.0	25
Nonprofit/secular	2.0	135	2.0	133
Community-based	1.0	83	6.0	82
Faith-based/segmented	1.0	69	10.0	69
Faith-based/integrated	2.0	48	13.5	48

*$\chi^2(5) = 9.12$, $p = .11$ (based on the Kruskal-Wallis H-test).
**$\chi^2(5) = 97.96$, $p < .001$ (based on the Kruskal-Wallis H-test).

fer significantly in the use of volunteers. The median number of volunteers per month reported by the community-based and faith-based programs—especially the faith-based/integrated programs—was much greater than what the nonprofit/secular programs reported (6, 10, and 13.5 per month versus only 2 per month, respectively). This was the case despite the much larger size of the nonprofit/secular programs. Volunteers were almost nonexistent among the government and for-profit programs.

These findings, however, do not substantially change the earlier conclusion of the dominance of government and nonprofit/secular programs in the welfare-to-work field. Virginia Hodgkinson and Murray Weitzman estimated the average number of hours put in by volunteers at 4.2 hours a week.[78] If one makes use of this estimate, the median faith-based/integrated program would receive 227 volunteer hours a month, or the equivalent of 1.4 full-time employees; the median faith-based/segmented program would receive 168 volunteer hours a month, or the equivalent of 1.1 full-time employees; and the median community-based program would receive 101 volunteer hours a month, or 0.6 of a full-time employee. If one adds the volunteer equivalents of full-time employees to the actual full-time employees of the community-based and faith-based programs, the numbers in table 12 change only slightly. The final conclusions are that the use of volunteers needs to be taken into account in assessing the relative size of the various program types but that doing so does not change the fact that the community-based programs and the two types of faith-based programs are still overshadowed in size by the government-run and nonprofit/secular programs.

Yet the presence and use of volunteers in the community-based and faith-based programs may say something very good about their ties to their local communities, and these ties, in turn, may make their programs more effective. Also, program clients may be more responsive to volunteers than to paid staff, simply because they know volunteers are freely giving their time to help them. The claim by some that religion is a motivating factor in volunteering receives support from the fact that the faith-based programs had more volunteers than the community-based programs, with the most explicitly religious (faith-based/

integrated) programs having more volunteers than the less explicitly religious (faith-based/segmented) programs.

Table 14 shows the median number of clients served and the median budget for the six program types. Again, we see the pattern of government and nonprofit/secular programs generally being larger than the other programs. The community-based and faith-based programs had the smallest budgets and fewest clients. However, even among the government programs, 16.1 percent had fewer than 100 clients. Government programs did not always equate to large, bureaucratic programs. A number of branch public libraries, for example, had small literacy or ESL (English as a second language) programs that catered to welfare recipients. As I pointed out earlier, however, these budget and client figures must be treated with some caution.

Based on the size of the programs, it is clear that government welfare-to-work programs continue to dominate the realm of welfare-to-work in the four cities studied, despite all the talk in public policy circles of devolving social services to nongovernmental providers. The large nonprofit/secular providers also make a large contribution. As measured by the number of full-time employees (table 12), the nonprofit/secular and government programs combined provide over 80 percent of the services. The for-profit, community-based, faith-based/segmented, and faith-based/integrated providers are small players. This fact raises serious questions about whether or not nongovern-

TABLE 14. Median Budget and Number of Clients Served, by Program Type

Program Type	Median Budget*	N	Median Number of Clients**	Percentage of Programs with Less than 100 clients	N
Government	$500,000	87	580	16.1	118
For-profit	$500,000	17	290	24.0	25
Nonprofit/secular	$890,000	123	400	15.9	138
Community-based	$200,000	73	200	30.9	81
Faith-based/segmented	$90,000	53	200	31.9	69
Faith-based/integrated	$114,082	40	110	38.3	47

*χ^2 (5) = 92.28, $p < .001$ (based on the Kruskal-Wallis H-test).
**χ^2 (5) = 31.94, $p < .001$ (based on the Kruskal-Wallis H-test).

mental providers outside of the large, professionalized secular nonprofit organizations have the capacity to meet anything more than a very small portion of the pressing need for welfare-to-work services. But this is not a complete picture. To complete it, one needs to look not only at the relative size of the various types of welfare-to-work programs but also at their relative rates of growth and their plans and desires to expand. Perhaps the potential capacity of the very small programs is greater than their current capacity. Table 15 shows the reported rates of growth from 1996 to 2001 for the six program types. There were no significant differences in the rates of growth for the various types of providers. All six types of providers experienced growth.

Tables 16 and 17 are more revealing. Table 16 shows the expansion plans of the various program types. When asked about their expansion plans, all six program types more frequently chose the "expand somewhat" alternative than the other alternatives they were given. Nevertheless, there were some significant differences among the different

TABLE 15. Growth in Clients Served, 1996–2001, by Program Type

Program Type	100%+ Increase in Clients (%)	21–99% Increase in Clients (%)	0–20% Increase in Clients (%)	Serving Fewer Clients (%)	N	Total (%)
Government	28.9	23.7	25.0	22.4	76	100.0
For-profit	42.9	21.4	21.4	14.3	14	100.0
Nonprofit/secular	42.6	26.6	18.1	12.8	94	100.1
Community-based	29.4	33.3	13.7	23.5	51	99.9
Faith-based/segmented	27.9	20.9	25.6	25.6	43	100.0
Faith-based/integrated	37.0	25.9	29.6	7.4	27	99.9

$\chi^2 (15) = 15.17, p = .44$.

TABLE 16. Expansion Plans, by Program Type

Program Type	Expand Greatly (%)	Expand Somewhat(%)	Stay Same Size as Now (%)	Reduce Size of Program (%)	N	Total (%)
Government	18.2	43.0	27.3	11.6	121	100.1
For-profit	28.0	48.0	12.0	12.0	25	100.0
Nonprofit/secular	28.8	43.9	15.8	11.5	139	100.0
Community-based	29.3	43.9	18.3	8.5	82	100.0
Faith-based/segmented	18.6	47.1	27.1	7.1	70	99.9
Faith-based/integrated	40.4	51.1	6.4	2.1	47	100.0

$\chi^2 (15) = 25.74, p < .05$.

types of providers. More faith-based/integrated providers stated they plan to expand greatly than did any other type of provider, and 91.5 percent said they plan to expand either greatly or somewhat (again, more than any other type of provider). Similarly, table 17 shows that when asked about the desire to expand, the faith-based/integrated programs, with 61.7 percent saying they wished to expand greatly and another 36.2 percent that they wished to expand somewhat, ranked higher than the government, nonprofit/secular, community-based, and faith-based/segmented providers.

Perhaps proving that the American entrepreneurial spirit is not dead, the for-profit providers indicated an even greater desire to "expand greatly."

In the visits to faith-based/integrated providers, it became clear that their reported expansion plans were more than fond hopes; time and again, persons we interviewed were able to cite concrete plans that their organizations were actively pursuing. The executive director of one faith-based/integrated group in Los Angeles, for example, spoke of plans to develop either a thrift store or a coffee shop that will offer employment to their clients and enable them to learn job skills. A pastor in a Philadelphia faith-based group revealed his organization's plans to start a Christian junior college in cooperation with a local four-year Christian college, to develop and enlarge a charter school already in existence, to add other education options, and to do more in housing and economic development in the neighborhood. He tied these plans directly into his organization's faith-based mission: "We see ourselves as an organization that will continue to grow around cer-

TABLE 17. Expansion Desires, by Program Type

Program Type	Expand Greatly (%)	Expand Somewhat (%)	Stay Same Size as Now (%)	N	Total (%)
Government	49.6	43.9	6.5	123	100.0
For-profit	72.0	24.0	4.0	25	100.0
Nonprofit/secular	49.3	47.1	3.6	138	100.0
Community-based	42.7	52.4	4.9	82	100.0
Faith-based/segmented	40.0	51.4	8.6	70	100.0
Faith-based/integrated	61.7	36.2	2.1	47	100.0

$\chi^2 (10) = 14.59, p = .15$.

tain key services that define who we are. And all of that will continue as an expression of who we are as an organization, which is a call to be of service to those around us."

This leaves the question of the capacity of small community-based and faith-based organizations in terms of their ability to partner with government, given the latter's attendant complex regulations and reporting requirements. The questionnaire did not attempt to explore this issue, due to its inherently subjective, hard-to-quantify nature. The general impression that my associate researcher and I received from our total of 24 site visits to faith-based and community-based programs in the four cities is that most appear to have the capacity to handle the paperwork and other demands put on organizations receiving government funding, especially with some guidance from government officials. This was not always the case, however. In the Los Angeles area, we visited a very small, new program that was struggling: its board was not very involved, its treasurer had just resigned, and its only full-time employee had recently decided to return to school for her master's in social work. That program would not be a good candidate for partnering with government. Such programs were the exception, however. We generally came away impressed with the skills and abilities of the persons with whom we met in small, community-based and faith-based organizations, and we suspect that even those organizations whose current ability to handle complex governmental partnership arrangements is doubtful could in time develop an ability to do so.

In summary, the capacity of the community-based and faith-based programs in terms of current size is very limited. Their capacity in terms of skill and ability in handling complex government regulations is usually but not always present. Nevertheless, they—especially the faith-based/integrated programs—plan and desire to expand. Many already have, and others could develop the skill and abilities needed to handle a government partnership. There is a potential that is greater than what is now in existence. If policymakers should decide to move in the direction of relying more heavily on community-based and faith-based providers, they would find providers who are eager to expand and to serve their communities more fully.

Public Policy Implications and Observations

The findings reported in this chapter, as well as previous research, lead to a number of especially noteworthy implications for public policy. They cast new light on the Bush administration's faith-based and community initiative and on the broader ongoing debate over public-private partnerships. First, this study demonstrates—as others have before it—that there are many faith-based groups providing social services. One-quarter of all the welfare-to-work programs studied were faith-based. Also, this current study has shown that among the faith-based programs, there is a clear division between those that keep faith elements implicit and separate from the services they provide and those that make faith elements explicit and integrate them into the services they provide. Public policy advocates often make this distinction, either to argue against government funding for the faith-based/integrated programs or to argue that they are the very programs that are most effective and thus that they are deserving of funding on the same basis as other faith-based or secular programs. Whatever one's position is on this issue, it is clear that in considering government partnerships with faith-based organizations, the distinction between faith-based/segmented and faith-based/integrated groups is real and sharp and needs to be taken into account.

This study also clearly demonstrates something that few other studies have considered: that community-based welfare-to-work programs can be identified and that they differ from the other nonprofit, secular programs. The community-based programs are smaller and—as measured by lower educational levels of their staffs and greater reliance on volunteers and part-time workers—less professionalized. Thirty-seven percent of the secular nonprofit programs fall into the community-based category. Many questions must be answered before one can make a case that public policy should seek to make greater use of these community-based entities, but this study shows that the concept of community-based programs can be operationalized to identify a distinct group of social service programs that match the characteristics many are identifying as those of grassroots, community-based programs.

It is also clear that in some important ways, the community-based and two faith-based program types fall into one camp, and the other three program types fall into another. This is true in terms of size, educational levels of staff, and use of volunteers and part-time staff. Thus, public policy efforts that link community-based and faith-based groups together as special objects of attention are warranted in the sense that these two types of groups share a number of characteristics. This link has been made, for example, in President Bush's White House Office of Faith-Based and Community Initiatives and in the 2003 CARE Act that was introduced by Senators Santorum and Lieberman, which contained a Compassion Capital Fund intended to help community-based and faith-based programs.

However, community-based and faith-based programs also differ in some respects. In my study, this was found to be the case in the proportion of programs in which both the staff and clients were overwhelmingly African American. Here, the two types of faith-based programs were more likely to be African American, and the community-based programs were similar to the government, for-profit, and nonprofit/secular programs. This means that public policy efforts to make greater use of programs with roots deep in the African American communities of large urban centers need to emphasize faith-based programs. Otherwise, most of the overwhelmingly African American programs will be missed. Also, although the community-based programs had more volunteers than the government, for-profit, and nonprofit/secular programs, the faith-based programs tended to have even more volunteers than the community-based programs. The faith-based/integrated programs reported over twice as many volunteers as did the community-based programs.

These differences between the community-based and faith-based programs are significant because they indicate that religion itself is in some respects making a difference in the nature of the welfare-to-work programs. Faith-based and community-based programs share a number of basic characteristics, most important size. Thus, when they differ, there is a presumption that the one key characteristic in their background and origins that they do not share—namely, religion—is underlying the differences.

Another finding that has public policy—and, indeed, political—

implications is that most of the faith-based/integrated programs were in the conservative, or evangelical, Protestant tradition. From this study and others, such as the Green and Sherman study cited earlier in this chapter, it is becoming clear that the day when most social service programs were linked to the Catholic or mainline Protestant traditions is passing and that the role of conservative Protestants is growing. This suggests, first, that government grant-making and contracting officials—if faith-based/integrated programs are to be included in government partnerships—will need to work with a religious tradition with which they may not have worked in the past. This shifting pattern also has political implications and may help explain why President Bush, a conservative president with personal and political roots in the conservative Protestant tradition, has been strongly advocating more government partnerships with faith-based—including faith-based/integrated—social service programs.

Another finding with major public policy implications is that the divide between faith-based/segmented and faith-based/integrated programs does not run between programs sponsored directly by religious congregations and programs sponsored by legally separate entities. The study found that the latter were as likely as the former—and even slightly more likely—to be integrally religious. One of the big objections raised by opponents of President Bush's faith-based initiative claims that it would explicitly allow government to fund the social service programs of religious congregations. But these objections often seem to be based on the assumption that programs run directly by religious congregations are more integrally religious than those sponsored by legally independent nonprofits. This assumption did not prove to be accurate in this study. In addition, the Green and Sherman study and my earlier 1996 study also found many separately organized nonprofits that were explicitly and integrally religious in nature. The pattern is clear and consistent. I am not necessarily saying here that it is improper for government to help fund integrally religious social service programs, only that limiting government funds to 501(c)(3) nonprofits and other legally independent nonprofits will not meet the objections of those opposed to funding integrally religious programs.

This study also confirms the observation by other scholars that most faith-based programs are very small. One can add that the community-based programs are also very small. Combined, faith-based and community-based programs served only a very small percentage of the persons in need of welfare-to-work services in the four cities under study. For-profit firms also served relatively small numbers of clients. Government-run and nonprofit/secular programs are currently serving the vast majority of those taking part in welfare-to-work programs in the four cities. This poses a huge challenge to those who believe that government and large secular nonprofit programs are often ineffective and that the for-profit, community-based, and faith-based programs are more creative, more flexible, and, ultimately, more effective. How does one grow the now very small community-based and faith-based programs? Perhaps even more difficult to answer, how does one grow the now small community-based and faith-based programs without losing the very qualities that are now making them effective (if they are indeed effective)? In the case of for-profit firms, how does one answer the critics of using the profit motive to improve services to the poor?

An upside of using community-based and faith-based programs to meet a larger proportion of the need for social services is the fact that in the welfare-to-work area they have the interest and desire to meet a much larger portion of the need than they are now meeting. Strong majorities of all three of the very small providers—community-based, faith-based/segmented, and faith-based/integrated—stated they had both plans and desires to expand. Seventy-five percent of these three types of providers said they had plans to expand either greatly or somewhat, and 94 percent said they had a desire to expand either greatly or somewhat. While these numbers are generally not significantly higher than those for the other, larger providers, they do demonstrate that the potential capacity of these three types of providers is greater than their current capacity. Should public policymakers decide to move in the direction of making greater use of them, there are community-based and faith-based providers willing—and even eager—to play a larger role in the provision of welfare-to-work services. The same is true of the for-profit providers.

To make a case for the greater use of nongovernmental providers and especially for the greater use of the currently underutilized for-profit, community-based, and faith-based providers, one needs to ask whether or not they are providing welfare-to-work services any differently than are the big two providers: government and nonprofit/secular programs. If they are not, it is hard to develop a rationale for shifting welfare-to-work services in their direction. If they are, there is a potential case to be made that they are providing more effective services or, if not that, at least that their services should be a part of a pluralistic mix of services. The next chapter considers what evidence exists indicating whether or not for-profit, community-based, and faith-based programs provide welfare-to-work services any differently than do government and nonprofit/secular providers.

III The Services Provided

There is no lack of opinions on how various types of providers deliver social services. Some commentators argue that government social service agencies are large, uncaring, and inflexible and do not hold their clients accountable. In contrast, they often claim that small, community-based nonprofits and faith-based organizations are more flexible and innovative, are in closer touch with the people they serve, and are more likely to hold clients accountable for their behavior (an approach sometimes called "tough love").[1] Some of these commentators take the further step to argue that large nonprofit organizations that regularly receive large government grants have come to exhibit many of the same pathologies they see in large, bureaucratic government agencies.[2] Other commentators emphasize the efficiencies that for-profit firms and competition will introduce into the human services field.[3] Yet other commentators see for-profit firms as unlikely candidates for providing efficient, caring services to the most needy among us.[4] They fear that the bottom line will take precedence over the caring provision of services. After all, they argue, all the financial pressures will be to cut services to the bone in an attempt to reduce costs and increase profits.

Most of these commentators, however, base their opinions more on predispositions, assumptions, projections, and hunches than on hard data. Although their writings abound with examples that illustrate the points they are seeking to make, they can cite the findings of only a handful of systematic studies.

This chapter can hardly claim to answer all of the questions concerning the nature and delivery of services provided by the six different types of welfare-to-work programs under study here. It does, however, throw light on the question of whether or not the different program types seek to move persons from welfare to self-sufficient employment in different ways. The next section presents key findings from the handful of systematic studies that have analyzed how various types of programs provide social services differently. The following three sections of the chapter explore differences and similarities in services offered by the six different types of welfare-to-work programs included in this study. The chapter concludes with a discussion of the public policy implications of the findings of this chapter.

Current Research Findings: Program Similarities and Differences

There are only a handful of studies that systematically compare different types of social service programs in terms of the services they offer, and these studies primarily focus on the distinction between faith-based and secular programs. Although these studies offer anything but definitive answers to the question of the nature of the services offered by different types of social service programs, they do suggest some answers to that question. More specifically, one can draw five tentative observations or conclusions from existing studies.

One conclusion is that *the specific types of social services offered vary from one category of provider to another.* As I noted in the previous chapter, Laudan Aron and Patrick Sharkey of the Urban Institute studied assistance programs for the homeless. They divided the organizations assisting the homeless and the programs they run into secular nonprofit, faith-based nonprofit, government, and for-profit categories.[5] Faith-based programs were defined broadly to include both religious organizations—which they apparently conceptualized as religious congregations—and religiously affiliated organizations.[6] Aron and Sharkey found that 47 percent of all the programs were run by secular nonprofits, 32 percent by faith-based nonprofits, 13 percent by government agencies, and 0.6 percent by for-profit programs. They were unable to determine what types of organizations were running the remaining 7 percent of the programs.[7]

Aron and Sharkey went on to examine what types of organizations were sponsoring various services for the homeless. Some of the key results are summarized in table 18. The government programs were more likely to be housing than any other type of program. Half of the small number of for-profit programs were housing programs, while one-fifth of their programs were feeding programs. The secular nonprofits also sponsored more housing programs than any other type of program for the homeless, but they had many food programs as well. A majority of faith-based programs aimed at helping to feed the homeless, but faith-based organizations also sponsored many housing programs. Most notable in these figures is the tendency of both secular nonprofit and faith-based organizations to offer many feeding and housing programs, but with the relative emphasis reversed between these two types of providers. The secular nonprofits offered more housing than feeding programs, while the faith-based nonprofits offered more feeding than housing programs. Also notable was the tendency of the government to sponsor many health programs, whereas the other three types of providers offered very few health programs.

It is sometimes asserted that in providing social services, faith-based organizations tend to take a holistic approach, one that deals with whole persons in their material, emotional, and spiritual needs. In the welfare-to-work field, this presumably means that, in addition to incorporating spiritual dimensions into the services provided, faith-based providers might provide more training in job readiness and other so-called soft skills than do secular programs. Soft skills consist of job-coping abilities, understanding workplace expectations, anger management, proper workplace attire, family-life skills, and other

TABLE 18. Types of Homeless Services and Sponsoring Organizations

Type of Service	Government (%)	For-Profit (%)	Secular Nonprofit (%)	Faith-Based Nonprofit (%)
Food	12.2	20.7	25.9	54.8
Housing	36.1	50.6	46.2	30.0
Health	23.3	6.4	5.5	1.0
Other	28.4	22.3	22.4	14.1
Total	100.0	100.0	100.0	99.9
N	5,324	251	18,764	12,593

Source: Data from Aron and Sharkey, *The 1996 National Survey of Homeless Assistance Providers and Clients,* 4, table 1.

such work-related living skills, while hard skills consist of computer proficiency, vocational skills, English language competence, job search skills, and other such work-related abilities. Philip Moss and Chris Tilly have distinguished between soft and hard skills.

> We define hard skills as cognitive and technical abilities. They include basic skills such as reading, writing, arithmetic and grammar; more abstract abilities such as problem solving or ability to learn; and technical abilities ranging from computer know-how to construction skills. . . . We define soft skills as skills, abilities, and traits that pertain to personality, attitude, and behavior rather than to formal or technical knowledge.[8]

Malcolm Goggin and Deborah Orth studied one government program and six faith-based programs in Grand Rapids, Michigan, that provide homeless families with services aimed at helping them to transition to employment and stable housing. A key conclusion of the researchers—based on in-depth interviews, site visits, and client focus groups—is that "FBOs' [faith-based organizations'] values extend beyond the goal of permanent housing for the homeless, and they are more likely to address clients' needs in a holistic way. . . . FBOs tend to promote spiritual health, church involvement, hope and dignity for clients, and social justice."[9]

A team of researchers recently studied welfare-to-work providers who held contracts in three counties with the state of Indiana under its Temporary Assistance for Needy Families (TANF) program.[10] They divided the providers into those where there was no faith influence, a moderate faith influence, and a strong faith influence. When they looked at job readiness, or soft skills, training, they found all three program types were providing about the same number of services (about nine such services).[11] In contrast, when they looked at hard skills training—such as job search, job development, and job placement—the strong faith influence programs were providing only about as half as many services as were the no faith influence and moderate faith influence programs. In short, the strong faith influence programs were putting a relatively stronger emphasis on soft skills than were the moderate faith influence and no faith influence programs.

A recent study by William Lockhart throws some additional light on faith-based and secular organizations' provision of training in soft skills.[12] He intensively studied three faith-based and three secular welfare-to-work programs in Raleigh, North Carolina, and Richmond, Virginia. The three secular programs included a government-run, a for-profit, and a nonprofit program. The three faith-based programs integrated numerous religious elements into the services they provided and would fall into the faith-based/integrated category being used in this book. All three were sponsored not by religious congregations but by legally separate nonprofit entities with 501(c)(3) status. Lockhart examined 17 soft skills, such as managing anger, setting goals, budgeting, and other life skills relevant to obtaining and holding a job. He found that the three faith-based programs had a slightly greater emphasis on these skills than did the three secular programs. The three secular programs put a strong emphasis on an average of 5.3 out of these 17 soft skills, while the three faith-based programs put a strong emphasis on an average of 6.3 out of these 17 skills.[13]

Lockhart makes a noteworthy observation that arises from various social service programs' efforts to teach soft skills, that is, from their attempts to change their clients' attitudes, values, and patterns of behavior. These efforts mean that many social service programs—faith-based and secular alike—are seeking not merely to teach marketable skills but to transform clients in their inner attitudes. He concludes that "both secular and faith-based programs were seeking to 'convert' the poor, not to a religion but to what is seen as the behaviors and attitudes suitable for success in the work place."[14] This can best be seen as a part of the emphasis on "new paternalism" in social welfare policy, about which Lawrence Mead has written. Mead defined this new paternalism as "social policies aimed at the poor that attempt to reduce poverty and other social problems by directive and supervisory means." He continued: "These measures assume that the people concerned need assistance but that they also need direction if they are to live constructively."[15]

In summary, there is evidence that faith-based social service providers offer a different mix of services than their secular counterparts do. They are not mirror images of each other. Some studies have found that faith-based programs may put a greater emphasis on training in soft skills and may in other ways focus more strongly on meeting the emotional and spiritual needs of their clients than do secular providers. The evidence for this is limited, however. Clearly, additional studies are needed.

A second conclusion that the available research seems to support is that *faith-based providers offer fewer and less complex services than do secular providers*. The study by Aron and Sharkey supports this conclusion. It asked the program administrators which of 59 potential needs of the homeless were being met by their organizations and whether they were being met on-site or off-site. Table 19 lists the 12 needs that were most frequently cited and whether they were being met on-site by the homeless agency itself or whether clients were referred to off-site programs for the meeting of those needs. Except for meeting the needs for food and clothing, the secular nonprofit programs were more likely to meet the identified needs on-site than were the faith-based programs. The faith-based programs were more likely to rely on off-site programs to meet the needs of their clients. The picture that emerges is one of the secular nonprofit programs offering a wider

TABLE 19. Faith-Based and Secular Nonprofits' Meeting of Major Needs of the Homeless, On-Site versus Off-Site

Major Need	Faith-Based Nonprofits		Secular Nonprofits	
	Percentage of Programs with Service Available On-Site	Percentage of Programs with Service Available Off-Site	Percentage of Programs with Service Available On-Site	Percentage of Programs with Service Available Off-Site
Food	85.2	37.3	75.4	44.0
Clothing	67.8	41.4	61.0	54.2
Money management	29.8	40.6	52.8	39.4
Conflict resolution	36.8	43.9	51.9	46.0
Needs assessment	40.6	52.2	74.0	39.4
Setting goals/service plans	33.3	47.5	69.5	34.1
Referrals	40.3	50.5	72.1	48.1
Follow-up	34.1	34.5	60.4	33.4
Locating housing	38.9	60.0	64.5	57.8
Financial assistance	37.2	59.2	45.9	60.8
Job skills assessment	19.7	58.5	33.5	64.7
Health assessment	18.2	57.8	28.8	61.1

Source: Data from Aron and Sharkey, *The 1996 National Survey of Homeless Assistance Providers and Clients*, 21–23, table 8.

range of services and more complex services. The two areas where the faith-based nonprofits met more needs on-site—food and clothing—are both services that tend not to involve long-term, continuing contacts. The very programs that involve longer-term, more intensive contacts—such as developing service plans, assessing needs, and locating housing—were the ones the secular nonprofits were more likely to offer on-site. Thus, one can argue that the faith-based homeless programs involved fewer personal, ongoing contacts than was the case for the secular nonprofit programs. These findings offer some support for the finding of Mark Chaves's study of congregations noted in chapter 2, namely, that religious congregations most frequently offer food, clothing, and housing programs. All of these tend to involve episodic, superficial contacts with clients rather than continuing, intimate contacts with clients. Such findings tend to run counter to the claims that faith-based organizations provide more caring, personalized services than do government or large nonprofit secular organizations.

One weakness of the study by Aron and Sharkey, however, is that it did not distinguish between programs provided by religious congregations and those provided by religiously affiliated organizations that are legally separate from any religious congregation or group. Most studies showing faith-based social service programs tending to provide more episodic, superficial services than secular nonprofit organizations have been based on studies of congregations, not faith-based nonprofit programs organized as legally separate entities. One is left to wonder whether the findings of Aron and Sharkey would be the same if they had distinguished between the programs of congregations and those of legally separate, faith-based nonprofit entities.

In fact, several studies have found that *faith-based nonprofit organizations tend to provide more complex, ongoing services than do religious congregations.* This is the third conclusion supported by existing research. For example, an exploratory study by Fredrica Kramer and her colleagues studied the provision of employment-related services by faith-based organizations in five cities: Baltimore, Fort Worth, Milwaukee, Pittsburgh, and San Diego. Their study has the big advantage of making the important distinction between programs run by religious congregations and those run by "nonprofit organizations with some religious or faith-based association."[16] Although they did not consider whether the faith-based organizations included any religious content in their programs, they were able to conclude that there was a difference between religious congregations and nonprofits with a religious orientation or connection. They found that most congregations that they contacted "do not provide programmatic or extensive services for employment-related needs of church or community members."[17] However, the researchers also concluded, "many faith-based social services organizations, whether independent of local affiliates or national networks, do provide employment-related assistance."[18]

Another study supporting the importance of distinguishing between services provided by religious congregations and those provided by faith-based nonprofit organizations is the 15 state study by John Green and Amy Sherman. They examined faith-based programs funded under four federal social service programs regulated by charitable choice guidelines. Green and Sherman sorted out the programs into those involving either extensive or limited interactions with clients. For example, faith-based organizations involved in job training or substance abuse programs were judged to have extensive interactions; those involved in operating thrift stores or providing emergency transportation were judged to have limited interactions. They found that 57 percent of the faith-based nonprofits fell into the extensive interaction category, while only 32 percent of the congregations did so; 68 percent of the congregations fell into the limited interaction category, while 43 percent of the faith-based nonprofits did so.[19]

Green and Sherman also asked the responding faith-based organizations which of the following six antipoverty strategies they pursued: advocacy, community development, spiritual growth/personal empowerment, training/education, support services, and referral services. Those that reported they engaged in at least five of these strategies were labeled "very broadly active," and the others were labeled "less broadly active." Green and Sherman found that 65 percent of the faith-based nonprofits fell into the "very broadly active" category and that only 35 percent of the congregations did so.[20]

Both the study by Green and Sherman and that by Kramer and her colleagues point to the importance of the distinction between religious congregations and faith-based nonprofits that are organized as legally separate entities. Clearly, studies only focusing on religious congregations or failing to distinguish between religious congregations and faith-based nonprofits miss an important part of the faith-based terrain.

Lockhart's study of six welfare-to-work programs clearly illustrates the fourth research finding, namely, that *many faith-based organizations integrate explicit religious elements into the services they provide.* Lockhart found that the religious programs differed from the secular programs in that "the religious programs tend to add explicitly religious elements to their teaching."[21] The explicit religious elements that the faith-based programs incorporated into their programs were such things as prayer, references to God and the Bible, personal testimonies, and invitations to become involved in the life of churches. He also found that messages similar to those found in secular programs were authenticated in the faith-based programs by appeals to the Bible or Christian teachings.

Lockhart found that the faith-based programs made use of many of the same elements for success as did the secular programs but that they went on to also include explicit religious elements. The secular providers used inspirational examples of former clients or even staff members who had made it; they emphasized the negatives of not working and the positive rewards of working, with the latter including material and psychological benefits to one's self and others. Lockhart comments, "the secular programs base the authority of their teachings on findings of experts and on the teachers' personal experiences, but the religious programs tended to connect the authority of their teachings to God's authority as revealed in the Bible while including personal experiences and some information from experts."[22] Lockhart summarizes the explicit religious message that the faith-based programs gave: "Thus we are invited to work because we have been created in the image of God, who is Himself a worker, for the purpose of working. If we want to reach our maximum potential, we should imitate God who works and calls us to work. And as we work we work 'as unto the Lord' as if God was the real boss."[23] A staff worker who had left a secular employment program to join one of the faith-based programs is quoted by Lockhart as emphasizing the importance of this religious motivation: "I think the religious element adds a real foundation. A motivation other than economic. I think that's more important than just about anything else."[24]

Lockhart also found the faith-based programs distinctive in that they presented God as a resource: "God is seen as the one who answers all sorts of prayers, including those for material resources."[25] Local congregations are also interpreted as resources, where clients can receive emotional and material support and encouragement.[26] Similarly, a researcher who studied Teen Challenge, a Christian residential drug treatment program, observed the strong emphasis put on building community or social ties.[27] This was achieved by creating mentoring relationships and building mutual support among the residents in the program.

A fifth conclusion one can reach based on past research is that *workers in faith-based programs tend to be especially marked by caring, compassionate attitudes.* Goggin and Orth reported, "Clients perceive front-line workers at most—but not all—of the FBOs as more caring than those at the government agency."[28] This finding must be tempered by the fact that only one government agency was used as a point of comparison, but this is the only study of which I am aware that has even attempted to address this question in a systematic manner. A related finding adds some additional credence to this one, however. The authors found that the organizations they determined to be most intensely religious in nature were the very agencies where the clients reported that the caseworkers were most likely to treat them as equals.[29]

Nevertheless, after examining the available studies related to the nature of the services provided by various types of social service providers, one is left with the overwhelming impression that this area is underresearched. What is known is very limited, and questions that have not even been studied abound. Most of the available studies are qualitative case studies, not extensive empirical studies. In addition, they only focus on the types and numbers of services offered by faith-based providers versus government or secular nonprofit providers. They do not focus separately on either small, community-based programs or for-profit programs. Much of what is explored in this chapter is new terrain.

The Nature of the Services Provided

This section explores what the four-city welfare-to-work study found in regard to the nature of the services offered by the six different types of providers. First, it is important to recall table 4 (in chap. 2), which lists 10 religiously based practices and the percentages of the faith-based programs that reported engaging in each of these practices. As I noted in chapter 2, the faith-based/integrated programs were distinguished by their engaging in many religiously inspired practices. A majority of those programs reported having religious symbols or pictures in their facilities, opening or closing sessions with prayer, using religious values in motivating their staffs, having voluntary religious exercises for their clients, using religious values to encourage clients to change attitudes, and encouraging clients to make religious commitments. In addition, 56.3 percent of the faith-based/integrated programs reported either giving preference in hiring to persons in religious agreement with the organizations or only hiring persons in religious agreement with the organizations. In short, the 40 percent of the faith-based programs and the 10 percent of all programs that fall into the faith-based/integrated category openly and explicitly introduce religious elements into the welfare-to-work services that they provide. This finding is similar to what Lockhart, Green and Sherman, and Goggin and Orth uncovered in regard to the religiously intensive, faith-based programs they studied.

I observed examples of the use of explicit religious elements at a Chicago program for homeless men run by a faith-based/integrated provider in the conservative Protestant tradition. It is a separate 501(c)(3) entity sponsored by a majority white congregation in a largely African American area of the city. Its staff is integrated, and a majority of its clients are African American. It is not a traditional homeless shelter but instead seeks to establish long-term relationships with the men and to help them move on to employment and permanent housing. It is hard to convey the extent to which the program has integrated Christian elements into its programming explicitly and directly yet in a manner that is accepting and nonthreatening, not condemning and judgmental. The spirit of this agency is reflected in the words printed on the cover of the program for its 2000 annual dinner: "Seeing Jesus in the face of a stranger." The first value listed in the agency's written statement of values reads as follows: "Respect for the dignity of our guests and participants. We believe all persons are created in the image of God and have infinite potential. We believe that respectful care of even the most disadvantaged and disturbed was taught and modeled for us by Jesus." The agency describes its mission in these words: "The mission of ——— is to provide our guests with services that will allow them to overcome the obstacles of homelessness through working with professional staff in a Christ-centered atmosphere." Both the explicitness of this Christian message and the positive, accepting manner in which it was conveyed are clearly evident in these statements.

One morning, I observed the use of religious exercises to accomplish this agency's mission. I was in a day lounge where 15 to 20 men were reading or visiting among themselves while several were doing their laundry in an adjoining room. At one point, a staff worker called the men to order and stated that they were now going to have their daily devotional time, that anyone who wanted to leave could do so, and that those choosing to stay needed to be quiet and respectful. One or two left, but almost all stayed. The worker then passed out a sheet with Bible verses printed on it, most of which stressed biblical promises of God's help or protection. Typical was "And we know that in all things God works for the good of those who love him, who have been called according to his purpose" (Romans 8:28, New International Version) and "For I am the Lord, your God, who takes hold of your right hand and says to you, Do not fear; I will help you" (Isaiah 41:13, NIV). The staff member would ask one of the men to read a verse and then would comment on that verse, stressing that God's promises apply to all. The session ended with group prayer. The devotional period lasted about 45 minutes; some of the men were very active and involved, while others were not.

In an interview with the head of the agency's employment programs, the use of religious values to change behavior and attitudes clearly came out. He was an enthusiastic young man, who had dropped out of seminary studies to work full-time at the agency. When asked what was his motivation for working at this agency, he replied: "God has called me to do this work; this is what I am supposed to be doing. But there are also challenging aspects of the job I enjoy. These are good folks; they will be good employees. I enjoy working with them." When asked what difference it makes that the program is faith-based, he replied: "We minister to their emotional needs, we minister to their employment needs, and we also minister to their spiritual needs. We believe it is that holistic approach which ultimately can make a person who has struggled in his life successful."

I also interviewed three of the program's clients (or "guests," as the program referred to them). One of them volunteered that this was the best program for the homeless in all of Chicago. When asked what makes it such a good program, he replied, "They talk about God here." When urged to be more specific about the program's virtues, the three men stated that the program provides good services—that it does not just provide a place to sleep but helps them get ahead. One used the term *tough love* to describe the times staff could be tough on them, but he went on to mention by name one staff member who was tough but also really cared about them.

Although the faith-based/integrated programs stood out in the extent to which religious elements were explicitly present in the services provided, one of the surprising findings my associate researcher and I uncovered in our 51 site visits was that the presence of religious elements was not uncommon in the secular programs.[30] An instructor in a government program in Philadelphia, for example, began a class with prayer and a reading from the Bible (those not wishing to participate were allowed to leave for this part of the class). The director of a community-based program in Los Angeles, when asked if her staff was guided at all by faith, responded: "Most definitely. We don't talk about religion here; however, people pray and fellowship together. . . . I know it is present—by the staff and their comments and their commitment here and knowing they want to make a difference. Sometimes they go beyond the scope of duties, so that is a higher calling, a higher order. It's the right thing to do." In a Dallas for-profit program, we found a framed copy of the Lord's Prayer and another religious plaque hanging in the reception area, and the director quickly made it clear that she is a Christian and that her faith motivates her to serve her clients and to expect the best from them. In a government welfare office in a very depressed area of Chicago, one direct service worker had a wooden carving of the name *Jesus* on her desk. At the same office, an assistant director, when asked what keeps her going on bad days, replied: "You have to be a little spiritual to understand this. You may not see the rewards in this lifetime." A government-run program in Dallas has a close working relationship with a church. The government program offers classes at the church in computer training and GED preparation, and the church provides space free of charge.

These are only a few examples of a frequently found pattern that my associate researcher and I came across even though we were not specifically looking for it. It cautions one not to assume that the distinction between faith-based and secular programs is absolute. In a society where religion continues to play a very prominent role, it may be inevitable that religion will be found in agencies that formally are secular in nature. Even with this qualification, however, the faith-based/integrated programs in the study were clearly distinguishable from the other program types by the extent to which they integrated explicit religious elements into the services they provided.

This leaves the broader question of whether or not the types of services provided by the six different categories of welfare-to-work programs differed. Did the smaller, community-based and faith-based programs offer only a few, limited services, while the larger government, for-profit, and nonprofit/secular programs offered a full range of services? Did faith-based groups tend to offer less intensive, less personalized services? Did congregations and nonprofit faith-based groups differ in the number and types of services they offered?

The study questionnaire explored questions such as these by asking the providers to examine a laundry list of 11 possible services and indicate which they provided. Table 20 shows what services each type of program provided (I will offer more discussion shortly on the distinction between job-oriented and life-oriented services). It demonstrates that the government and nonprofit/secular providers offered the greatest number of services (an average of about 6.5 services out of the possible 11). The for-profit and community-based providers offered an average of 5 services, and the faith-based groups offered even fewer—less than an average of 4.5 services. What is one to make of these figures? Clearly, the faith-based programs offered only about two-thirds as many services as did the government and nonprofit/sec-

TABLE 20. Services Provided, by Program Type

	Government (%)	For-Profit (%)	Nonprofit/Secular (%)	Community-Based (%)	Faith-Based/Segmented (%)	Faith-Based/Integrated (%)
Job-oriented services						
Job search	62.4	69.2	78.3	63.4	48.6	45.8
Education/literacy	62.4	26.9	50.7	39.0	38.9	35.4
Education/ESL	58.4	19.2	28.3	34.1	25.0	22.9
Education/GED preparation	60.8	26.9	47.8	23.2	33.3	29.2
Education/vocational training, work skills	65.6	57.7	58.0	42.7	31.9	27.1
Job placement	59.2	69.2	73.9	47.6	37.5	35.4
Job internships/apprenticeships	42.4	23.1	44.9	25.6	22.2	14.6
Client assessment	52.8	30.8	71.0	61.0	45.8	45.8
Life-oriented services						
Work preparedness	70.4	57.7	81.2	58.5	55.6	50.0
Life skills	64.8	69.2	77.5	54.9	58.3	60.4
Mentoring	37.6	46.2	39.1	35.4	43.1	52.1
Mean number of services offered	6.4	5.0	6.5	4.9	4.4	4.2
N	125	26	138	82	72	48

ular programs, but they nevertheless tended to offer multiple services and not merely one or two. They run extensive, multiservice welfare-to-work programs, although this is even more fully the case with their secular counterparts.

The fact that the government and nonprofit/secular programs offer the greatest number of services reflects their larger size. It strengthens the picture of government and nonprofit/secular programs dominating the welfare-to-work field. Not only are they the largest programs, but they also offer the widest variety of services. In the number of services offered, the community-based programs, while offering more services than the faith-based programs, are closer to the faith-based programs than to the government and nonprofit/secular programs. This reinforces the impression that the number of services offered is more a function of size than of secular or religious orientation. It also supports my observation in chapter 2 that by a number of measures, the community-based programs are more similar to the faith-based programs than to the secular programs.

Table 21 presents another way of looking at the issue. It divides the services offered between those that involved less intensive interaction with clients and those that involved more intensive, longer-term interaction with clients. Services that involved only classroom instruction or short-term contacts were placed in the "less intense" category, and those that tended to involve long-term and one-on-one interactions were placed in the "more intense" category. If one compares the mean number of less intense services provided by the six program types with the mean number of more intense services, the differences among the program types narrow as one moves from the less intense to the more intense services. The government programs offered an average of almost one more of the less intense than they did of the more intense services, and the nonprofit/secular and community-based programs offered an average of one-half more of the less intense than they did of the more intense services. In contrast, the for-profit programs offered a greater number of the more intense services than they did of the less intense services. The two types of faith-based programs averaged almost the same number of less intense and more intense services. (Note the row near the bottom of table 21 that subtracts the average

TABLE 21. Services Provided Divided by Intensity of Interactions, by Program Type

	Government (%)	For-Profit (%)	Nonprofit/ Secular (%)	Community-Based (%)	Faith-Based/ Segmented (%)	Faith-Based/ Integrated (%)
Less intense services						
Job search	62.4	69.2	78.3	63.4	48.6	45.8
Education/literacy	62.4	26.9	50.7	39.0	38.9	35.4
Education/ESL	58.4	19.2	28.3	34.1	25.0	22.9
Education/GED preparation	60.8	26.9	47.8	23.2	33.3	29.2
Job placement	59.2	69.2	73.9	47.6	37.5	35.4
Client assessment	52.8	30.8	71.0	61.0	45.8	45.8
Mean number of less intense services offered	3.6	2.4	3.5	2.7	2.3	2.1
More intense services						
Education/vocational training, work skills	65.6	57.7	58.0	42.7	31.9	27.1
Job internships/apprenticeships	42.4	23.1	44.9	25.6	22.2	14.6
Work preparedness	70.4	57.7	81.2	58.5	55.6	50.0
Life skills	64.8	69.2	77.5	54.9	58.3	60.4
Mentoring	37.6	46.2	39.1	35.4	43.1	52.1
Mean number of more intense services offered	2.8	2.5	3.0	2.2	2.1	2.0
Mean number of less intense services minus the mean number of more intense services	0.8	−0.1	0.5	0.5	0.2	0.1
N	125	26	138	82	72	48

number of more intense services that each of the six program types provided from the average number of less intense services they provided.)

All of this indicates that by this measure, the for-profit programs were much closer to the faith-based programs than to their secular counterparts. They seem to focus on a limited number of services, such as job search, job placement, vocational training, work preparedness training, and life skills training. This may be due to a tendency for government contracts to focus on such services.

Table 21 also demonstrates that a pattern some other researchers have found—that of religious organizations tending to offer temporary, episodic, or fleeting services—did not hold up in the case of welfare-to-work programs. In them, the faith-based programs, while not offering as many services as their secular counterparts, nevertheless offered a wide range of services. If anything, they tended to emphasize services of a more intense, continuing nature. A potential explanation rests on the fact that over two-thirds of the faith-based organizations offering welfare-to-work services were faith-based nonprofit organizations and not religious congregations. As I reported earlier, the evidence from some previous studies has demonstrated that faith-based nonprofit organizations tend to offer longer-term, more-intensive services than do congregations.

To test this theory, table 22 explores the question of the differences in the services offered by faith-based nonprofit organizations and religious congregations. It offers very little—if any—support for the conclusion that the former organizations offer more intensive, longer-term welfare-to-work services than the latter. The welfare-to-work programs that were run by religious congregations generally offered fewer services than those run by separate entities, but there was no tendency for the separate entities to be especially active in providing the more intense, longer-term services. It appears that if a faith-based organization decides to move beyond basic services (e.g., food pantries and clothing closets) to become involved in the more complex, challenging task of providing welfare-to-work services, it is as likely to emphasize more intense, ongoing services as it is to emphasize less intense, shorter-term services. This is equally true whether the organization is a faith-based nonprofit organization or a religious congregation.

Another important question is whether faith-based programs tend to offer more holistic services that deal with the whole person in his or her emotional, attitudinal, and behavioral makeup, while their secular counterparts emphasize job skills and job placements and stay away from the more value-laden areas of attitudes and patterns of behavior. Some studies that I noted earlier seem to suggest that this may be the case. One could theorize that community-based organizations, with their closer ties to the communities in which they are located, might fall somewhere in between the two extremes. To explore these issues, I distinguished between *life-oriented services,* or those that are largely concerned with attitudes, values, and modes of behavior, and *job-oriented services,* or those that are concerned with more instrumental, job-related skills. (See table 20 to see which services I placed in each category.) The life-oriented services are concerned with issues such as self-esteem, work habits, attitudes toward supervisors, and attitudes toward work itself. Among the questionnaire's list of 11 services, the

TABLE 22. Services Provided Divided by Intensity of Interactions, by Sponsoring Entity of Faith-Based Programs

	Religious Congregations (%)	Separate Faith-Based Entities (%)
Less intense services		
Job search	44.1	52.6
Education/literacy	32.4	34.6
Education/ESL	26.5	21.8
Education/GED preparation	32.4	34.6
Job placement	26.5	44.9
Client assessment	29.4	53.8
Mean number of less intense services offered	1.9	2.4
More intense services		
Education/vocational training, work skills	35.3	29.5
Job internships/apprenticeships	8.8	24.4
Work preparedness	52.9	55.1
Life skills	50.0	67.9
Mentoring	47.0	47.4
Mean number of more intense services offered	1.9	2.2
N	34	78

3 that fell into this camp are work preparedness training, life skills training, and mentoring. These aim at promoting what were defined earlier in this chapter as soft skills. The remaining, 8, job-oriented services relate to teaching certain marketable skills or to putting persons in touch with job opportunities. These services aim at promoting hard skills.

Table 23 shows the mean number of job-oriented and life-oriented services offered by each of the six program types. All six types provided approximately the same number of life-oriented services, but fewer job-oriented services are evidenced as one moves from government providers to, respectively, nonprofit/secular, community-based, for-profit, faith-based/segmented, and faith-based/integrated providers. This means that the faith-based programs offered a higher percentage of life-oriented services than did the three types of secular programs. This is seen in table 24, which shows the mean percentage of life-oriented services that the six types of providers offered. Almost 40 percent of the faith-based providers' services were life-oriented, while only 25 to 32 percent of the secular programs' services were. The differences here—while not dramatic—are significant and in the expected direction. Also, it is helpful to note that the nonprofit/secular and for-profit programs provided higher proportions of life-oriented services than did the government and community-based programs (an average of a little over 30 percent versus a little over 25 percent, respectively). The biggest differences, however, came between the two types of faith-based providers and the four types of secular providers. That the

TABLE 23. Mean Number of Job-Oriented and Life-Oriented Services Provided, by Program Type

Program Type	Mean Number of Job-Oriented Services	Mean Number of Life-Oriented Services	Mean Number of Total Services Provided[a]
Government (N = 125)	4.6	1.7	6.4
For-profit (N = 26)	3.2	1.7	5.0
Nonprofit/secular (N = 138)	4.5	2.0	6.5
Community-based (N = 82)	3.4	1.5	4.9
Faith-based/segmented (N = 72)	2.8	1.6	4.4
Faith-based/integrated (N = 48)	2.6	1.6	4.2

[a]Due to rounding, the total is not always the sum of the mean number of job- and life-oriented services.

smaller community-based providers differed markedly from the faith-based providers in the average proportion of life-oriented services suggests that the religious nature of the faith-based providers, not size or other factors, was contributing to their tendency to include many life-oriented services.

It must be kept in mind, however, that this higher percentage of life-oriented services among the faith-based providers was a result not of the faith-based programs offering more life-oriented services but of their offering fewer job-oriented services than the secular providers. Yet it is noteworthy that when the usually small faith-based providers had to decide which services to provide and which ones not to provide, they opted to provide as many life-oriented services as their larger secular counterparts and reduced the number of job-oriented services. Notably, the faith-based providers still offer more job-oriented than life-oriented services, thereby demonstrating an attempt to have a balance between the two types of services.

It is also worth noting that the faith-based/segmented and the faith-based/integrated programs did not differ in the mean percentage of life-oriented services they provided. This is somewhat surprising, given the fact that these two types of faith-based programs differ in many other ways that I have explored already and will explore further in chapter 3. This finding offers at least partial confirmation of a claim

TABLE 24. Mean Percentage of Life-Oriented Services Offered out of All Services Offered, by Program Type

Program Type	Mean Percentage of Life-Oriented Services Offered out of All Services Offered
Government ($N = 123$)	25.9
For-profit ($N = 26$)	30.9
Nonprofit/secular ($N = 135$)	32.0
Community-based ($N = 80$)	27.7
Faith-based/segmented ($N = 70$)	38.2
Faith-based/integrated ($N = 48$)	37.2

$F(5, 476) = 4.72, p < .001$.

made by many persons interviewed from faith-based/segmented programs in on-site visits, namely, that although their programs do not include many explicitly religious elements, their programs are nevertheless shaped by their faith commitment, and it is implicitly present in much of what they do. The director of programs for a faith-based/segmented provider in Philadelphia explained:

> We really see this as a ministry. . . . It's faith-based and it's faith run to be honest. . . . If you visit other programs, they are more what I guess I would call cookie-cutter. There they have the look of a program; they have the look of a school. It's colder; it has a colder feel. . . . When I talk to the people about [our] program, I let them know that I think we are more family oriented, I guess I want to say, because we are small; because our staff is small, we want to take a personal interest in our students.

At a Los Angeles faith-based/segmented program, a client who had been homeless and is now in her own apartment and working part-time was asked how the faith-based program differs from the ones at the local welfare office. She replied that at the welfare office, they just try to get you in and get you out, while at the faith-based program, they really try to help. She said that if the welfare office finds you a job, there is no follow-up, but the people of the faith-based program are still there for you; earlier, she had made the point that the staff would be willing to just sit and talk when she was feeling down. She summed it up: "When one is out of the workforce for a long time, they help one with the first steps. It is a comfortable, family-type situation where they really care about you." Both the staff member and the client used the analogy of family to describe the faith-based/segmented programs they were in. They seemed to be grasping for an idea present among many of the staff and clients at faith-based/segmented programs, namely, that the faith element is present even when it is more of a background, atmosphere-creating element than an up-front, explicit element. This may help explain the fact that the faith-based/segmented programs were as likely to emphasize life-oriented services as were the faith-based/integrated programs.

The Sense of Personalized Concern

The claim is sometimes made or implied that there is some sort of a hierarchy of caring or personalized concern for clients among the different types of welfare-to-work programs. The claim is that the faith-based programs' staffs are the most caring, followed by the community-based staffs, then the large, professionalized nonprofit/secular staffs, and, last of all, the government and for-profit staffs. It is especially sometimes assumed that a sense of personalized concern will be lacking within government and for-profit organizations—in government agencies due to their large size and rigid bureaucratic organization, in for-profit firms because of their drive to increase the profit margin. As I reported earlier, research by Goggins and Orth offers some support for there being a greater level of concern among workers at faith-based programs than at government-run programs.

The questionnaire for the study on which the present book is based did not attempt to test these assumptions quantitatively, but in our 51 on-site visits, my associate researcher and I questioned many staff members regarding their motivation for the work they were doing or the reward or enjoyment they obtained from their work. We were impressed by how often staff members gave altruistic responses to these inquiries. Repeatedly, they referred to caring deeply about their clients, rejoicing when their clients succeeded, and feeling disappointment when their clients failed. The following six comments from staff members are typical.

> Sometimes the students are on their last leg. I love being able to see them strengthen that leg and instill confidence in themselves. I have not missed a graduation. They come up and give you a hug and introduce you to their families.

> I enjoy the rewards when my clients make it—when they turn from a caterpillar into a butterfly! That is my reward.

> There's a passage in the Bible that says to whom much is given, much is required. And I've been given a lot, a lot of opportunity.

Some people just haven't had the same fortune that I've had—you know, a stable home, drug-free parents, and more. So one can't do better than to give some of that back—and we get paid to do it!

I take this job so serious—that, you know, we have beautiful souls inside and eventually it is going to be transformed outside as well, so the beauty is going to be outside/inside. Right now, it is inside. I tell people, "You know, . . . I see beauty already." . . . So people expect the best. I always say that we have a staff that is dedicated, committed, and our participants deserve the best.

I see it [i.e., the speaker's position] as a calling. I wage war on unemployment. I want to make issues and unemployment disappear. My riches are not in my paycheck but the thank-you's I receive. (Paraphrase)

This is my calling. This is where I am happiest. I'm best with people and to try to right conditions and to be an advocate and counselor. God must smile when we reach some of our participants and they finally "get it." I had a young lady who was very difficult to work with, but when she got it, she really took off! One day she bought a beautiful picture for me at a thrift store as a gift—it meant everything to me! (Paraphrase)

Based on the content of what they said about how they view their jobs or the clients with whom they work, it would be impossible to guess the types of organizations for which these staff members are working. In fact, the first one is from a government agency, the second from a for-profit firm, the third from a nonprofit/secular agency, the fourth from a community-based organization, the fifth from a faith-based/segmented provider, and the sixth from a faith-based/integrated program. Statements like these were much more nearly the norm than the exception in all six types of organizations.

It may be that anyone who is willing to work in a position that does not pay all that well, that involves working with persons who often will disappoint, and that even sometimes means working in surroundings not entirely safe is likely to be a person who is motivated in large part by altruistic ideals. If money or prestige is one's chief goal, there are much more promising arenas in which to seek one's fortune than the welfare-to-work field. In addition, of the 115 staff members we interviewed in the four types of secular programs, 10 percent mentioned—without being probed or asked leading questions—that some religious values or motivations were important for them. The third person just quoted—from a nonprofit/secular agency in Dallas—is an example of this. This may indicate that welfare-to-work service providers tend to attract staff members who have a sense of personal commitment, often even rooted in religious values, no matter in what setting that person works.

These expressions of altruistic motivations were, of course, not universally present among staff members in the programs visited. When asked about motivation, one supervisor in a government office responded that she enjoys working with the subcontractors. She mentioned clients only to say that they help make her appreciate what she has. An instructor in a for-profit program only mentioned that the job site is within walking distance of his home and that since he teaches some travel agent skills, he is able to obtain some good travel deals. However, these two examples were the exception; they were by far outnumbered by statement after statement from staff members emphasizing a concern for their clients and referring to the satisfaction the staff members receive when their clients make progress.

Another claim often made is that for-profit companies will not exhibit the same sense of compassion and caring as will government agencies and nonprofit providers (whether faith-based or secular). For-profit providers, so the claim goes, will put the bottom line over personalized, compassionate help. This study cannot directly confirm or disprove such claims, but the visits to seven for-profit welfare-to-work programs raise questions about them. When we asked the directors or supervisors of for-profit programs about the charge that they will put profits before serving people, they usually made the plausible retort that they in fact have strong incentives to serve people effectively, since not doing so would mean that they would not have their contracts renewed and would be out of business. Some asserted that they are held to higher standards because they are for-profit agencies. Therefore, they claim that they are under more pressures to produce than are nonprofit providers. An official with a large for-profit company in Los Angeles who had also worked for a nonprofit argued:

> And we do work under, I feel, like a different set of rules. We are scrutinized more [than the nonprofits]. We are looked upon more as professionals. The performance [standard] seems like it is higher. . . . With the two contracts [that we have], maybe we have to do 100 registrations and they [the nonprofits] have to do 100 registrations. But if we do 99 we get a hand slap, and if they do 80 . . . it is like "Oh well, they are a nonprofit agency. It is OK." You see that. . . . I think that when we look at providing services, we are looked at under a microscope every single day.

I have already mentioned the sense of dedication we often found among staff members of all six types of welfare-to-work programs, including for-profit ones. One staff member who works directly with clients at a large, Philadelphia for-profit firm reported that he sometimes continues to work with clients even after they have been employed successfully for six months. Since his company is not reimbursed for spending time with clients after they have been employed for six months, he was asked if he had ever been told by a supervisor not to spend time with clients once they have achieved their six months of employment. He replied: "No, never! I do it all the time. People will call me, et cetera, and I do what I can to help them. I see that as part of my job."

These findings regarding workers' sense of concern and commitment toward the clients with whom they work are admittedly anecdotal in nature. Limited confidence should be put in them. But they raise some doubts about what is often conventional wisdom, and they suggest that what Goggins and Orth found in their Grand Rapids study may not be the norm. Clearly, additional, systematic research on the motivations and attitudes among workers in the various types of social service programs is very much needed.

The Issue of Sectarian Worship, Instruction, and Proselytization

The language of charitable choice stipulates: "No funds provided directly to institutions or organizations to provide services and administer programs under subsection (a)(1)(A) shall be expended for sectarian worship, instruction, or proselytization."[31] An executive order issued on December 12, 2002, by President Bush similarly states that faith-based agencies receiving federal funds may "not use direct Federal financial assistance to support any inherently religious activities, such as worship, religious instruction, or proselytization."[32] Such provisions raise the question of whether or not faith-based programs studied here were engaging in "sectarian worship, instruction, or proselytization," or, in the words of the 2002 executive order, in "inherently religious activities, such as worship, religious instruction, or proselytization." This question is especially relevant in the case of faith-based/integrated programs, since they are, by definition, the programs that are in fact bringing explicit religious elements into the programs they are offering. Also, as I noted earlier, a majority of the faith-based/integrated programs are from the conservative or evangelical Protestant tradition, a tradition noted for its sometimes strong commitment to making new converts. As I documented earlier in this chapter and in chapter 2, faith-based/integrated programs clearly introduce religious elements into their welfare-to-work services, and they do so openly and explicitly. As table 4 (in chap. 2) makes clear, approximately 80 percent of the faith-based/integrated programs open or close at least some sessions with prayer, 60 percent have voluntary religious exercises, 96 percent use religious values to encourage clients to change their attitudes, and 65 percent urge clients to make personal religious commitments.

Do such activities constitute "sectarian" worship, instruction, and proselytization within the meaning of the law? Or do they constitute "inherently religious" worship, instruction, or proselytization within the meaning of the Bush executive order? In other words, do sectarian activities constitute another distinguishing mark of the faith-based/integrated programs? This question has many public policy implications. Some claim that these are the very sorts of practices that make faith-based programs effective, since they deal with matters of the heart and spirit. To eliminate such practices would be to strip these programs of their most effective tool. Yet the use of these practices raises legal and First Amendment questions if the programs that use them are to partner with government. In light of this study and others, three basic observations can be made in responding to the question about whether the activities of faith-based/integrated programs constitute "sectarian" or "inherently religious" activities.

The first observation is that the meaning of the phrases "sectarian worship, instruction, or proselytization" and "inherently religious activities, such as worship, religious instruction, and proselytization" are anything but self-evident. The word *proselytization* is a case in point. The *Merriam-Webster Unabridged Dictionary* defines the verb *proselytize*, or *proselyte*, as "to make or attempt to make proselytes"; the noun *proselyte* is defined as "one who has been converted from one religious faith to another." A secondary definition of the verb *proselytize* or *proselyte* is "to recruit members for an institution, team, or group especially by the offer of special inducements." Both definitions clearly involve not merely changing values or attitudes but recruiting persons to join a particular religious group or a particular institution, perhaps with the offer of enticements of one type or another.

Based on the dictionary definition of the word *proselytize*, using religious values and beliefs as a motivation for changing attitudes toward work or to instill a greater sense of self-esteem or responsibility does not constitute proselytization so long as the goal is not to recruit or pressure persons to join some religious group. As documented by this study and others, faith-based programs will often seek to change client attitudes or behavior patterns by using religious perspectives and values to assure clients that they are of great value and worth, that God loves them and has a plan for their lives, and that work is not merely a means to earn money but a way to honor God. This is what John Orr has called "life style evangelism."[33] But this is far removed from the dictionary understanding of proselytization just cited.

Closer to the standard definition of proselytization would be efforts to encourage persons to attend church services or to accept Jesus into their lives. Even here, some questions could be raised if these efforts are not aimed at recruiting new members for a particular church or to a particular tradition within Christianity and if they are done gently and without pressure or material enticements. But it certainly comes a lot closer to the normal meaning of proselytization, and it clearly needs to be distinguished from efforts to use basic Christian values to change clients' attitudes and patterns of behavior. A lack of clarity remains.

Similar issues arise in defining the phrase "sectarian worship, instruction, and proselytization" used in charitable choice provisions. The adjective *sectarian* is defined by the *Merriam-Webster Unabridged Dictionary* as "of, relating to, or having the characteristics of one or more sects especially of a religious character"; the noun *sect* is defined in a number of ways: "a dissenting religious body," "a group within an organized religion whose adherents recognize a special set of teachings or practices," "an organized ecclesiastical body . . . outside one's own communion," and "a comparatively small recently organized exclusive religious body." All of these definitions carry the idea that being sectarian requires having involvement with a specific, even narrow or exclusive, religious body of some kind.

However, the Supreme Court has sometimes seemed to use the adjective *sectarian* as a synonym for *religious*. In a decision dealing with governmental financial support for faith-based K–12 schools, the Court stated: "At the religious schools here—as at the sectarian schools that have been the subject of our past cases—'the secular education those schools provide goes hand in hand with the religious mission that is the only reason for the schools' existence.'"[34] In a more recent decision, though, a plurality of the Supreme Court explicitly rejected the use of the term *pervasively sectarian* as "born of bigotry" and one that "should be buried now."[35] The plurality of four justices reached this conclusion on the basis that *pervasively sectarian* was a term created in the late nineteenth century to refer to Roman Catholic schools, which were labeled sectarian (i.e., narrow and closed-minded) in distinction from the broadly Protestant public schools.[36] In that context, *sectarian* was a pejorative word meaning "Catholic."

Compounding the confusion, Congress has sometimes used the terms *religious* and *sectarian* in an ambiguous way. Questions remain about whether Congress is using the terms interchangeably or to refer to distinguishable things. For example, an act providing funding for college and university buildings reads that the funds are excluded for "any facility used or to be used for sectarian instruction or as a place for religious worship."[37] Why the switch from *sectarian* to *religious* in the same sentence? Is Congress implying that there is a difference between sectarian instruction and religious instruction, with the former forbidden but the latter permitted in facilities built with government funds? When it comes to worship, the presumably broader term, *religious,* is used. Was this Congress's intent, and if so, what exactly is the difference? Confusion and uncertainty run rampant.

Thus, when charitable choice legislation refers to sectarian worship, is it referring to all prayers or devotional exercises, no matter how broadly based? Or does it refer only to prayers and devotional exercises that are peculiar to a specific, narrowly conceived religious tradition? Similarly, is sectarian instruction meant to include only instruction in the specific tenets and doctrines of a narrowly conceived religious tradition? Or is it any instruction with any religious elements present? Similarly—as seen earlier—does proselytization refer to any efforts to use religious values to change attitudes or patterns of behavior or only to efforts to present the opportunity to join a body of believers?[38] Or does it only refer to heavy-handed efforts to pressure or entice persons to join some particular religious congregation or denomination?

President Bush's 2002 executive order using the phrase "inherently religious activities, such as worship, religious instruction, or proselytization" adds some clarity. The adverb *inherently* carries the idea of something that belongs to the essential, inner nature of a thing. Presumably, activities whose very inner natures—or cores—are religious would be excluded from government funding; activities that may have some religiously based values or references as peripheral or secondary aspects would not be excluded.

Remaining questions about the meaning behind the language of charitable choice legislation have important public policy implications because, as will shortly be seen, whether or not the faith-based welfare-to-work programs studied here would have trouble partnering with government depends on how these questions are answered. Before directly dealing with this issue, however, it is helpful to make a second observation.

The second observation is that almost all of the programs studied here—whether government or private, for-profit or nonprofit, faith-based or secular—attempt to change the attitudes, values, and behavior patterns of the clients with whom they are working. This effort frequently revealed itself in numerous ways during the site visits. Frontline workers often reported that among the biggest barriers faced by their clients were possessing low self-esteem, having given up and having no hope for the future, possessing poor crisis management skills, lacking a true work ethic, or engaging in patterns of self-destructive behavior. Many workers would hasten to make two additional points: that structural problems—such as a lack of transportation, jobs in inaccessible suburban locations, or no dependable child care—also play a role and that the problematic attitudes and forms of behavior were understandable given the life circumstances out of which their clients had come. Nevertheless, they were also convinced that without attitudinal and behavioral change, improvements in their clients' economic situation would be very hard to achieve.[39]

A manager in a Los Angeles community-based program, when asked about the services the agency provides, observed: "Life skills are absolutely crucial. Unless or until you can change a person inside, or help them to see and understand who and what they are inside, and . . . help them fill their basket with positive things about who they are, you are not going to do anything. We do extensive life skills training." Countless similar examples could be cited. An instructor at a Los Angeles government-run program for noncustodial parents (largely young men with children to support) said that most of her students are stuck developmentally, that they are deeply affected by past broken relationships. Thus, her first task is to get them to accept responsibility. A frontline job developer at a Chicago nonprofit/secular provider described the challenge in these words: "The problem is those who never got 'it.' I don't know exactly what 'it' is, but it drives you to be self-sufficient. These women are comfortable in this setting. They come from families that, generation after generation, have been on welfare. They lack motivation to do anything else." The head of a job retention effort at a Dallas nonprofit/secular agency reflected on the interplay between economic conditions and clients' attitudes when asked about the challenges of job retention.

Obviously, the market today—after 9/11, you know—right now we have a lot of weird things in the culture going on. But apart from that, I think that a lot of it is attitudinal on the client's part. We have second- and third-generation TANF recipients, and to go out and work for $7.50 an hour when they have three children to support is going to cause a whole cascade of events. . . . We try to go at it from self-esteem; we try to go at it from long-term gains.

As part of the efforts to change attitudes and behavior, inspirational posters or sayings were usually present in the classrooms and reception areas of the programs we visited. In a nonprofit/secular program in Dallas, for example, the walls of a classroom had posters with appropriate pictures and these captions: "Soar on your own wings," " 'What lies behind us and what lies before us are tiny matters compared to what lies within us' (Oliver Wendell Homes)," and "The future belongs to those who believe in the beauty of their dreams." These can be viewed as secular counterparts to the religious icons or sayings often present on the walls of faith-based programs—both are aimed at encouraging and inspiring the inner person.

The faith-based/integrated programs pursue similar goals but by means of explicit Christian messages. Recall that table 4 (in chap. 2) shows that nearly 96 percent of the faith-based/integrated programs reported using religious values to encourage clients to change attitudes. An example of what this means is revealed by an account from the head of the employment program in a Chicago faith-based/integrated program that works with homeless men.

> We are spiritual creatures, and that spiritual focus gives the men even more resources upon which, hopefully, to get over the things they struggle with. . . . Scripture would teach that all work has dignity, no matter what level of work it is. It has dignity before God. . . . So we try to instill that in the men—that all work does have dignity. And that if they will do it unto God, then God will bless that. You know, Scripture says, "Do everything unto the glory of God"; whatever you do. And we also believe that if they can take that perspective with them, those are

the exact attitudes that will make them successful. If they are invested in their work no matter what it is, and [if,] because they are invested[,] they're willing to show initiative and drive, and [if] that work has a purpose, then ultimately that's what's going to make them successful in their employment. Because [now] they are waiting for this perfect job to drop into their laps, and they don't have initiative, and they're not invested; they don't give a crap, because they believe they are not going to be successful.

Other studies have also found both secular and faith-based programs working to change client attitudes and patterns of behavior. Goggin and Orth report that the government program included in their study of transitional housing programs "aims at least in part at changing clients' attitudes." They continue: "According to the director, this entails 'mothering'—constantly saying, 'You need to learn these things.' . . . Case managers also try to change self-defeating behavior."[40] As I reported earlier, Lockhart concluded from his case study of six welfare-to-work programs that "both secular and faith-based programs are seeking to 'convert' the poor, not to a religion but to what is seen as the behaviors and attitudes suitable for success in the workplace."[41]

This second observation is important from a public policy perspective because it makes clear that what distinguishes faith-based from secular welfare-to-work programs is not that one seeks to change attitudes and patterns of behavior while the other does not. Rather, faith-based programs use religious values and perspectives to change attitudes and patterns of behavior, while secular programs use nonreligious values and perspectives toward this purpose.

The third observation I wish to make focuses on the nature of the religious appeals that faith-based programs make. One stereotype of religious antipoverty efforts assumes that these efforts view poverty as the result of sin and perhaps even as God's judgment on persons who have failed to live by his rules. Thus, it is assumed that major components of faith-based programs with an explicit religious content include both a highly judgmental attitude that holds persons responsible for their own problems and the force-feeding of religious doctrines. It is unknown how many outside observers in the media and among scholars hold to this stereotype, but it is probably still present in society. It may be rooted in the assumption that today's religiously based antipoverty efforts are closely related to the Charity Organization Society of the late nineteenth century, which had chapters in all major cities and was led by several prominent clergymen. Walter Trattner has described the basic philosophy of this movement: "Leaders of the movement believed in the individualistic-moral concept of poverty; they accepted the prevailing economic and sociological philosophy that attributed poverty and distress to personal defects and evil acts—sinfulness, failure in the struggle for survival, excessive relief-giving, and so on."[42]

To the extent that this image of faith-based welfare-to-work programs is still lingering in some persons' minds, my study and other recent studies clearly indicate that it needs to be replaced by a quite different image. This includes welfare-to-work programs sponsored by conservative Protestant, or evangelical, groups. Much closer to today's reality than the old stereotype is the picture painted by one of the directors of a faith-based/integrated program in Dallas, quoted already in chapter 2: "We are faith-based—we strive to be the hands of Christ for the homeless. Our desire is to touch them as if they are Christ himself. We don't preach to them; we don't require them to attend any church services. But everything comes from a biblical perspective." Countless similar quotations could be culled from printed materials and interviews we conducted with the personnel of faith-based/integrated programs. The director of one such program put it this way: "Our call is for life transformation; we do not proselytize, do not say if you get saved everything will be OK. But we say you are precious—you reflect God's image and . . . you need to find the good work that God created for you to do." This was a recurrent theme, especially among the more religiously conservative programs. The assistant executive director of a Dallas program put it this way: "What we have here is an extension of our individual faith. We as a group do not feel we need to go evangelize or proselytize. If someone asks questions, we will talk to them about faith matters. We do not hide it. But neither do we lead with it. That is not our purpose. When we take this approach, there is no hidden agenda to shove your beliefs onto others."

More than once, we were quoted the saying "Preach the gospel always; use words only when necessary," to make the point that acts of love, mercy, and assistance are at the center of what the programs are all about. The staff members of these programs came much closer to the attitude of "There, but for the grace of God, go I" than to one of harsh judgmentalism.

Also typical is a moving paragraph from a 2001 Christmas letter written by the director of a faith-based inner-city program in Chicago.

> Where I am, in the so-called inner city, I've heard hundreds of prayers, midst the weeping and wailing, for our cities and for our nation [after 9/11]. We pray that God will bless America and that America will bless God. But there's something else that burns in our souls. Every year about 10,000 young men and women, mostly one by one, get slain on our streets. Within 200 feet of our church, one man was axed to death, another was shot as he sat on the back steps of the church, and a third one, 23 years old, died of a drug overdose. So we cry out for the nation not only but for this street corner, for the people sitting in darkness, for hope to be rekindled, for justice and mercy to flow wildly, for God to walk real close to us humbled people.

The examples could be multiplied. The slogan of one faith-based/integrated program in Los Angeles reads, "Where love embraces life." Another Los Angeles faith-based/integrated program has the following belief statement: "God calls people of faith to minister to His Children emotionally, physically, mentally, socially and spiritually. This is done through a realization that we all have needs to fulfill and each one of us has strengths to appreciate." A Dallas faith-based/integrated program states its goal in these words: "With outstretched hands and hearts, the people of this ministry bear witness to Christ's love and grace." The mixture of approaches is described in another sentence: "Support, accountability, and faith guide each family member back to a functional and productive lifestyle." The same flyer mentions the organization's job search program and describes it as breaking "down the barriers which prevent the homeless from obtaining employment." What are these barriers? The very next sentences give the answer: "Free childcare is available for infants through school-aged children while parents are at work or seeking employment. In addition, —— provides professional attire and assists with transportation costs."

Goggin and Orth found a similar pattern in their study of transitional housing programs. For example, regarding one of the two most integrally religious programs they studied, they report: "The nonprofit housing corporation espouses three core values: treat residents with respect, residents deserve the opportunity to press toward a greater housing goal, and beauty is a gift of God. According to the executive director, this means that the organization is 'a ministry of what God calls us to be,' and requires staff members to avoid being judgmental or moralistic."[43] As I noted earlier, in interviewing focus groups of clients, Goggin and Orth found that the clients of the most integrally religious programs were also the clients most likely to report that they were treated as equals.[44]

Lockhart reports that the faith-based programs he studied tried to bring their clients into the churches that were sponsoring the programs. Proselytization of a sort was going on. But he found this to be a quite different sort of proselytization than a stereotypical high-pressure, judgmental effort: "My observation of when the Christian gospel was presented in the faith-based programs, it was done in a gentle, winsome manner, with soft voices, inviting questions and responses. There was no heavy 'fire and brimstone' preaching or altar calls."[45]

Based on my study and on evidence from other studies, one can reach three conclusions concerning the nature of the religious values and perspectives that faith-based programs—especially the faith-based/integrated programs—weave into the welfare-to-work services they provide. First, religious values and perspectives are often used in attempts to raise self-esteem and to change self-defeating attitudes and patterns of behavior. Second, some programs attempt to persuade persons to attend or join religious bodies associated with the programs. Third, both of these efforts are made in a gentle, affirming manner and as an added source of help in extremely difficult circumstances, not in a harsh or condemning manner.

From a public policy perspective, the three foregoing observations have much significance—but they also raise more questions than they answer. The available evidence reveals that the religious worship and instruction that takes place in faith-based social service programs—while almost always specifically Christian in nature—are not specific to certain traditions within Christianity. The devotional exercise described earlier in this chapter cannot be cast within any particular denominational or doctrinal framework. Is it, then, sectarian worship? Given the ambiguities surrounding the legal definition of the term *sectarian,* it is hard to say. It certainly is inherently religious; it thus would not be eligible for government funding under President Bush's 2002 executive order and would need to be voluntary in nature and held at a time or in a place separate from government-funded activities (as in fact it was).

Similarly, if appeals to religious values are used to encourage clients to change certain attitudes and values that are hindering them from becoming economically self-sufficient, is this either sectarian or inherently religious instruction? Some could make that case. But such appeals would surely not be sectarian in the more specific, narrow sense of the word. The sort of faith-based appeals made in the programs we observed are a thousand miles removed from instruction in the stances different Christian traditions take on such esoteric theological issues as predestination, forms of baptism, and transubstantiation. Instruction in such doctrines would clearly fall into the camp of sectarian instruction. But such instruction is obviously not an issue in the welfare-to-work programs we observed.

In addition, are appeals to secular values and perspectives any less sectarian than the sort of religious appeals being made? As with religious values, secular values are broadly, but not universally, shared and, by their very nature, are not subject to empirical proof. Nor do the sort of religious appeals being made seem to fall under the concept of inherently religious. The appeals being made deal, at the core, with attitudes toward work, personal responsibility, individual hope, and self-esteem, not with religious doctrine. Religious values and perspectives are brought in to bolster the case for certain forms of behavior or certain attitudes that are functional for finding and keeping employment. Thus, they would seem to be playing a supportive role and not an inherent or intrinsic role. But others may disagree.

Similarly, is a staff member engaged in proselytization if she responds to a client's question by explaining how she has found strength to go on in a "personal relationship with Jesus Christ" and by urging the client to reestablish connections with a church in which the client has previously been active (a different church than that of the staff member)? Or is it proselytization if a welfare-to-work program presents God as a potential source of strength in overcoming the scars of a past filled with domestic abuse, as long as there is no pressure to join a particular church? Or is it even proselytization if a church and its members are presented as a potential source of support and help? Is this any more proselytization than a staff member at a secular agency urging a client to join a self-help support group for women who have suffered domestic abuse? Simply posing such questions demonstrates—at least in my mind—the difficulty in confidently giving clear-cut answers.

In brief, it is a lot easier to assemble a picture of the sort of religious instruction and worship that is taking place in many faith-based welfare-to-work programs included in this study than it is to label them. A host of legal, public policy questions and uncertainties remain. In chapter 5, I offer some suggestions on how to deal with these.

Public Policy Implications and Observations

The differences and similarities in welfare-to-work services being provided by the six types of providers reported on in this chapter contain many important public policy implications. In summarizing the key differences and similarities, it is clear, first, that there are significant differences in the mix of welfare-to-work services that the six program types provide. The different program types are not clones of each other. The government and nonprofit/secular programs tend to offer more services than do the for-profit, community-based, faith-based/segmented, and faith-based/integrated programs. The faith-based/integrated programs include many explicit religious elements in the services they provide, although they do so in a positive, affirming manner. Faith-based programs—both the segmented and integrated—offer a higher proportion of training in life-oriented, soft skills than do the four types of secular programs.

However, this research cautions against seeing the services provided by the six program types as being completely different. There are also many similarities among their services. Most notably, compared to the secular programs, the faith-based programs do not offer less complex services marked by shorter-term, less intense contact with clients, as some earlier research indicated might be the case. Also, this study supports the proposition that the workers in all six program types are motivated by a similar sense of compassion and concern for the needy with whom they are working. In addition, the study found that even the distinction between faith-based and secular programs is not absolute, with many of the secular programs containing some religious elements and with the faith-based programs offering many of the same services as the secular programs. All six program types tend to seek to change client attitudes and patterns of behavior, but the faith-based/integrated programs support these efforts by explicit religious references, while the other program types do not. In short, this chapter reports that there are measurable differences in the types of services delivered by the different program types, yet there are also notable similarities and overlap among them.

This chapter also examined in some detail the nature of the faith-based practices in which many faith-based programs engage. Whether or not they fall under practices that government is forbidden to fund remains an open question, given the many legal uncertainties in this area.

Based on the findings presented in this chapter, there are three observations that are particularly relevant from a public policy perspective. One is that if it makes good public policy sense to encourage more public-private partnerships, it seems to make good sense for those partnerships to be formed with all six types of welfare-to-work programs. There does not seem to be any reason, based on the types and mixes of services the various programs provide, to exclude any program type from partnerships with government. Given the diversity of clients and client needs, given the diversity of approaches taken by different providers, and given the lack of firm evidence pointing to the superiority of any one approach of working with welfare clients, it seems imprudent to limit government contracting or other collaborations to only one or two types of nongovernmental entities. To rule out for-profit firms, small community-based, or faith-based providers simply because they are for-profit, small, or faith-based is unwarranted. The problem of usually fractured families seeking to move ahead in a cold, highly competitive world, often with multiple barriers blocking their ability to move ahead, is so deep a challenge that—from the perspective of a public policy that is seeking to move such persons into the economic mainstream—working with a wide variety of approaches and providers makes good sense. Underlying this observation is the finding that no one type of welfare-to-work program appears on the surface to be doing a bad job of providing services. They provide many similar services, and all do so with at least a basic level of concern and caring. In fact, one could make the case that the faith-based programs—the very ones some believe should be excluded from government funding—bring especially valuable resources to their welfare-to-work task, in the form of a greater emphasis on life-oriented services and a presentation of faith as an added resource. This may especially hold true for clients for whom faith plays—or has once played—an important part in their lives.

A corollary of this first observation is that government ought to respect and make use of the differences in the various program types, not seek to make them all conform to one mold. Accountability—in the sense of good record keeping and as good an account as is feasible of program outcomes—is of course essential. But beyond that, a variety of approaches appears to make good public policy sense. If this is the case, government ought to respect program differences in their partners, not see them as anomalies to be eliminated. This is also consistent with the concept of the quasi autonomy that pluralist theory suggests should mark the various social structures in a free society. This means there is a need for creative partnerships, based not on preconceived notions of which specific agencies or which type of agencies are most effective but on proven track records, the quality of proposed plans, and the background and merit of the entities willing to partner with government. In chapter 5, I will consider how this may be accomplished.

A third observation is the compelling need for legal clarification as to what government partnerships with faith-based organizations means for those organizations. What can and cannot be done with government funds? How closely can privately funded religious practices be linked to government-funded services? To answer these questions, the legal use of such terms as *proselytization, sectarian worship,* and *sectarian instruction* need to be defined much more precisely than is the case now. Until that is done, many faith-based programs may feel that they would be in a highly ambiguous situation if they were to partner with government in providing welfare-to-work services. Again, in chapter 5, I will offer more on how this can be accomplished.

All this leaves crucial questions in regard to the extent and nature of present-day relationships between the government and nongovernmental entities providing welfare-to-work services. This is the topic considered in chapter 4.

IV The Government-Provider Relationship

Most of the controversy surrounding the use of nongovernmental providers to deliver essential social services centers on issues of governmental funding and regulation of the nongovernmental providers. Hardly anyone suggests that it is inappropriate for nonprofit providers to deliver social services to those in need. We are moved and humbled when we read of someone who has devoted a lifetime of unheralded service to others in a nonprofit agency when he or she could have been making much more money and achieving more recognition in some other field. We admire those who contribute time or money to private charities. Controversy arises when it is suggested that these nonprofit entities should receive tax dollars to help cover the costs of the services they are providing. Alternatively, it may arise when a nonprofit organization is faith-based and claims it should be free of government regulations to which their secular counterparts are subject. Or controversy may emerge when for-profit firms insist they have as much right to partner with government in providing social services to the needy as do nonprofit organizations. In other words, the most contentious issues in the area of public-private partnerships appear at the points of contact between government and nongovernmental entities, whether for-profit, nonprofit, or faith-based.

It is this contentious area—the government-provider nexus—that I explore in this chapter. The first three sections of the chapter give an overview of what past research has shown regarding this connection in three areas: government funding of social services programs of nonprofit and for-profit providers; government regulation of nongovernmental providers; and informal ties of consulting, referrals, and information sharing. The following three sections present what the study reported in this book found in regard to the government-provider relationship. The last section considers a number of public policy implications based on the findings of this chapter.

Current Research Findings: Government Funding

This section considers what previous research has found in regard to government funding of nongovernmental social service programs. In the case of nonprofit providers, both secular and faith-based, there is a long tradition of government funding. Observers are in unanimous agreement on this point. Carol De Vita has written:

> Government, at every level provides very few human service programs directly. Instead, government provides funding for an array of services and programs, such as employment and training, health care, child care, foster care, food and nutrition, senior citizen centers, social services, and many more. The actual delivery of services is generally achieved through the use of nonprofit, and sometimes for-profit, service providers.[1]

Similarly, Mark Carl Rom has noted: "since the 1960s, more federally funded employment and training services have been contracted out than not. The contracts have been for a wide range of services, including intake and eligibility determination, training, and job placement, among others. Most of the contractors for these programs have been nonprofit or public organizations."[2]

Lester Salamon found that approximately 36 percent of the income of nonprofits as a whole comes from government sources.[3] In the social services field, he found that 37 percent of the income of nonprofit agencies comes from government sources.[4] Countless other studies could be cited, but the point is clear: nonprofit social service agencies depend on the government for much of their funding.

A key question is whether this funding relationship extends to faith-based nonprofits or is limited to secular nonprofits. Research shows that very frequently it extends to faith-based nonprofits. Ana Greenberg, for example, reports that such large faith-based organizations as Catholic Charities and the Salvation Army "receive a substantial amount of their revenue from government sources, mainly contracts for service." She specifies, "For instance, in 1996, Catholics Charities USA received $1.3 billion or 64 percent its total income, the Salvation Army received $245 million or 16 percent of its total income and the YMCA received $203 million or 16 percent of its total income from government sources."[5] An earlier national study of mine showed that of the faith-based child and family care agencies, 82 percent reported receiving government funds, as did 70 percent of the faith-based international aid and relief agencies and 97 percent of the faith-based colleges and universities.[6]

Although some claim that government funding only goes to faith-based programs that separate out their religious elements and offer purely secularized social services, there is limited, but clear and persuasive, evidence that government funds often extend to faith-based organizations that integrate religious elements into the services they are providing. In fact, the Child Care and Development Block Grant of 1990 (amended in 1996) explicitly allows government vouchers to be used to pay for child care in programs that integrate religion into their child care services: a voucher "may be used for child care services provided by a sectarian organization or agency, including those that engage in religious activities, if those services are chosen by the parent; it may be used by providers for any sectarian purpose or activity that is part of the child care services, including sectarian worship or instruction."[7] My previously cited study found that among the integrally religious child and family care agencies, 67 percent reported receiving government funds; among the integrally religious international aid and relief agencies, 69 percent did so; and among the integrally religious colleges and universities, 97 percent did so.[8]

In short, a number of studies document that faith-based social service organizations—including integrally religious faith-based organizations—receive significant amounts of government funding. The studies also demonstrate, however, that fewer faith-based organizations than secular organizations receive government funding and that the faith-based organizations receiving funding tend to receive less government money than do their secular counterparts. As Greenberg reports, "Congregations and small religious groups receive minimal levels of government funding for the service delivery they do engage in."9

Tables 25 and 26 tell a similar story. Table 25 is drawn from two tables from Aron and Sharkey's national study of homeless programs, mentioned in previous chapters. The study found many faith-based homeless programs receiving government money, but it found that a much higher percentage of secular programs were receiving government funds (76.8 percent versus 38.5 percent). Among those that received government funds, the secular programs tended to receive much more money (60.2 percent of the secular programs received at least one-half of their funding from government, while only 12.1 percent of the faith-based programs did so). Table 26 is from my earlier study of child and family agencies. Ninety-six percent of the secular programs received government funding, compared to 82 percent of the faith-based programs. Also, 83 percent of the secular programs received 40 percent or more of their funding from the government, compared to 51 percent of the faith-based programs. Although the family and child care agencies received more government funding than did the homeless programs in Aron and Sharkey's study, the relative patterns were the same.

John Green and Amy Sherman studied faith-based organizations in 15 states that had received government funding under the charitable

TABLE 25. Percentage of Funding from Government, Faith-Based and Secular Homeless Programs

	None	1–24%	25–49%	50–74%	75–99%	100%	N
Secular	23.2%	7.6%	9.0%	15.1%	23.2%	21.9%	17,271
Faith-based	61.5%	17.9%	8.6%	5.3%	4.1%	2.7%	11,902

Source: Data from Aron and Sharkey, *The 1996 National Survey of Homeless Assistance Providers and Clients,* 31–32, tables 14 and 15.

TABLE 26. Percentage of Funding from Government, Faith-Based and Secular Child and Family Agencies

	None	1–19%	20–39%	40–59%	60–79%	80%+	N
Secular	4%	8%	5%	9%	20%	54%	133
Faith-based	18%	19%	12%	9%	17%	25%	11,902

Source: Data from Monsma, *When Sacred and Secular Mix,* 68.

choice provisions that have been included in four federal social service programs.[10] Their study showed that faith-based groups were receiving significant proportions of their budgets from the government (see table 27). Thirty-three percent of the social service programs received less than half of their program budgets from government, 27 percent received 75 to 99 percent from the government, and another 18 percent received all of their program budgets from the government. Green and Sherman did not gather comparable data from secular nonprofits receiving funds in the 15 states, but the fact that these figures are higher than those found in the two previously cited studies indicates that there may be more government funding available under charitable choice than in some other areas. A study of faith-based programs providing employment-related services in five cities (Baltimore, Fort Worth, Milwaukee, Pittsburgh, and San Diego) found that of the 43 programs included in the study, 22 (51 percent) received some government funding.[11]

Another important question is whether or not government funding of nonprofit social services leads to governmental domination of the recipient nonprofit agencies. Stanley Carlson-Thies has used the term *vendorism* to describe a relationship where the government turns nonprofit agencies with which it contracts into vendors, who become, in effect, extensions of government.[12] Many persons are convinced that vendorism is common, even though hard data is scarce. Steven Smith and Michael Lipsky concluded that nonprofit-government contracts have led to "regulations, obligations, and restrictions that accompany

TABLE 27. Percentage of Funding from Government, Faith-Based Programs Funded under Charitable Choice

	Percentage of Budgets from Government Funds
Less than 25%	18
25–49%	15
50–74%	22
75–99%	27
100%	18
N	389

Source: Data from Green and Sherman, *Fruitful Collaborations*, 13.

contracts," have "created rules and regulations for private agencies that otherwise would not be subject to government control," and have "resulted in unprecedented involvement of government in the affairs of nonprofit organizations."[13] In particular, many faith-based organizations reportedly fear that with government money will come government control—that is, that there is truth behind the statement "With government shekels come government shackles."

My earlier study shows that these fears may be overstated, since few faith-based organizations receiving government money reported interference with their religious missions as they had defined them.[14] Green and Sherman similarly report very high levels of satisfaction with government from the faith-based organizations that had received government contracts in their 15-state study. Table 28, taken from their study, shows that overwhelming majorities of the 389 faith-based organizations with government contracts ranked their experience of working with government positively, felt that officials monitoring the contracts were largely not intrusive, and considered the reporting requirements tolerable.

Two remaining issues concern the extent to which government

TABLE 28. Assessments of Relationship with Government by Faith-Based Organizations with Government Contracts under Charitable Choice

	Percentage Citing the Indicated Assessment
Experience with government	
Very positive	47
Somewhat positive	46
Somewhat negative	5
Very negative	2
Intrusiveness of officials monitoring contract	
Very little intrusion	62
Some intrusion	32
Considerable intrusion	5
Great intrusion	2
Burden of reporting requirements	
Very little burden	27
Some burden	44
Considerable burden	20
Great burden	9

Source: Data from Green and Sherman, *Fruitful Collaborations,* 28.

funds, first, secular community-based nonprofits and, second, for-profit firms providing social services. There is almost no systematic research to guide one in examining these issues. In the case of community-based organizations, there are reports of various barriers they have faced,[15] but I know of no studies that have looked at this issue systematically. It would be logical to presume that due to their small size and lack of strong professionalization, community-based organizations would have a hard time navigating the challenging field of governmental contracting and grant writing, but one cannot say this with assurance by referring to existing research.

It would appear that for-profit firms receive almost all of their social services funding—at least in the welfare-to-work field—by way of government-funded contracts or voucher-type programs. Although there is little research formally documenting this fact, it only stands to reason, since there are unlikely to be any other funding sources. User fees are unlikely, given the poverty and unemployed status of most welfare beneficiaries and many others seeking social services. Corporate and individual donations are unlikely, given the profit-seeking nature of for-profit firms. Of course, some employment and training programs run by for-profit vocational institutes or colleges may include both fee-paying students and students whose fees are paid via a government training program for the disadvantaged. This means there may be some programs that are funded both by user fees and by government-provided funds. This is an area that has seen almost no systematic research, leaving this study almost no prior research on which to build.

In summary, one can put forward, with reasonable confidence, five conclusions in terms of government funding of nongovernmental social service programs. First, secular nonprofit social service programs receive significant amounts of government funding for the services they provide. Second, faith-based social service programs also receive significant amounts of government funding, although they tend to receive less than do secular nonprofits. Faith-based programs that integrate religious elements into the services they provide also frequently receive government funding. Third, the available evidence is mixed on whether or not the autonomy of faith-based and secular nonprofit organizations in partnerships with government has been unduly compromised. Fourth, community-based nonprofits probably receive less funding than the larger, more professionalized, secular nonprofits. Fifth, almost all of the funding for for-profit social service programs comes from the government.

Current Research Findings: Government Regulation

In a chapter aptly entitled "Strings without Money," Charles Glenn, considering the role of government regulation of organizations providing education and social services, sees the hand of government regulation as heavy even in the absence of governmental funding. He writes:

> There seems, however, to be a natural tendency for government's oversight to become increasingly comprehensive, intrusive, and detailed. . . . Nor is the problem merely one of bureaucratic encroachment; over the past several decades a wide range of groups in society have managed to have their agendas written into laws and regulations in ways that—in many instances—affect organizations that do not accept public funding.[16]

Glenn goes on to suggest: "the most significant form of government intervention into the activities of faith-based organizations that do not seek public funding involves their licensing or accreditation. Whether or not a particular activity requires licensing is a decision that government itself makes, and the range of activities regulated in this way seems to expand constantly."[17]

Despite observations such as these, it is hard to find systematic data measuring either the actual or perceived amount—and onerousness—of government regulation of nongovernmental social service providers. The topic generally only comes to public notice when there is an outcry from a social service provider over what it perceives as unreasonable, constricting governmental regulations.

Government regulations usually take one of three different forms. One form consists of health and safety standards and deals with items such as fire safety standards, facilities for cooking and storing food, rest room facilities, availability of drinking water, and the presence of dangerous substances, such as lead paint or asbestos. Areas used by the public need to meet basic health and safety standards, yet some nonprofit and for-profit social service providers can feel they are being asked to meet very expensive, less-than-essential standards. For example, one Chicago faith-based organization included in this study is located on a church campus. At one time, it ran into problems because it is housed in several separate buildings with no central fire alarm system. Similar controversies have periodically arisen over such issues as health and safety standards for child care centers. Usually these controversies arise in conjunction with small church-based or community-based nonprofit organizations that are perceived by many—including themselves—as providing an important service to the community, yet they believe government regulators are setting such high, impossible-to-meet standards that their organizations are virtually being closed down.[18]

Closely related to health and safety regulations are legal requirements designed to prevent discrimination against certain groups in the population that have been subjected to discrimination in the past. The Americans with Disabilities Act—in its attempt to protect the right of persons with disabilities to function as fully participating members of society—is one example of a law that can add enormous costs to nongovernmental entities, as they seek to remodel often very old buildings to conform to the law's requirements. Civil rights laws against discrimination based on race, ethnicity, or gender—and, often more importantly, the reports and documentation used as part of the enforcement mechanisms—can add additional paperwork that is especially onerous to small nonprofits and that can pull limited staff resources away from direct service provision. But given the very large size of the nonprofit sector,[19] the large number of for-profit social service providers, and the basic values of equity and fair play, it is hard to argue that nongovernmental organizations should be exempt from these legal requirements.

There is one clear instance, however, where existing law explicitly excludes faith-based organizations from having to meet a regulatory requirement that other organizations have to meet. Section 702 of Title VII of the federal Civil Rights Act of 1964[20] provides that religious organizations are allowed to make hiring decisions based on religion, even though other, secular organizations are not allowed to do so.[21] The reasoning is that if a faith-based organization is to be able to maintain its religious character, it must be free to hire persons whose religious beliefs are compatible with the goals and mission of the organization. Otherwise, it would soon cease to exist as a faith-based organization. As Senator Sam Ervin colorfully put it during a 1972 Senate debate over the addition of an amendment that strengthened Section 702, "In other words, this amendment is to take the political hands of Caesar off of the institutions of God, where they have no place to be."[22]

The Supreme Court has upheld the constitutionality of this exemption in *Presiding Bishop v. Amos,* which involved a maintenance person who lost his job at a Mormon recreation center in Salt Lake City due to his no longer being a member in good standing of the church. In its decision, a unanimous Supreme Court ruled that the law allowing religious organizations to favor coreligionists in hiring "is rationally related to the legitimate purpose of alleviating significant governmental interference with the ability of religious organizations to define and carry out their religious missions."[23] In a concurring opinion, Justice William Brennan was even more explicit on what was at stake:

> Determining that certain activities are in furtherance of a [religious] organization's religious mission, and that only those committed to that mission should conduct them, is thus a means by which a religious community defines itself. Solicitude for a church's ability to do so reflects the idea that furtherance of the autonomy of religious organizations often furthers individual religious freedom as well.[24]

In other words, the Supreme Court has held that allowing faith-based groups to favor their coreligionists in their hiring is not a violation of the First Amendment but is a crucial means by which an organization defines itself and thereby protects its autonomy. This holds true even in the case of employees—such as the maintenance person in the *Amos* case—who are not directly involved in the teaching or sacramental activities of a religious organization.

A third type of governmental regulation is perhaps the hardest of the three with which to deal. It is the requirement that agencies providing certain types of social services must pass certain accreditation standards, or that the staff members providing certain social services must possess professional credentials thought to be important. There are two issues here for some providers. One is the simple matter of costs. To hire professionally trained and credentialed staff or to bring facility, staffing, and record-keeping standards up to those demanded by certain accreditation agencies may be prohibitively expensive for some providers.

Even more fundamentally, there may also be deep differences of opinion on the best programmatic approaches to dealing with the social problems with which an agency is seeking to deal. These differences of opinion may in turn be rooted in profound differences of opinion on the root causes of certain social ills. In discussing faith-based drug dependency programs, a representative of a professional association once stated before the Senate Judiciary Committee: "[The Association for Addiction Professionals'] concern is not with who provides care, but rather by what clinical standards that care is provided. We are committed to the application of science-based best practices." He went on to state that for his organization, the "salient issue is the clinical competency of the treatment provider."[25] The Web site for this same organization declares that "science has shown that addiction is a brain disease that responds well to treatment," and it advocates "public policy initiatives that ensure access to effective, clinically appropriate, science based treatment for chemical dependency disease for all in need of treatment."[26] This professional association clearly holds to certain underlying assumptions and defends certain treatment modalities. Many would agree with it; others would disagree. Faith-based agencies that believe illegal drug dependency is at root a moral or lifestyle problem—not a "treatable brain disease"—may very well feel that they are being asked to sell their very souls if they are forced into a treatment modality that they believe fails to deal with what they see as root causes. Meanwhile, those who are convinced that the science-based treatment modalities being taught in the best professional schools are the most effective and only responsible way to provide treatment for drug dependency may be convinced that to allow less professionalized, faith-based agencies to operate on the basis of their assumptions is to allow malpractice and put needy persons in danger.

As Ram Cnaan has pointed out, most professional schools of social work are thoroughly secularized and give short shrift to religiously based approaches to social ills.[27] It is no wonder that some faith-based groups feel that governmental regulatory attempts to impose certain professionalized credentialing and accreditation standards are an exercise of undue governmental power.

These issues are not purely academic. For example, President Bush's interest in and support for the delivery of faith-based social services can be traced back to his days as governor of Texas and to a controversy that arose over credentialing standards for the San Antonio Teen Challenge program.[28] The Texas Commission on Alcohol and Drug Abuse ruled that Teen Challenge—a residential faith-based drug treatment program—needed to meet state credentialing standards. The state at one point threatened to withdraw Teen Challenge's license and to close it down if it did not have certified chemical dependency counselors and other such professional staff. Out of this controversy, then Governor Bush appointed a special commission to study this issue and other related issues of state partnerships with faith-based organizations. This commission ended up recommending that alternative credentialing or certifying processes be created for certain faith-based organizations.[29]

The bottom line is that all nongovernmental providers—whether secular or faith-based, community-based or large and professionalized, nonprofit or for-profit—live in a world of government regulations and restrictions. No one would argue that government does not have a responsibility to protect the health and safety of the staff members and clients of these providers. It also has a responsibility to prevent civil rights violations of their staffs and clients and to work to prevent dangerous, fraudulent practices. But it is also important for the basic autonomy of nonprofits to be protected. The issue is one of seeking the correct balance between governmental protections and nongovernmental providers' freedom of action. Although it is possible to frame the issue of "strings without money," very little research has sought to explore the nature of the current balance. There is a dearth of systematic information about the extent and perceived level of onerousness of government's regulatory role in the lives of nongovernmental social service providers.

Current Research Findings: Provider Networks

This leaves the question of what past research has revealed concerning the existence of informal networks of social service providers. Most social services are not simply provided by government agencies or any other single set of organizations. Instead, they are provided by a confusing array of government agencies; for-profit firms, such as Maximus and Lockheed Martin; large, professionalized, secular nonprofits; small, nonprofessionalized, community-based, grassroots organizations; faith-based organizations providing largely secularized services; and faith-based organizations providing services pervaded with religious elements. In such a situation, one could easily suppose that these various organizations are often at loggerheads with each other as they compete for limited resources, put forward competing visions of effective social services, and struggle to maintain "market share" (to use a term borrowed from market economics). Alternatively, one could imagine that these various social service organizations are bound together into a more or less rational, informal network of services in any one city or community. These networks would consist of many channels of communication facilitated by more formal, periodic meetings or collaborations and many informal, ad hoc consultations, referrals, information exchanges, and cooperative ventures.

Here again, the available insights from previous research are thin. Greenberg has reported the existence of informal, cooperative networks: "State and local initiatives in welfare reform, such as Family Pathfinders and Faith in Families, are built upon voluntary and informal relationships between local agencies, nonprofits, businesses, and congregations."[30] She goes on to cite a number of other examples of such networks in cities around the country. But the extent and exact nature of such cooperative networks remain unexplored.

Government-Provider Relationships: Funding

This section considers what the study on which this book is based revealed concerning financial partnerships between government and nongovernmental welfare-to-work programs. Table 29 shows the percentage of organizations that reported receiving no government funds for their welfare-to-work programs. It clearly reveals that as one moves from nonprofit/secular, to community-based, to faith-based/segmented, to faith-based/integrated programs, more and more programs receive no government funding. Almost 60 percent of faith-based/integrated programs stated that they operate without any government funding. Two of the 25 for-profit programs reported receiving no government funds, placing them slightly above the nonprofit/secular programs in terms of operating without any government funding.

Table 30 shows the percentages of programs without any government funding in the four cities included in the study. With one or two exceptions, the pattern noted earlier—that of programs with no government funding increasing as one moves from nonprofit/secular, to community-based, to faith-based/segmented, to faith-based/integrated in program types—holds true in all four cities. The exception is Chicago, where more faith-based/segmented programs than faith-based/integrated programs reported operating without government

TABLE 29. Types of Programs Receiving No Government Funds

Program Type	Percentage Receiving No Government Funds	N
For-profit	8.0	25
Nonprofit/secular	4.3	139
Community-based	28.9	83
Faith-based/segmented	44.4	72
Faith-based/integrated	58.3	48

$\chi^2 (4) = 79.07, p < .001.$

TABLE 30. Percentage of Programs Receiving No Government Funds, by City and Program Type

	Chicago		Dallas		Los Angeles		Philadelphia	
Program Type	%	N	%	N	%	N	%	N
For-profit	12.5	8	10.0	10	0.0	4	0.0	3
Nonprofit/secular	2.0	50	13.3	15	2.0	51	8.7	23
Community-based	23.3	30	42.1	19	16.7	24	50.0	10
Faith-based/segmented	35.3	17	59.1	22	29.4	17	50.0	16
Faith-based/integrated	10.0	10	66.7	12	90.0	10	62.5	16

funding. Also, the community-based and faith-based/segmented programs in Philadelphia had the same percentage not receiving government funding.

In an interview for this study, the director of a Protestant faith-based program in Chicago stated her feeling that due to the longstanding, strong Catholic influence in Chicago politics, there is a friendlier atmosphere toward government funding for faith-based organizations there than in some other cities. She felt that her program, even though in the Protestant tradition, also benefited from this atmosphere. Her observation is partly borne out by looking at the percentages of all faith-based groups operating without any government funding in the four cities (i.e., by taking the faith-based/segmented and faith-based/integrated programs together). Chicago, at 26 percent, had the fewest programs without any government funding. There is a large jump to the next closest city, Los Angeles, at 52 percent without government funding, which is followed closely by Philadelphia at 56 percent and Dallas at 62 percent. It is interesting to note that the two cities associated with political leadership strongly and publicly in favor of government partnerships with faith-based providers—Philadelphia under Mayor John Street and Dallas under Texas's former governor George W. Bush[31]—are the two cities with the most programs receiving no government funding. This may say something about the difficulty elected officials face in turning entrenched patterns in their preferred directions. Despite these differences among the four cities, however, the similarities among them are far greater than the dissimilarities.

Table 31 includes only the programs that reported receiving government funding and shows for the five program types the average percentages of government funding out of the programs' total budgets. The pattern is clear. The faith-based/integrated programs that did receive public funding reported receiving the least amount of government funding (30.1 percent), with the faith-based/segmented reporting the next smallest amount of government funding (50 percent). Both faith-based program types were easily outstripped by the nonprofit/secular and community-based programs in the average amount of government funding reported (76.4 percent and 65.9 percent, respectively).

Before commenting at greater length on these findings, it is helpful to take note of the for-profit programs and the fact that the government funds they received for their welfare-to-work programs constituted less than 100 percent of their budgets. Eight percent of the for-profit programs reported receiving no government money at all, and those that did receive government money received an average of 60.2 percent of their program costs from the government. I had expected both figures to be higher. The explanation seems to lie in the nature of some of the for-profit organizations running welfare-to-work programs. My associate researcher and I made site visits to seven for-profit organizations. All but one of the programs that did not receive 100 percent or nearly 100 percent of their funding from the government were proprietary trade or vocational schools that also had paying students.[32] One, for example, was a school teaching computer skills. Most of their students paid out of their own pockets for the training, but a number were also sent over by the local Workforce Investment Board, and the charges for those students were paid out of tax dollars. Most of the public policy debate surrounding the use of for-profit companies to deliver welfare-related services has focused on the use of large firms, such as Maximus and Lockheed Martin, to deliver a full range of comprehensive services. But this study has revealed a type of for-profit firm that is largely being ignored in the policy debate: vocational schools that are providing skills training, sometimes, but not always, along with some other supportive services (such as training in résumé writing and life skills).

TABLE 31. Mean Percentage of Budgets from Government Funds, by Program Type

Program Type	Mean Percentage of Budgets from Government	N
For-profit	60.2	20
Nonprofit/secular	76.4	122
Community-based	65.9	52
Faith-based/segmented	50.0	36
Faith-based/integrated	30.1	18

Note: The calculations in this table include only data from programs receiving government funds.

$F(4, 243) = 13.44, p < .001$.

Returning to the question of the disparities in government funding for secular and faith-based nonprofit programs, the old question of whether the glass is half empty or half full emerges. Compared to the nonprofit/secular and community-based programs, the faith-based programs were faring much worse in terms of receiving government funding. That is the half-empty perspective on the glass, and I will return to it in a moment to explore why this is the case.

There is, however, also the half-full perspective. In fact, a majority of the faith-based/segmented programs reported receiving government funding, and the amounts received were significant: on the average, they received one-half of their budgets from the government. Even among the faith-based/integrated programs, over 40 percent received government funds, and they averaged just over 30 percent of their budgets from government—again, a significant amount. Here, it is important to recall from chapter 2 the types of religious practices engaged in by the faith-based/integrated programs. Table 4 (in chap. 2) reveals that a majority of faith-based/integrated programs open or close sessions with prayer, use religious values to motivate staff, have voluntary religious exercises, use religious values to encourage clients to change their attitudes, and either give preference in hiring staff or only hire staff who agree with their religious beliefs. Nevertheless, many were able to secure government funds, often in significant levels. The glass is indeed half full.

But the glass is also half empty. Some 44.4 percent of the faith-based/segmented programs received no government funding at all, and those that did receive government funds received an average of one-half of their budgets from the government. The corresponding figures were much lower for the faith-based/integrated programs. Just over 58 percent of them did not receive any government funds, and those that received government funds received an average of only 30.1 percent of their budgets from government sources. These figures are in sharp contrast with those from their secular nonprofit counterparts. A mere 4.3 percent of the nonprofit/secular programs received no government funds, and those that received government funds averaged 76.4 percent of their budgets from the government. Especially instructive are the community-based programs, since they are very similar to the faith-based programs in size and sophistication. Only

28.4 percent (compared to 44.4 percent and 58.3 percent for the faith-based/segmented and faith-based integrated programs, respectively) received no government funds, and those that received government funds averaged 65.9 percent of their budgets from the government (compared to 50 percent and 30.1 percent for the faith-based/segmented and faith-based/integrated programs, respectively). Apparently, factors related to the religious nature of the faith-based welfare-to-work programs resulted in their being more likely to receive either no government funds or smaller amounts of government funding than the secular welfare-to-work programs.

The preceding figures are generally in line with those from earlier studies of government funding of social welfare services. Compared to the funding of homeless programs as documented by Aron and Sharkey, both the faith-based and the secular welfare-to-work programs in the current study tended to receive somewhat more government funding. Compared to my earlier study of child and family service agencies and to Green and Sherman's study of social service programs receiving government funding under charitable choice, the welfare-to-work programs tended to receive somewhat less government funding (cf. tables 25, 26, and 27 with tables 29 and 31). As one moves from homeless programs, to welfare-to-work programs, to child and family service programs, to programs funded under charitable choice, the amount of government funding increases. But a basic pattern—one of extensive government funding for both secular and faith-based nonprofits, but with secular nonprofits receiving significantly more government funding than faith-based nonprofits—holds true across all four studies.

This is clearly illustrated by table 32, which compares the amount of government funding documented by Green and Sherman's study with what was found by the current study of welfare-to-work programs. The faith-based programs in Green and Sherman's study were clearly receiving greater percentages of their budgets from the government than were the faith-based welfare-to-work programs included in the current study. However, the current study's secular nonprofit programs were receiving even greater proportions of their budgets from the government than were the faith-based programs in either Green and Sherman's study or the current study. In summary, various studies that have explored the amount of funding received by faith-based and secular nonprofit social service programs have found differing proportions of the nonprofits' budgets coming from the government, yet the relative amount of government funding for secular and faith-based nonprofits has not varied, with secular nonprofits consistently receiving greater percentages of their budgets from government sources than have their faith-based counterparts.

Previous studies have not broken the secular nonprofit programs down into larger nonprofit programs and smaller, community-based programs. Thus, no comparisons can be drawn between what I found here and earlier studies.

This leaves the question of why the faith-based welfare-to-work programs and, to a lesser degree, the community-based programs tended to fair so much worse than the large, secular nonprofits when it comes to government funding. Is this due to discrimination against faith-based and community-based providers on the part of government funders, as some claim? Or are there other explanations? The current study throws light on this question. Table 33 shows the reasons that the four types of nonprofit programs not receiving government funding gave for not doing so. The nonprofit/secular, community-based, and two types of faith-based programs tended to give distinctive answers to the question of why they do not receive government funds. These answers reveal three significant patterns.

TABLE 32. Percentage of Budgets from Government Funds

	Secular Nonprofits (%)[a]	Green-Sherman Study (%)[b]	Faith-Based Programs (%)[c]
Less than 25%	8	18	42
25–49%	10	15	15
50–74%	17	22	13
75–99%	43	27	15
100%	22	18	15
N	174	389	53

[a]Includes both nonprofit/secular and community-based programs, but only programs receiving government funds.
[b]Data from Green and Sherman, *Fruitful Collaborations*, 13.
[c]Includes both faith-based/segmented and faith-based/integrated programs, but only programs receiving government funds.

In the first pattern, every one of the handful of nonprofit/secular programs that do not receive government funding said the reason for not doing so was that this was "just the way things have worked out." This alternative was put on the questionnaire (see app. C, Q14) as a residual category for those programs that had not really thought about government funding or that had felt no need for it. The picture of the large, secular nonprofit welfare-to-work programs being very closely allied with government is strengthened by the consistent pattern of these responses.

A second pattern can be found in the responses of the community-based programs, which divided three ways on the question. About one-fourth reported that they have a self-conscious policy against accepting government funds, and another one-fourth indicated that they had inquired about government funds and decided not to apply. Close to half reported, as did all the nonprofit/secular groups, that this is just the way things have worked out. The picture that thus emerges is that about one-half of the small community-based programs were scared off government grants—either out of fear of government control or by intimidating application procedures—and that about one-half did not feel the need for or had not given any thought about government funding. The executive director of one Los Angeles community-based organization, for example, told the story of her father, who had headed up the nonprofit organization and had never wanted or received government funding, due to fear of red tape and rigid conditions: "I have been working in this field for a very long time. I grew up in it. My father founded ——. He created an organization that never received government funding, because of the stipu-

TABLE 33. Reasons for No Government Funds, by Program Type (percentage citing reasons given)

Program Type	Self-Conscious Policy (%)	Applied, Did Not Receive	Inquired, Did Not Apply (%)	Way Things Worked Out	N	Total
Nonprofit/secular	0.0	0.0	0.0	100.0	5	100.0
Community-based	26.1	8.7	21.7	43.5	23	100.0
Faith-based/segmented	40.6	21.9	9.4	28.1	32	100.0
Faith-based/integrated	40.7	18.5	22.2	18.5	27	99.9

$\chi^2(9) = 17.41, p < .05$.

lations in there—the red tape and the guidelines and the reports and all of that." Her organization now receives some government funding, but she seeks to keep it only a small part of her budget by pursuing as many other sources of funds as possible. Her big fear is that her agency might become overly dependent on government money and that government restrictions might thereby become intrusive. This finding means that any public policy initiative that seeks to increase the participation of community-based welfare-to-work programs in government financial partnerships will need to deal with the issues of intimidating application processes and of rigid, constricting program criteria.

The two types of faith-based programs present a third pattern. About 40 percent of both types of faith-based programs reported a self-conscious policy against accepting government funds, which is a much higher proportion than either the community-based or the nonprofit/secular programs gave for not accepting government funds. Also noteworthy is the fact that among the faith-based/integrated programs that reported they either have a self-conscious policy of not accepting government funds or had inquired about government funds but decided not to apply, 65 percent also reported a desire to expand greatly.[33] Clearly, their decision not to pursue government funding was not due to a desire to remain small. Also noteworthy is the fact that about 20 percent of both types of faith-based programs reported having applied for government funds and having been turned down. Compared to the nonprofit/secular and community-based programs, much smaller percentages of the faith-based programs reasoned that they did not have government funding because that was just the way things had worked out.

Do these patterns support the claim some are making that there are many barriers preventing faith-based nonprofit organizations from accessing government funds? A prima facie case can be made that discrimination is occurring. In addition to the simple fact that the faith-based groups were receiving much less funding than the secular groups, two other facts help bolster the case that discrimination is present. First, when compared to the community-based providers—who, as I showed in chapter 2, are similar to the faith-based programs in terms of size and level of professionalization—the faith-based providers still received much less government funding. Thus, the smaller size and lower levels of professionalization of the faith-based providers cannot in themselves explain the low levels of government funding. Second, 21 percent of the faith-based programs had applied for funding and been turned down, compared to none of the nonprofit/secular programs and only 8.7 percent of the community-based programs. All this suggests that the playing field of distributing limited government resources to nonprofit organizations is indeed not level. It does not, however, constitute conclusive proof that government funders have been favoring secular providers over faith-based providers simply because the faith-based providers have a religious dimension. Possibly, there may be other factors in play.

Therefore, in visits to those faith-based programs that do not receive government funds, my associate researcher and I probed further in regard to the reasons for their not receiving public funds. Time and again, fear for their religious freedom; a more general fear of cumbersome, time-consuming government regulations; fear of being unable to pursue the programs they feel called to pursue; or a combination of these fears were cited. For example, one assistant director of a Dallas faith-based/integrated program that does not accept government funds reflected two of these fears.

> One day we got a check for $10,000 from the government and, along with it, a big box filled with the paperwork that needed to be filled out. [The director] packed it all up and sent it back! There seems to be so much red tape involved with government. We probably could take some money for some programs, but then we would have to be so careful about when we talk about Christ. [The director's] philosophy is that if we do not have to have it, it is better to get along without it.

The senior pastor of a Philadelphia church that is heavily involved in inner-city ministries and that does not receive government funds said that the church "would be very cautious in regard to any arrangement with the government that would in any way compromise the autonomy of our ministry and especially our message." The pastor continued: "To us the message is everything. Word and deed are both important. The word message is essential to the action—we do not want to compromise that." The head of a Los Angeles faith-based program that had applied for but not received government funding insisted, "we don't want to compromise parts of our program for governmental sources of funding." In short, the seemingly endless paperwork and a fear of not being able to pursue certain desired programs seem to play as large a role in staying away from government funding as does the fear of compromising faith-based practices. All three are important. These considerations go a long way toward explaining the almost two-thirds of the faith-based/integrated programs that expressed a desire to expand greatly but either have policies against accepting government funds or inquired about them and decided not to apply for them.

As was found to be the case with community-based programs, any public policy initiative seeking to enable faith-based welfare-to-work programs to partner more frequently with government will need to address issues of overly complex application and reporting processes and of rigid, constricting program criteria. In addition, in the case of faith-based programs, potential limitations on faith-based practices will also have to be addressed.

Government-Provider Relationships: Informal Networks

In addition to inquiring about government funding, the questionnaire used in the study also inquired concerning other types of contact with government. The results are shown in table 34. The most striking aspect of this table is the fact that very few nongovernment programs reported no contacts with government. Right across the board, the programs reported multiple contacts with government. Majorities of all five types of nongovernmental providers reported receiving referrals from government. Near majorities reported making referrals to government, and—perhaps most significantly—majorities reported having "had informal consultations or exchanges of information with government offices" (see app. C, Q17). Even though there were very large differences in the receipt of government funds among the five program types, there were almost no differences among them in the number and types of contacts with government.

TABLE 34. Types of Contact with Government, by Program Type (percentage reporting various types of contacts)

Program Type	No Contact (%)	Referrals from Government (%)	Referrals to Government (%)	Informal Consultations (%)	Clients in Government Jobs (%)	Licensed by Government (%)	Safety Health Inspections	Other Contacts (%)	N
For-profit	4.2	79.2	41.7	54.2	16.7	29.2	29.2	20.8	24
Nonprofit/secular	3.7	81.5	46.7	55.6	30.4	21.5	31.9	15.6	135
Community-based	10.3	62.8	37.2	62.8	7.7	11.5	19.2	16.7	78
Faith-based/segmented	13.4	52.2	41.8	56.7	6.0	14.9	32.8	9.0	67
Faith-based/integrated	6.3	60.4	47.9	56.3	10.4	8.3	37.5	22.9	48

Table 35 gives some added insight by revealing how many of table 34's seven different sorts of contact the five nongovernmental programs types reported having with government. There was a slight tendency for for-profit and nonprofit/secular programs to report having more government contacts than did the community-based and the faith-based programs. If one combines the programs having three to four types of contact with those having five or more types of contact, one finds that over half of both the for-profit and nonprofit/secular programs had three or more types of contact. Almost 60 percent of the nonprofit/secular programs had three or more types of contact. This compares to about 40 percent of the community-based and faith-based programs having three or more types of contact with government. These results reinforce the picture that emerged from the funding patterns that also showed the large, professionalized nonprofit/secular programs in partnership with government. But whatever differences there were among the five different program types were by far overshadowed by the similarities. All five types of welfare-to-work programs had multiple contacts with government.

The range and variety of contacts between government and welfare-to-work programs that receive no government funding is illustrated by the following sampling of written comments made on the questionnaire by respondents from programs that receive no government funding.

- A respondent for a Los Angeles community-based program wrote, "All local government officials support our work vocally and financially (private contributions)."

TABLE 35. Number of Types of Contact with Government, by Program Type

Program Type	No Contact (%)	1–2 Types of Contact (%)	3–4 Types of Contact (%)	5–7 Types of Contact (%)	Total (%)	N
For-profit	4.2	45.8	29.2	20.9	100.1	24
Nonprofit/secular	3.7	37.8	44.5	14.1	100.1	135
Community-based	10.3	50.0	35.9	3.9	100.1	78
Faith-based/segmented	13.4	46.2	32.8	7.5	99.9	67
Faith-based/integrated	6.3	47.9	31.3	14.6	100.1	48

- A respondent for a Dallas faith-based/integrated program wrote. "We work cooperatively with government."
- A respondent for a Los Angeles faith-based/segmented program wrote, "We were invited to attend workshops provided by government officers."
- A respondent for a Chicago community-based program wrote, "We put up fliers in government offices."
- A respondent for a Chicago faith-based/segmented program wrote: "We have received resource material from government offices. We have attended conferences sponsored by government offices and congressmen."
- A respondent for a Los Angeles faith-based/integrated program wrote, "Police, parole officers, and social workers refer clients to us."

In site visits to programs, the host of cooperative relationships that cut across various types of entities were frequently evident. In Los Angeles, for example, a community-based organization that is working to place women in nontraditional job positions uses the buildings and classrooms of a public community college free of charge. A faith-based/integrated program in Los Angeles does not receive government funding, but it does have several Americorp volunteers. These relationships often appear to be two-way, cooperative relationships. A Philadelphia faith-based/integrated program reported, "[Government] officials visit us and ask us to promote their work in the community."

Most of the nongovernmental programs viewed these relationships with government positively. After the programs were asked about the number and types of contacts they had with government, they were asked whether or not they found their contacts with government to be satisfactory. Table 36 gives the results by program type. Overwhelming majorities—in the area of 70 percent—of all five program types reported they were very or usually satisfied with their contacts with government. It is worth noting that although 67.4 percent of the faith-based/integrated programs reported they were very or usually satisfied with their contacts with government, 16.3 percent indicated they were usually unsatisfied with their contacts with government.

TABLE 36. Satisfaction with Government Contacts, by Program Type

Program Type	Very Satisfied (%)	Usually Satisfied (%)	Neither Satisfied nor Unsatisfied (%)	Usually Unsatisfied (%)	Very Unsatisfied (%)	N	Total (%)
For-profit	17.4	52.2	30.4	0.0	0.0	23	100.0
Nonprofit/secular	13.1	63.1	16.2	6.9	0.8	130	100.1
Community-based	25.7	44.3	18.6	11.4	0.0	70	100.0
Faith-based/segmented	28.1	52.6	14.0	5.3	0.0	57	100.0
Faith-based/integrated	18.6	48.8	16.3	16.3	0.0	43	100.0

Even though the latter figure represents a small minority, it is higher than the figures exhibited for this category by the other program types, and it may signal some tension between government officials and a minority of the more explicitly religious faith-based programs.

Our site visits led to a somewhat less sanguine view of government contacts. Both faith-based and secular nonprofit providers presented a recurrent theme: the individuals in government with whom they deal are good, understanding, helpful persons who truly care for the poor (whom both the governmental and the nongovernmental providers are seeking to serve), but the bureaucratic structures are difficult to deal with because decision-making authority is diffused through several levels. Thus, when dealing with a government organization, one has to go to one person to get his or her approval, then one also needs to go to several supervisors up in the hierarchy, since they, too, need to sign off on the decision. All this takes enormous amounts of time and effort. This perspective was summarized neatly by the director of a Dallas faith-based inner-city ministry when he reported many contacts with the "U.S. attorney's office, school officials, housing authority, city council members, etc., etc." He explained: "On the individual level, without exception, these contacts are delightful and helpful. On the bureaucratic level, it just doesn't move!"

In brief, the picture that emerges is not of nongovernmental welfare-to-work programs working in isolation from government but of their being woven into a web of cooperative relationships that most of the programs find satisfactory in nature. This was true whether they were for-profit or nonprofit, secular or faith-based, and whether they received government funding or not. It is not a misnomer to speak of a "network" of welfare-to-work programs and services in the four cities.

The questionnaire did not inquire extensively concerning the regulatory arm of government and its impact on the operation of the welfare-to-work programs included in the study. The question that asked about various possible contacts with government listed as two options "We have undergone health or safety inspections by the government" and "We are licensed by a government agency" (app. C, Q17). Table 34 shows that about 10 to 35 percent of the programs reported either one or both of these contacts with government. Many—but a minority—of welfare-to-work programs were dealing with government on the regulatory level. I suspect these figures would be higher for other types of social service programs, especially those that provide health care or drug dependency services, involve residential programs, or deal with children. In these areas, governmental regulatory rules understandably tend to be more numerous. From written comments on the questionnaires and from site visits, it appeared that regulatory contacts with government officials hardly seem to appear on the radar scopes of the welfare-to-work programs included in the study. Among some 78 questionnaire comments concerning contacts with government, only 2 mentioned a regulatory issue. In extended conversations with staff at 51 programs, the issue of regulatory problems hardly ever came up (although we did not specifically probe for them). One of the very few exceptions was the previously mentioned faith-based/integrated program in Chicago that is housed in several separate buildings on a church campus, where an issue had come up in regard to the lack of a central fire alarm system.

Government-Provider Relationships: Shekels without Shackles

What has thus far been reported in this chapter clearly points in the direction of the existence of pervasive, ongoing partnerships between government and a variety of nongovernmental entities. The findings also point in the direction of most of the nongovernmental entities evaluating most of their contacts with government positively, although some express frustrations due to delays in getting final answers from complex governmental bureaucracies. This leaves the question of the many financial partnerships between government and nongovernmental welfare-to-work programs. Popular expectations would suggest that if one is to find unhappiness and tensions in this partnership, one would surely expect to find it in the financial area. Are the nongovernmental entities satisfied with the state of the financial partnerships with government? Or are these partnerships marked by dissension, tension, and resentment? Are they true partnerships, with both of the partners having a healthy measure of independence? Or are they marked by government dominating and subverting the entities with which it is partnering so that they have become little more than unwilling clones of the government? It sometimes is assumed that government is an oppressive force under whose bureaucratic weight any partner would struggle to survive. Whether or not this is the situation will be explored in this section.

For those programs receiving government funding, the questionnaire posed a list of 10 possible results of their receiving public funds and asked which of them they had experienced. Five of these results were positive in nature, and 5 were negative. Table 37 lists these 10 results in order of the frequency with which they were cited—with the 5 positive results listed first and the 5 negative results listed next. The table gives the percentage of organizations that indicated each result was a consequence of their receiving government money. The positive results were clearly selected much more frequently than the negative results, except for the perennial complaint about too much paperwork.

Table 38 reveals that the generally positive assessment of government funding cuts across the various program types. For each program, I subtracted the number of negative results cited from the number of positive results cited. Thus, if a program cited as many negative results as positive results, it would have a score of zero; if it cited more

TABLE 37. Results of Receiving Government Funds (percentage indicating they have experienced each result)

	Percentage Reporting Indicated Result
Positive results	
Expanded the number of clients we are able to serve	48.7
Hired staff with stronger qualifications and more experience	27.5
Provided services more professionally/effectively	26.9
Hired staff with higher levels of education	26.3
Improved facilities to better serve clients	24.0
Negative results	
Put more time and effort into paperwork than should be necessary	31.6
Became more "bureaucratic," less flexible and creative	15.7
Became less efficient	2.2
Cut down on religious emphasis/practices	1.8
Received fewer private gifts and volunteer hours than we otherwise would	1.2
N	336

positive results than negative results, it would have a positive score; if it cited more negative results than positive results, it would have a negative score. Table 38 shows that although there were significant differences among the five program types receiving government money, all of them were largely positive in judging the results of receiving that money. If one takes into account all of the programs that reported more positive than negative results of receiving government funds, one finds that 71.4 percent of the for-profit programs, 70.7 percent of the nonprofit/secular programs, 83.6 percent of the community-based programs, 61.8 percent of the faith-based/segmented programs, and 61.1 percent of the faith-based/integrated programs reported more positive than negative results of government funding. From this perspective, the community-based programs were the most positive, and the two categories of faith-based programs were the least positive.

Table 39 gives a little different perspective on the responses to this question. It gives the exact percentage of times the five different program types cited each of the 10 possible effects of receiving government funds. Here, it emerges that the nonprofit/secular programs were both the most positive and the most negative in judging the effects of government funding. In the case of 4 of the 5 positive effects, the nonprofit/secular programs cited those effects as frequently or more frequently than did any other program type. In the case of the 5 negative effects, 1 did not apply to the secular nonprofits, and 2 were cited by very few of any of the programs. However, of the remaining

TABLE 38. Positive versus Negative Results of Government Funds, by Program Type

Program Type	3–5 More Negative than Positive Results (%)	1–2 More Negative than Positive Results (%)	Same Number of Negative and Positive Results (%)	1–2 More Positive than Negative Results (%)	3–5 More Positive than Negative Results (%)	N	Total (%)
For-profit	0.0	9.5	19.0	61.9	9.5	21	100.0
Nonprofit/secular	1.6	22.2	5.6	31.8	38.9	126	100.1
Community-based	0.0	10.9	5.5	52.8	30.8	55	100.0
Faith-based/segmented	0.0	14.7	23.5	29.4	32.4	34	100.0
Faith-based/integrated	0.0	16.7	22.2	50.0	11.1	18	100.0

$\chi^2(16) = 35.90, p < .01.$

TABLE 39. Results of Government Funding, by Program Type

	Percent Reporting Indicating Result				
	For-Profit	Nonprofit/ Secular	Community-Based	Faith-Based/ Segmented	Faith-Based/ Integrated
Positive results					
Expanded number of clients we are able to serve	76.2	76.2	74.5	67.6	61.1
Hired staff with stronger qualifications and more experience	28.6	46.0	47.3	35.3	16.7
Provided services more professionally/effectively	14.3	46.8	41.8	32.4	44.4
Hired staff with higher levels of education	28.6	47.6	45.5	35.3	16.7
Improved facilities to better serve clients	19.0	40.5	38.2	32.4	27.8
Negative results					
Put more time and effort into paperwork	47.6	56.3	43.6	38.2	55.6
Became more "bureaucratic," less flexible and creative	19.0	31.0	18.2	11.8	16.7
Became less efficient	0.0	4.8	3.6	0.0	5.6
Cut down on religious emphasis/practices	NA	NA	NA	8.8	0.0
Received fewer private gifts and volunteer hours	0.0	4.0	1.8	0.0	0.0
N	21	126	55	34	18

2 negative effects, the nonprofit/secular programs cited those effects more frequently than did any other program type.

In summary, in terms of the theoretical framework set down in chapter 1, the evidence presented here supports the proposition that nongovernmental organizations that enter into financial partnerships with government are able to do so without surrendering their autonomy. The pluralism of social structures is able to survive even financial partnerships with government. But this is only the beginning of the exploration I intend.

This leaves, first of all, the issue of faith-based organizations and their ability to maintain their autonomy. They have the added potential disadvantage of having religious orientations and practices to protect from government interference, a situation not faced by the secular nonprofits. The starting point in addressing this issue is to note that only 3 of 54 faith-based agencies receiving government funding cited the negative result of having to reduce their religious emphases or practices. In fact, not one of the 18 faith-based/integrated programs receiving government funds (the very programs one would expect most likely to have run into this problem) reported having to curtail any of their religious practices. Many directors of faith-based programs that receive government funding bore witness to the fact that they have been able to do so without compromising their religious commitments and goals. The director of one Chicago program that receives government funds stated: "We have monthly reports and all that, but it's never been a matter of great tension, you know, of church and state. . . . We've been amazingly free of any debate, disputes, or challenges."

It is instructive to compare the findings reported in table 38 with those of Green and Sherman reported earlier in this chapter (table 28). Direct comparisons cannot be made, because questions were worded differently, but it appears that the findings are very similar: faith-based organizations receiving government money are generally happy with their partnership with government. In both studies, one-third to two-thirds of faith-based organizations reported positive results from receiving government funds, and only a relatively few negative results were reported. When one looks at the faith-based/segmented and faith-based/integrated programs separately, the latter are somewhat less positive and somewhat more negative. But even among them, the overall assessment is positive. They seem to believe the partnership works: they are able to serve more clients with better services due to receiving government money, and most of them are able to do so without suffering undue restrictions on their religiously inspired practices or other programming efforts.

From extensive interviews with directors and staff members in 20 faith-based programs in four different cities, one comes away with the clear impression that as long as persons of all faiths or of none are welcomed and provided with services and as long as proselytizing is not a direct, overt part of the program, few or no problems are experienced. Neither of these conditions pose much of a problem for either type of faith-based welfare-to-work program. As table 4 (in chap. 2) reveals, only 1.4 percent of the faith-based/segmented and 2.1 percent of the faith-based/integrated programs (which comes to 2 of the 120 faith-based programs) gave preference to clients of the program's own faith, and as I reported in chapter 3, almost all of the faith-based programs we visited saw proselytizing as, at most, an indirect or secondary goal. It was viewed more as a happy and hoped-for by-product of their welfare-to-work efforts than as a direct, explicit goal. This was also true of the conservative Protestant programs, where one might most likely expect to see strong proselytizing efforts.

Many may be surprised at the lack of reported government limitations on religious practices in programs it helps fund. There are probably two explanations for the lack of complaints. One is that government officials may be willing to cut some slack for welfare-to-work programs that are willing and able to tackle very difficult social ills and work with an often very challenging clientele with whom not many others are eager to work. The director of a Chicago faith-based program closely associated with a predominantly African American congregation told this story: "The only time someone from the government told me not to involve Christ in our work is when I was over at the church, but the gentleman [the government official] who said this said: 'I couldn't care less. I'm just going to tell you what the rules are because I know you are a good person.'" One suspects that the rules of the game as they work themselves out in practice in the inner cities of major metropolitan areas often bear little resemblance to Washington and academic debates over government funding. I was introduced to a healthy dose of reality by an assistant director of a Dallas faith-based program that receives government funding and has done so for years, when he said: "My theory is that in the inner city, nobody really cares what you do. One can evangelize et cetera without persons asking questions. This is different in the suburbs—there the ACLU would be all over you. . . . The political alliances are different here in the inner city. The ACLU and we are on the same side on many issues, not at odds. This helps." The executive director of another Dallas faith-based program stated that the attitude of government officials seems to be that they need all the help they can get, so as long as what the program is doing works, they are satisfied. She also mentioned the fact that since many of their students come from Christian backgrounds, questions of faith naturally come up in their classes. This, she felt, also helps.

A second reason for the lack of government-imposed limitations—despite very frequent concerns—lies in the ability of program directors to finesse and manage potential problems. The director quoted in the previous paragraph also related the story of a time when an official questioned the presence of a cross in the building where the program's services were being given: "You know, one time they wanted me to cover up the cross of Christ, but they did not push that too much. I wasn't going to cover up any cross of Christ. No way! I don't care how much money they gave me. I'm not going to do that!" The government official backed off. When the executive director of a Chicago faith-based agency that receives limited government funding discussed the ambiguity surrounding government money and what the agency may and may not do that is of a spiritual nature, I suggested that perhaps the policy was "Don't ask, don't tell." She responded, "Exactly!" and went on to compare the situation to that of the city building code, which is workable only because it is usually not enforced in all its particulars. Similarly, she suggested that as long as the agency welcomes persons of all faiths and does not require participation in religious exercises and as long as she maintains a good working relationship with the government officials, questions are not raised about the agency's faith-based practices.

All this should not be interpreted, however, as meaning that there are no problems or concerns in this area. Almost all the directors of faith-based program and especially those of the faith-based/integrated programs expressed some sort of a concern or had some story of their having to finesse a potentially troubling situation. The existence of deep concerns was illustrated when the director of a Los Angeles faith-based/integrated program that had recently been granted some state funding asked me to turn off the tape recorder when I asked her about the faith elements in her program. Nevertheless, despite a frequent sense of caution or concern, almost all of the faith-based programs in all four cities that were receiving government funds reported no problems of government forbidding them to engage in practices of a faith-inspired nature that they thought important.

These findings lead to a puzzle. Anyone who has read claims frequently made in more popular writings or who has talked to any number of faith-based social service program directors that do not now receive government funding will have noted the strong fear of forming financial partnerships with government. The fear is that doing so will inevitably lead to the weakening of the religious elements in the organizations' programs. They believe that this has often happened in the past with other organizations that once were faith-based but that now show little evidence of a faith once deeply held. Yet researchers who have talked to or surveyed the directors of programs already receiving government funding have generally come back with reports that, in fact, government money tends not to lead to the undermining of faith-based agencies' religion mission. Why is this? Why does perception seem to diverge from actual experience? I cannot give a definitive answer to that question, but there are four factors that I suspect contribute to this situation.

One factor that may send warning signals to many faith-based agency directors and popular writers concerning government funding is the belief that there are many faith-based groups that started out integrally religious, then accepted government money, and now are thoroughly secular. It is true that many now thoroughly secularized organizations once started out as integrally religious. Of the 226 secular nonprofit programs in my study, 53, or almost one-fourth, indicated that they at one time had a religious orientation but now are largely secular in nature. It is easy to jump to the conclusion that a prime factor in this secularization was government funding, along with government limits and pressures against the faith elements in the program. However, Charles Glenn and others have argued that there are many other factors involved in this secularization process, such as increasing professionalization, United Way and foundation demands, and—maybe most important—a lack of clear thinking and strong commitment to the religious orientation on the part of the faith-based organizations' leaders themselves. Glenn concluded, "government interference may be less significant than loss of conviction or lack of clarity [on the part of the organizations' leaders] about the significance in practice of religious convictions, insights, and actions."[34]

A second factor that may feed the impression that with government money comes severe limitations on the religious practices of faith-based organizations is the uncertain legal situation in which faith-based programs receiving government funds in fact find themselves. As I noted in chapters 1 and 3, this legally uncertain situation is real, even though most faith-based nonprofits seem to navigate it successfully. There has been only one decision by the Supreme Court since 1900 that deals with faith-based nonprofit social service programs. Thus, there are almost no direct precedents to guide either the nonprofit organizations or the government officials enforcing government grants or contracts with faith-based nonprofits. Meanwhile, a series of decisions dealing with the funding of K–12 schools and colleges and universities could—depending on how they are interpreted and applied—be very troubling to the freedom of faith-based organizations to live out their religious commitments. As I discussed in chapter 3, even such crucial terms as *proselytization, sectarian worship,* and *sectarian instruction* have been left undefined. Also perhaps affecting this situation are a spate of lawsuits that have been filed in recent years and are now in the lower courts.[35] Once they are finally decided—and especially if some of them make it all the way to the Supreme Court—greater clarity may be gained. In the meanwhile, faith-based organizations understandably may fear that accepting government funding may put their religious missions in jeopardy.

A third factor may help explain the disjunction between frequent fears of government financial partnerships and actual practice as reported here and elsewhere. This factor rests on the fact, reported in chapter 2, that most faith-based social service programs that integrate religion into the services they provide are in the conservative, or evangelical, Protestant tradition. Political conservatism does not necessarily correlate with theological conservatism, and there are a number of politically moderate or liberal evangelicals. But that tradition is predominantly marked by persons who are politically conservative.[36] This leads them—as is the case with conservatives generally—to have a deeply ingrained suspicion of government. Thus, the natural inclination in the absence of strong countervailing information may be to assume that with government money will come strong, negative government controls.

There is a final factor that may explain the disjunction between, on the one hand, the fears that with government money will come a loss of religious practices and, on the other hand, the reality reported by most religiously oriented organizations that have received government money. It lies in the fact that the vast majority of programs that receive government money receive only a portion—usually even less than 50 percent—of their budgets from government. This gives these faith-based organizations a huge advantage in maintaining their autonomy from governmental domination. Yet when faith-based groups receiving government funds are discussed, it is often assumed that one is talking about 100 percent funding of the funded programs.

The partial funding that faith-based programs typically receive from government means they have a flexibility and an independence that organizations with all or nearly all their funding coming from government just do not have. There may even be more here than immediately meets the eye. Most obviously, organizations with their own independent sources of funds do not have to fear the loss or reduction of government funding as does an organization almost totally dependent on government funds. In addition, they are not limited in their programming to what government is willing to fund. If they see a need not covered by their government contract or grant, they can meet it out of existing funds or go out and try to raise money to meet this need. For example, a Dallas faith-based/segmented organization that receives 40 percent of its funding from government sources and 60 percent from private donations moves into new fields to meet new needs as they recognize and define them. The assistant executive director, explaining to me that there are now fewer single mothers on welfare in their area, reported: "former welfare recipients who are single moms are now working one or two jobs trying to make it. Their kids are left to wander the neighborhood, so now we have shifted our programming to provide a safety net for unsupervised children." In a similar vein, the head of a Philadelphia faith-based/integrated, inner-city program that receives government funding expressed strong opinions about what she saw as the harshness of the government regulations requiring the sanctioning of clients and her program's use of private funds to overcome them: "They [the government] make it difficult for us to do what you know people need, because they tell people they have to leave [the program after a period of time]. . . . in the interest of continuity, we have programs set up for continuity."

In addition, faith-based and community-based organizations that need to raise a large portion of their own funds tend to have a certain mind-set and a capability that helps protect their independence. It is a certain entrepreneurial, can-do, fund-raising mind-set, which leads to the maintaining of contacts with foundations and large donors and mailing lists of small donors. An organization that has become largely or entirely dependent on government funds will soon lose the mind-set and the ability to raise independent funds.

If this last point is correct, it raises questions about the amount of autonomy or freedom possessed by the secular nonprofit programs. It is often assumed that faith-based organizations are especially vulnerable to co-option by the government due to their faith-based nature, but I am convinced that, in fact, the nonprofit/secular organizations are more vulnerable to a loss of autonomy, because of the much higher percentages of their budgets that come from government sources. Of the large nonprofit/secular welfare-to-work programs, 96 percent of them reported receiving an average of 76 percent of their budgets from the government. If government shackles indeed come with government shekels, the nonprofit/secular programs may be much more vulnerable to being shackled than are the faith-based and community-based programs.

As I reported earlier in this section, the nonprofit/secular programs are the ones that were not only the most positive but also the most negative in assessing the effects of government funding. An interview with the executive director and education director of a Philadelphia nonprofit/secular program was not promising on this score. The previous year they had had 200 students; in the first two months of the current year, they were down to only 14 students. Why? It was explained to me that they receive 90 percent of their funding from government sources and that the government had adopted new rules that resulted in the precipitous drop in students they were serving. The directors stated that they had not been consulted before the new rules were adopted. When asked if they were frustrated by the new rules, they replied: "Yes, more than a little! What is the background of the people making these decisions? . . . How do they come up with their rules? . . . But they are not willing to listen to us."

Earlier, the organization had been a community-based group that had been privately funded. When I asked the executive director if—in light of her frustration with the new rules that had been imposed on them—she thought it would be better if they had stayed with more community involvement and no government money, she replied:

> No, I don't think it would be better. You can't replace the level of government money with private money. There is no way we would be able to serve the number of people that we serve unless we had our government funding. . . . I would never go back and be a small nonprofit with a budget of a couple hundred thousand dollars a year, which is what we could raise from private sources. . . . We would be doing a disservice to do that. The need is so great that turning down public money would fly in the face of our trying to serve.

This interview illustrates a basic dilemma that many programs heavily financed by government funds face. With government funding, they are able to serve much larger numbers of persons in desperate need of help, but with that same government funding comes program mandates and restrictions that the programs often find constricting.

Frequently, the 10 nonprofit/secular programs we visited expressed a perspective that was similar, even if not as dramatic. The perspective was most evident in the unarticulated assumption that if there were no government contracts for a certain program, there was simply nothing the organizations could do. The fund-raising efforts of the organizations often seemed to consist of determining their qualification for government contracts or grant programs. For example, when visiting a Dallas nonprofit/secular agency that receives 100 percent of its welfare-to-work funding from government contracts, I interviewed several staff members who work directly with welfare recipients. They told me that basic life skills are very much needed by their clients. When asked if they favor more spending on life skills classes, they responded: "Yes! On budgeting, saving, and buying what they need before luxuries; on nutrition, cooking instead of snack foods. Self-esteem training is needed. . . . Many have no knowledge of nutrition—their kids get too much sugar, and therefore they are hyper at school and the teacher wants to medicate them. One thing leads to another." When asked why such classes are not offered, the staff members simply responded that there are no government grants available for such classes.

The vice president of a Los Angeles nonprofit/secular agency gave an even more explicit example of this pattern.

> The meeting I just came out of is an example of that. We had done English as a second language for teaching to refugees and immigrants but got out of it when the school districts took it over—I would guess seven, eight years ago. Now they are linking this to naturalization. Well, we provide naturalization services. And the funding for naturalization services that we've gotten through the state is being cut by the governor. So WIA, the Workforce Investment Act, is a new stream of money coming down, kind of grabbing a lot of bizarre programs, in my opinion, that do not have a whole lot to do with workforce investment. One of them is naturalization. So we're looking at trying to jump in and set out a program. . . . So that's what we are looking at. We try to figure out where the needs are and how we can come up with funding to hire people to do that.

These are good persons, doing good work. But they are closely tied to government contracts and grants. As a result, there is a danger that programming will follow the money instead of identified community needs.

In summary, the strong majority of the secular nonprofits seemed to be highly satisfied with their relationship with government. This does not alter the fact that they have lost their independence. When they are told a certain program is ending, it ends; when told a program is changing, it changes; when told there is no money to meet a perceived need, that need is not met. Usually, the secular nonprofits felt that the government program priorities and conditions were appropriate. This is what saves the situation and assures that, most of the time, most nonprofit/secular program directors will respond positively to their financial partnership with government. But this does not change the fact of who is in charge.

Public Policy Implications and Observations

Many public policy debates are currently swirling around the Bush administration's faith-based and community initiative or other proposals to make greater use of for-profit and nonprofit organizations in the delivery of social services. Most of these debates center on issues of government funding of nongovernmental entities. Thus, the research findings related in this chapter contain a number of vital implications for current public policy issues. Here, I highlight six especially significant observations with public policy consequences.

First, the findings reported here help put current discussions and debates over funding of faith-based and community-based nonprofit organizations into a more accurate context. Proponents of faith-based and community initiatives often seem to claim that theirs is a wholly new policy initiative, on the basis that government currently only partners with large, secular nonprofit organizations or, at the most, with large, professionalized faith-based organizations (e.g., Catholic Charities or Lutheran Social Services). Opponents often seem to operate out of the same assumption. They claim that the guidelines for the separation of church and state would be violated in new ways if charitable choice provisions or faith-based initiatives were implemented.

The research reported here demonstrates that, at least in the welfare-to-work field, both sides are wrong. From a public policy perspective, the issue should not be framed in terms of whether or not public policy ought to take a new turn. Instead, it should be framed in terms of whether an existing policy ought to be expanded and pursued more broadly and in terms of what standards should govern that policy. Those are the issues. This means that advocates of faith-based and community initiatives need to explain why they believe current practice ought to be expanded. In addition, they need either to defend the existing standards under which current practice operates or to explain what modifications in the standards should be implemented. Those who oppose faith-based and community initiatives need to clarify whether they are only opposing the expansion of current practice or if they wish to alter the status quo so that current forms of governmental partnerships with faith-based organizations are either eliminated or fundamentally altered. If they are opposing expansion, they need to explain why they oppose the expanded form of a policy that they are willing to support in its current form. If their goal is to alter the status quo, they need to acknowledge and make a case for the fact that they wish to eliminate current partnerships or, at the least, to alter the rules under which those partnerships now exist. I reach these conclusions on the basis that both my current study and a number of prior studies all agree that there is much government funding of faith-based social service programs, including many that integrate religious elements into the services they provide. Also, many small, community-based organizations receive government funding. As research accumulates, these conclusions are becoming harder and harder to deny.

A second observation deals with the apparent existence of certain barriers that prevent faith-based and community-based programs from partnering with government to the same degree that the large nonprofit welfare-to-work programs do. This study has not revealed systematic data that constitute conclusive proof of discrimination against faith-based and community-based welfare-to-work programs. But there is circumstantial evidence that faith-based and community-based programs face barriers that the large, professionalized nonprofits do not face. Although more research is clearly needed, the playing field does not appear to be level. If the goal of public policy is to form public-private partnerships with a wide variety of welfare-to-work programs, ways to draw more community-based and faith-based programs into such partnerships need to be found.

Although many financial partnerships already exist between government and faith-based and community-based organizations in the welfare-to-work field, many faith-based and community-based organizations continue to harbor a host of fears and suspicions toward governmental partnerships. These fears lead to a third public policy observation. As a result of these fears, many community-based and faith-based organizations hesitate to enter into partnerships with the government. If those advocating faith-based and community initiatives are to succeed, they must address these fears and suspicions and their underlying causes. Forty percent of the faith-based welfare-to-work programs and one-fourth of the community-based programs have a self-conscious policy of not accepting government funds. They have taken themselves off of the playing field, fearing what a financial partnership with government would entail. About another 20 percent of these organizations have inquired about government funding but have backed off after those initial inquiries. That many of these programs eschew government funds out of fears over partnering with government is revealed by the fact that many of them made a self-conscious decision not to pursue government funds even while expressing a desire to expand their services. Given the small size of most faith-based and community-based programs, those players now on the sidelines need to be brought into partnerships with government, if these programs are to make a sizable contribution to meeting pressing welfare-to-work needs.

Sometimes, opponents of faith-based and community initiatives picture these groups as eager to get at the public trough to gobble up tax dollars, and they will refer to government grants or contracts that reimburse programs for providing social services to needy persons as aid to those groups. One can question who is aiding whom. If this public policy initiative is to work, government will often have to play more the role of the pursuer than that of the pursued. It is asking programs to deal with persons who may have drug and alcohol dependence or criminal histories or who may have been subjected to domestic violence or for other reasons may have been defeated and beaten down by the vicissitudes of life. Welfare-to-work programs need to encourage and support such persons, giving them hope and empowering them to get their lives squared away and to find employment—in a very tight job market where the only jobs may be miles away from where the person lives. This is not a task for the fainthearted or easily discouraged. It is understandable that many faith-based and community-based groups already feel overwhelmed and are not all that eager to take on added responsibilities, even if they will be partially reimbursed by government for their efforts. (Government normally only partially reimburses faith-based and community-based programs.)

Policymakers must take these realities into account and craft public policies in response to them. At the very least, the application process for obtaining government funds should be simplified, and the continued flexibility and independence of the faith-based and community-based programs receiving funds require safeguarding.

The findings reported in this chapter also indicate that a clarification of the rules governing faith-based practices would help reassure the faith-based groups that are now hesitating to enter into partnerships with government. It is clear that they now often feel they are in a vulnerable position that requires diplomatic skills and a certain caution—rooted in the fact that they can never be fully sure what is and is not permitted. The fact that almost all feel they have navigated these waters successfully may be more a result of government officials who wish them to continue as partners and of church-state watchdog groups that, until recently, have not monitored existing practices very closely. At the least, much uncertainty remains. Congress and the president have already partially responded to this need by adding charitable choice provisions to four different pieces of legislation. The same rules or modified versions of them could be adopted to cover other social service areas, but even these provisions leave some questions unanswered. If faith-based programs are to be encouraged to enter financial partnerships with government, there is a need for a clarification of the standards.

A fourth public policy implication requiring examination holds that true public-private partnerships—with government and nongovernmental entities sharing equally in the delivery of social services—are endangered by too high a level of government funding. If, as I believe, there are advantages to nongovernmental entities maintaining a significant degree of autonomy, the findings reported in this chapter point in the direction of the advantages of government funding programs at less than 100 percent. Vendorism is a very real potential problem. It is hard to conceive of a true partnership (with each party in the partnership maintaining a measure of independence) if one of the partners—namely, government—is putting up all of the finances. If, however, government is putting up, for example, 40 or 67 percent of the funding while its partner is putting up 60 or 33 percent of the funding, there is more likely to be the balance of power or control that one would expect in a true partnership. Because of this factor, this chapter reports a paradox: one would expect that due to potential restrictions on their religiously inspired practices, faith-based programs would be especially burdened by financial partnerships with government, but faith-based programs seem less burdened by such partnership than are the large, professionalized nonprofit organizations who usually receive the strong majority of their funding from government. Overreliance on government for funds seems to be a greater impediment to maintaining a strong measure of autonomy than does having a religious mission that one is seeking to protect.

A fifth public policy observation is that a network of cooperative, informal contacts and collaborations between government and the various types of nongovernmental welfare-to-work programs exists. This network seems to be one of the strengths of the existing scheme of welfare-to-work programs. Yet policymakers rarely acknowledge this strength or develop policies and practices to build on it. Possible initiatives include more formal consultative bodies made up of representatives of a wide diversity of welfare-to-work providers, more regularized channels for sharing program information and encouraging referrals, and more coordinated responses to changing political challenges.

A sixth and final public policy observation is that in the public-private nexus, there seem to be very few problems due to the regulatory role of government. In the past, there have been a few, well-publicized controversies dealing with health and safety standards, civil rights disputes, or licensing and credentialing issues, but such issues are not in the forefront of the concerns of the welfare-to-work programs included in this study. Here, the responsible government agencies and the welfare-to-work programs seem to have worked out a satisfactory modus operandi.

This chapter and chapters 2 and 3 have each ended by making a number of public policy observations. None of these chapters, however, has suggested to what concrete public policy conclusions these observations would lead. The final chapter takes up this task.

V Public-Private Partnerships
Public Policy Issues

There is always a gap between factual description and policy application. That is true here also. There is no clear, readily identifiable, and unanimously accepted line connecting the findings reported in this book with the public policy conclusions to which they lead. In making that connection, underlying assumptions, ingrained proclivities, and intuitive insights play as much a role as do the basic facts. Public policy-making and prudent, responsible advocacy remain much more an art than a science.

Therefore, this chapter is of necessity more personal than were the earlier chapters. Yet I judge it worthwhile to lay out what I see as the key public policy implications of the findings of my study of welfare-to-work programs in four large, metropolitan areas, as supplemented by the work of other scholars. I do not expect unanimous agreement on what I write here—far from it. My hopes are twofold: first, to broaden the scope of agreement in utilizing public-private partnerships to provide vital social services; and second, even when agreement is not attained, to frame the relevant issues in such a manner that a more thoughtful, fact-based conversation may result. I thereby hope to advance the always essential cause of democratic discussion. Out of informed discussion may emerge more viable public policies and a broader consensus on them.

This chapter is divided into four sections. The first section summarizes the findings of this book around the four public policy questions that I initially raised in chapter 1. In the second section, I discuss the key underlying assumptions that have shaped my more specific policy proposals, which I then present in the third section. The brief fourth section makes several suggestions for further research, in areas that appear to be the most crucial for advancing our knowledge of public-private partnerships in the delivery of social services to those in need.

Summary of Key Findings

Near the end of chapter 1, I outlined five key public policy issues or questions relevant to a consideration of government expanding its practice of forming partnerships with nongovernmental entities in the welfare-to-work field. The last issue—that of the relative effectiveness of different types of welfare-to-work programs—was not considered in this book. The other four issues were. I summarize here the findings of this study as they relate to those four issues.

Public Policy Issue Area 1: What is the capacity of nongovernmental entities? Here, the issue is whether or not for-profit, nonprofit, community-based, and faith-based programs are willing and able to take on the provision of welfare-to-work services to additional clients. Their ability to do so is governed by two distinguishable questions: first, do these nongovernmental entities have the current or potential size to take on additional clients; second, do they have the requisite skills, experience, and sophistication needed to form financial partnerships with government? The information gathered by this study offers a qualified yes to both of these questions, although difficulties and challenges are present.

Perhaps the programs best positioned for government to rapidly increase its reliance for providing welfare-to-work programs are the for-profit programs. A number of sizable for-profit programs that are already providing services are eager to expand their services, and most seem to have the sophistication and experience needed to partner with government. Hiring for-profit firms to provide welfare-to-work services is a controversial proposal for other reasons, but a lack of capacity—both current and potential—does not appear to be a major limiting factor.

Nonprofit/secular providers are also positioned to expand the number of welfare-to-work clients with whom they are working. They tend to be large, they generally have the desire to expand, and government already largely funds them. Thus, they have already demonstrated their capacity as government partners. As is often the case, it is easier to expand existing relationships than to build new ones. Objections can be raised, however, to doing so. Expanding government's partnerships with the large, professionalized nonprofits would not overcome whatever weaknesses there may be in this type of provider—and some observers have argued that there are real weaknesses in them—nor would it expand the range of options available to welfare recipients in their efforts to achieve self-sufficiency. But a lack of capacity does not appear to be a problem in relying more heavily on the nonprofit/secular providers.

In the case of community-based and both types of faith-based programs, there are capacity issues to be faced. All three program types tend to be very small, and many have not previously partnered with government. For many of them, size as well as experience and skill in working with government are open to question. If there are persuasive public policy reasons to make greater use of them, some very small programs would have to grow significantly beyond where they are now, and some would need help in meeting record-keeping and reporting requirements. However, they are eager to expand, and many of the faith-based/integrated programs in particular already have concrete plans to do so. All three program types already offer many services involving complex, ongoing work with clients. In addition, over half of them are already in financial partnerships with government, meaning there already is a base of public-private partnerships that could be expanded. In short, their potential capacity is great, even though their current capacity is limited. It would take some concerted public policy efforts to realize that potential.

Public Policy Issue Area 2: Do for-profit, large nonprofit, community-based, and faith-based providers deliver social services any differently than do government providers? This is a crucial question. If nongovernmental providers deliver welfare-to-work services in the exact same manner as do governmental providers, it is hard to imagine what case can be made to justify the effort to shift the provision of more welfare-to-work services to nongovernmental providers. Moreover, if community-based and faith-based providers deliver services in the same manner as the large, secular nonprofits, there would appear to be no public policy benefits to be gained by making a concerted effort to develop more government partnerships with the former. However, if community-based and faith-based providers provide different welfare-to-work services or provide the same services in a different manner, a case can potentially be made that the goal of moving more welfare recipients toward greater self-sufficiency would be served by partnerships with a wider variety of providers.

This study demonstrates not only some similarities in the services that different types of providers offer welfare-to-work clients but also notable differences. The six program types are not clones of each other. In particular, the services of the faith-based programs—both segmented and integrated—are clearly distinguishable from the services offered by the other four program types. They tend to offer a higher proportion of life-oriented services than do the other program types. Also, a large number of the faith-based programs are largely run by and serve African Americans. The faith-based/integrated programs introduce many explicit religious elements into the welfare-to-work services they provide. The government and nonprofit/secular program types are very similar to each other by a number of measures, such as the mean number of services made available, the mean number of more intense and less intense services offered, and the mean number of job-oriented and life-oriented services provided. Thus, this study does not strengthen the case for shifting more welfare-to-work services from government providers to large, professionalized, secular nonprofit providers. In addition, this study did not find differences among the six program types in the sense of dedication or concern expressed by their workers—all seemed largely to possess a strong commitment to the persons with whom they were working.

Public Policy Issue Area 3: What are the extent and nature of public-private partnerships that already exist, and are there currently barriers to community-based and faith-based organizations partnering with government? A host of public-private partnerships abound in the welfare-to-work area. The for-profit and the large, professionalized nonprofit/secular agencies in particular have formed close partnerships with government. Most of the money for the welfare-to-work services they provide comes from government coffers. The basis on which to question whether or not these are true partnerships arises from the fact that the government is in such a dominant position that the for-profit and non-profit/secular entities are in a largely subservient position, with little independence of action. They may still be doing good work, but there is little doubt about who is determining program priorities and emphases—and it is not the for-profit and nonprofit entities. Even many of the government-run programs are run not by stereotypic welfare offices but by community colleges and other government entities that are independent of the centralized social services or welfare bureaucracy. Many function similarly to the large, professionalized nonprofit/secular agencies, competing for contracts and seeking to fit their programs to the latest directives of the funding agency.

The situation is more complex when it comes to community-based and faith-based welfare-to-work programs. One fact is clear: upwards of three-fourths of the community-based and one-half of the faith-based programs receive government funding for their programs. Those that receive government funds receive more than a token amount of money—the community-based programs average two-thirds of their budgets from government sources, the faith-based programs one-third. While these numbers are sizable, they are much less than the numbers for these programs' for-profit and nonprofit/secular counterparts. Some additional facts indicate that the lower levels of funding for faith-based programs may be due to discrimination against them by government funders. They receive less funding than the community-based programs (which are similar to the faith-based programs in size and professionalization), and more faith-based programs have been turned down for funding than is true of either the community-based or the nonprofit/secular programs. But this evidence, while impressive, is circumstantial, not conclusive. It is also clear that other factors play a role, such as faith-based providers' fears of losing religious freedom or program independence and complex application processes. The latter two factors also seem to play a role in many community-based programs eschewing government funds. Public policy will need to deal with all three of these factors if public-private partnerships are to be expanded among faith-based and community-based programs.

Chapter 4 also found that most welfare-to-work programs in financial partnerships with government were largely satisfied with their relationship with government. This held true for all program types.

A final important feature of current government-private relationships in the welfare-to-work arena is the existence of a comprehensive network of service providers, bound together by ties of mutual referrals and informal consultations, no matter the type of private agency and no matter whether or not there is a financial relationship.

Public Policy Issue Area 4: Is it possible to construct public-private partnerships without the private entities losing their autonomy? The evidence of this study indicates that programs heavily subsidized by government funds—that is, programs run by government entities, for-profit programs, and nonprofit/secular programs—have lost much of their freedom to establish their own priorities and to make their own programming decisions. Their almost complete dependence on government funds means they are bound by government-established programs and priorities. They have so few independently raised funds that their independence is largely bound by their success in lobbying governmental funding agencies to grant them additional funds or to change existing program guidelines. The community-based and faith-based programs—receiving either no or limited government funds—seem usually to have greater control over their programming. A supporting constituency and other contacts with private funding sources is a great resource in terms of maintaining agency autonomy.

At present, there may, however, be a cruel trade-off. The community-based and faith-based programs have been largely successful in safeguarding their autonomy by maintaining a source of funds independent from government, but as a result, they also have generally remained very small. The nonprofit/secular agencies have lost much of their autonomy by entering deeply into financial partnerships with government, but that same government money has enabled them to grow to the point where they can serve large numbers of the needy. Autonomy with small size or loss of autonomy with large size seems to be the trade-off. The public policy challenge is, first, to wean the large nonprofit/secular agencies away from some of their government money while enabling them to replace the government money lost with private money and, second, to help the small community-based and faith-based agencies to expand with additional government funding without losing the private funds they are now able to raise. It would seem that the for-profit and government-run programs, due to their natures, will necessarily continue to be almost totally dependent on government funding. Even here, however, perhaps public policies that will increase their autonomy can be found.

Assumptions on Which the Policy Recommendations Rest

In the next section of this chapter, I make a number of public policy recommendations. Before I set out these recommendations, I think it will be helpful for me to lay out the eight basic assumptions that underlie my efforts to apply the results of research to current policy. Most of these assumptions are largely noncontroversial, but as will be seen later, they are crucial in shaping the policy recommendations to come.

My first assumption is that *government funds for antipoverty programs in general and for welfare-to-work programs in particular will continue to be severely limited.* With the war on terrorism having no end in sight, with federal government tax cuts already programmed to come into effect in future years, with budget deficits on both the federal and state levels a fact of life, and with antipoverty programs traditionally low on most policymakers' priority lists, one can best assume that money for welfare-to-work programs will continue to be sparse. This means that any public policies in the welfare-to-work area must seek to get the most effect for the least expense. What dollars are available must be stretched to obtain the greatest benefit for those who need to escape the clutches of poverty and welfare dependency.

My second basic assumption is that *a libertarian, hands-off approach by government is unlikely to lead persons out of poverty and welfare dependence.* Some have argued that government's welfare and antipoverty programs have done more harm than good, that they have created a dependence mind-set on the part of many of the poor. The next step thus appears self-evident: the best antipoverty program is no program at all. If government would only get out of the welfare and antipoverty business, nonprofit and faith-based groups would step in to fill the gap, and persons would turn away from self-destructive behavior and learn self-reliance. That is the libertarian position.

It is assumed sometimes that various calls for greater reliance on faith-based and community-based groups to meet the needs of the poor are in reality thinly disguised libertarian efforts to get government out of the poverty-fighting business. One cannot judge the inner motives of political leaders who are calling for greater reliance on faith-based and community-based organizations. But two points need to be made. First, President George W. Bush, as the most public and highest-ranking advocate of faith-based and community initiatives, has frequently gone out of his way to distinguish his position from the libertarian position. For example, in his January 2001 executive order that established the White House Office of Faith-Based and Community Initiatives, he clearly stated: "Faith-based and other community organizations are indispensable in meeting the needs of poor Americans and distressed neighborhoods. *Government cannot be replaced by such organizations,* but it can and should welcome them as partners."[1] Second, there is abundant evidence—including evidence contained in this book—that nonprofit and faith-based programs cannot begin to meet the needs of the poor on their own. Only government has the financial resources and the power to play the needed coordinating and stimulating roles. The policy recommendations in this book are not based on some imaginative world in which nongovernmental entities can take over the role of government in meeting the needs of the poor.

My third assumption is that *no one method of helping persons to move from welfare dependence to economic self-sufficiency has been demonstrated to be the most effective for all persons.* This assumption rests on two basic facts. One is that the life situations of persons receiving welfare assistance varies from one person to another; there is no one stereotypic welfare recipient. Some recipients are recently unemployed persons who only need some good leads to be successful in the job market. Others are third-generation welfare recipients with no work experience and with no understanding of the world of work. Some are single moms with several children; others are noncustodial fathers who have not taken responsibility for their children. Some have a strong support network in the form of family and friends; others have almost no support network at all. Some have job skills that are in demand; others are functionally illiterate. One could go on and on. The point is that it is foolish to think that a "one-size-fits-all" approach will ever work. Persons and needs differ; thus, programs must differ.

A second fact underlying this third assumption is that there is no one well-established, proven approach to moving persons from welfare dependency to economic self-sufficiency. Currently, the emphasis throughout the nation is on the "work first" approach. The idea is that welfare recipients ought to be encouraged or forced into some sort of employment immediately. If these efforts fail, assessment is done to determine what correctable barriers caused those persons to fail in finding a job. This approach has some things to recommend it, and it has worked well under some circumstances. It has its supporters; it also has its detractors. Neither this approach nor any other has been demonstrated to be *the* most effective way to help people on welfare. This fact and the fact that welfare recipients and their needs largely differ are strong reasons for encouraging a variety of welfare-to-work providers to offer a variety of approaches to meeting welfare recipients' needs.

My fourth assumption is that *a persuasive rationale for public-private partnerships depends on permitting the nongovernmental partners to maintain their independence and their distinctive approaches to ending welfare dependency, while at the same time allowing government to enforce appropriate accountability standards.* If the nongovernmental entities in partnership with government would be forced into a single template for providing welfare-to-work services, it is hard to develop a rationale for such partnerships. But it is equally hard to develop such a rational if these partnerships would mean that government would make large sums of money easily available to almost any entity to pursue almost any approach to ending welfare dependency. To do so would, at best, risk pouring money into efforts almost certain to fail. At worst, it would encourage a host of charlatans to join the queue for government money. The sad fact is that the poor would be the losers in either case.

What is needed is a balance that allows—and even encourages—experimentation and a creative flexibility on the part of the nongovernmental entities, as well as on the part of independent governmental entities, such as local community colleges. The balance would need to encourage such experimentation and flexibility within certain bounds set by accountability and program responsibility. Accountability is crucial, because whenever money is involved, waste and outright fraud are ever present dangers—and being in the self-giving antipoverty business or even in the faith-based antipoverty business is no guarantee against waste and outright fraud. Similarly, certain program boundaries are in order. This is where many judgment calls come in, but the goal is to allow for new approaches to old or emerging needs (i.e., for some experimentation) but also to rein in proposals that are totally untried and, from all appearances, seem doomed to failure. It may prove hard to maintain this approach without veering into the ditch on either side of the road, but this ought to be the goal.

My fifth assumption is that *it is vital for individual welfare-to-work programs and the overall welfare-to-work structure to respect and strengthen the human worth and dignity of the program clients.* Persons on welfare are often victims of an overwhelming number of challenges that life in modern society can inflict on them, some of which are forced onto them by outside forces and others of which are self-imposed by past mistakes. Some are victims of domestic abuse. Others are products of failed school systems. Many come from unstable home environments with few positive parental role models. Many succumbed to sexual temptations and were caught up in single parenthood at a young age. Drug dependence and criminal convictions are far from unknown among welfare clients. Poor health is often both a cause and a result of the poverty in which they find themselves. Whatever the source of their problems, it is important that antipoverty, welfare-to-work efforts start with the clients where they are now, assert their worth and dignity by word and deed, and move on from there. I say this for two reasons. One is that persons who are poor and dependent on welfare are in fact persons of great worth and dignity. Both the Jewish and Christian religious traditions assert this. Many of the frontline workers and volunteers with whom I met during the course of this study remarked on how much they respected those with whom they were working, how much resilience they demonstrated, and how much they often learned from them. Second, if persons are to act responsibly and learn new habits of self-reliance and initiative, they need to be treated as responsible persons, capable of becoming self-reliant and making decisions. Sometimes, as was pointed out to me on occasion, one may need to show respect for a client by way of "tough love"—by saying clearly, "You can do better than this, and I expect you to do better." Setting the bar high is one way of showing confidence in a person and his or her abilities. Other times may require giving clients some real choices—making sure they are in control of their own lives and not simply being acted on, as a child would be.

My sixth assumption rests on the distinction between two different kinds of social capital: bridging capital and bonding capital.[2] *Bonding capital* emphasizes ties to family, ethnic, or religious groups or other in-groups of which one is a member. It is inward looking and tends "to reinforce exclusive identities and homogenous groups."[3] *Bridging capital* is what ties persons to broader groups in the community. It is inclusive in nature and reaches across divisions and groups in society. Building on this distinction, my sixth assumption asserts that *both bonding and bridging capital are important resources in helping persons to move from welfare dependence to economic self-sufficiency.* The poor often seem to be persons who are lacking in both types of social capital. They often do not have in place strong support networks based on family, church, or neighborhood on which to draw. This is a lack of bonding capital. Thus, problems concerning child care, transportation, and backup in case of illness or other of the crises life constantly generates become catastrophes, since there is no support network to fall back on. The poor also often lack bridging capital. They often do not have contacts outside their immediate community that are needed to find job or educational opportunities. Especially in Chicago, I was told many stories of the poor living isolated lives in "the projects," lives so isolated that it becomes difficult to develop the contacts one needs to move with confidence in the wider world. In order for many persons to move from welfare to work, they need programs that will develop both the bonding and the bridging capital of their clients.

My seventh assumption is that *church-state separation is an important value that is rightly enshrined in both the First Amendment and in the values of the American people.* It needs to be respected. However, it is also important to understand the underlying goal of church-state separation, which, I believe, is to achieve the greatest religious freedom for all, including the right to be free of religion. "Religion," in the words of one legal scholar, "is to be left as wholly to private choice as anything can be. It should proceed as unaffected by government as possible."[4] In a free society, all persons face a choice to believe or not believe, to observe or not observe. Government should, by its actions, do as little as possible to influence that choice, either for or against religion, making it neither easier nor harder for persons to choose any particular system of religious belief or to chose one religious or one secular belief system over another. In short, public policy should be religiously neutral, by affecting choices for or against religion as little as possible. That is the true purpose underlying church-state separation.

My final assumption may be the most surprising and thus the most controversial of the eight. It rests on a trend that has been growing in the American religious scene for some time, but this study is one of the first studies to document some of its public policy consequences. This assumption is that *there is a new, potentially valuable, largely untapped resource in the social service arena in the form of conservative, or evangelical, Protestant programs.* As I noted in chapter 2, the standard wisdom is that the mainline Protestant churches are actively engaged in providing social services and that conservative, or evangelical, Protestant churches are largely inward looking, caring only for their own members. This view poses a problem for the argument that religion might play a robust role in the provision of social services, since the mainline Protestant churches are, in Robert Putnam's words, "dwindling, aging, and less involved in religious activities."[5] Meanwhile, "the fraction of all church members who belong to evangelical churches has risen."[6]

Yet my study has shown that a majority of all of the faith-based welfare-to-work programs are rooted in the conservative Protestant tradition. The site visits in particular helped to document that many of these programs are vigorous and growing. This is what has led to my eighth assumption. There appears to be a major shift occurring in the welfare-to-work field in the four cities studied. This shift is away from mainline and toward conservative Protestant churches and their members and allied organizations in providing most of the faith-based welfare-to-work programs. If, indeed, there is a major movement within conservative Protestantism toward active social involvement, this may prove to be a positive development. As the vigor and social activism of the mainline churches decline, the social activism of the evangelical churches may be increasing.[7] If this trend can be encouraged and strengthened, a new resource for fighting poverty in the United States would be brought online.

Key Public Policy Goals and Policies That Support Them

In this section, I put forward four basic goals of public policy as they relate to governmental partnerships with for-profit, nonprofit, and faith-based social service organizations. These goals are (1) to encourage more community-based and faith-based organizations to enter into financial partnerships with government agencies, (2) to protect and increase the independence of for-profit and secular nonprofit organizations that already are in financial partnerships with government agencies, (3) to protect and enhance the dignity and choice of clients who are receiving services from governmental and nongovernmental service providers, and (4) to meet the fears of those who see legal-constitutional and practical dangers and problems in public-private partnerships. I will consider each of these four goals in order, describing them in greater detail, explaining the ways in which they are supported by the research reported in this book and by other recently completed research, and suggesting 12 specific policy initiatives that will help to achieve these goals.

Before detailing these four goals and some specific public policies to which they lead, it is important to make clear that all four rest on the underlying belief that it makes for good public policy to expand and regularize the already existing practice of government frequently partnering with nongovernmental entities for the provision of welfare-to-work services. Public-private partnerships make good public policy sense in the welfare-to-work field. There are three basic reasons why I hold to this belief. One is that there are existing welfare-to-work programs being run by all six types of organizations on which this study has focused. Of all of the welfare-to-work programs included in this study, 75 percent were nongovernmental in nature. With few exceptions, they appear to be doing good work, with dedicated staff members, often under very difficult situations. To cut back on government's collaborative relationships with these programs is unwarranted. To do so would mean that government agencies would have to create new programs, hire staff, develop the needed infrastructure of buildings and community contacts, and in other ways build programs from scratch. It clearly seems best for government to build on and strengthen what is already in place, instead of ignoring already existing programs or, worse, undercutting them by creating competing programs.

This is not a strategy of government simply putting money into whatever programs are already out there. Rather, this is a strategy of true partnership, with government and its partners together developing the best strategies and approaches. Thus, government would play a directing and coordinating role, making sure essential services are available for all who are in need and qualified to receive them. But government should not play a dominating role, setting strategy, dividing responsibilities, and dictating program content. The key is partnership, with both of the partners having a say in what is to be done and how it is to be done.

A second reason for continuing and expanding government's partnerships with nongovernmental entities is to strengthen and empower civil society in communities facing severe social needs. It is a recipe for failure for government agencies alone to seek—without the support of a vital civil society—to stabilize and turn around a community facing severe economic dislocations, depressingly high crime rates, high rates of out-of-wedlock births, and other such challenges. Government agencies simply cannot meet severe needs or overcome pressing challenges by themselves. Large city police departments have learned this lesson. It is no less true of government agencies seeking to deal with social needs and problems—whether those needs and problems are ones whole communities are struggling to overcome or are matters individuals are facing. The appropriate role of government is to supplement—not supplant—families, houses of worship, self-help associations, block clubs, community development corporations, and other manifestations of civil society. Otherwise, government is left with an impossible task for which its resources and its will are almost certain to be inadequate. Thus, whenever public policies strengthen civil society, they make the task of government more manageable. This study has demonstrated that there are a plethora of nongovernmental entities in the welfare-to-work field that have roots deep in the communities they are serving. By partnering with and empowering existing welfare-to-work programs, public policy strengthens civil society. The needy, their communities, and society as a whole all benefit.

A third reason why expanding and regularizing governmental partnerships with nongovernmental entities in the welfare-to-work field makes good public policy sense is that it helps provide a way out of the dilemma mentioned at the beginning of this book: the fact that Americans tend to want to help those in need but also tend to view large government programs with extreme distrust. If government works with and through welfare-to-work programs run by for-profit, nonprofit, and faith-based entities, there is likely to be higher and more sustainable public support for helping those in need than if government itself runs the programs.

One additional observation is that government ought not to partner with or otherwise fund organizations that are teaching hatred or violence or that are in other ways violating the basic rules of a democratic society. This stipulation is more hypothetical than practical. In my four-city study, I did not come across any welfare-to-work programs that would fit into this category. But some may exist.

With the expansion and regularization of public-private partnerships as the underlying objective, I now examine in greater depth the four specific public policy goals I enumerated at the beginning of this section, along with specific public policies that would help achieve them. The first goal is **to encourage more community-based and faith-based organizations to enter into financial partnerships with government agencies.** At times, both proponents and opponents of easing the entry of community-based and faith-based nonprofit groups into financial partnerships with government picture such groups as being eager to get at federal tax dollars. This study has demonstrated that the reality is quite different. Many of these groups are fearful of what they perceive as a protracted process of mind-numbing complexity even to apply for government funds, not to mention severe program limitations and an avalanche of intricate reporting requirements that go with the receipt of such funds. Many are small programs, serving a small population in need, by way of a program they have evolved and find effective. They have a lot invested in their programs. It ought not to be overly surprising that they are not necessarily beating on the doors of government funding agencies, eager to go through the complex process of seeking government funds and, if successful, adding more clients, many of whom are anything but easy to work with. There will be money for more staff, but many organizations may feel that the added burdens they will be taking on more than outweigh the staff resources they will be able to add. As I reported in chapter 3, many of the faith-based and community-based welfare-to-work organizations are willing and even eager to expand, but they are not sure that acquiring government contracts and grants is the best way to do so.

If government is to work more closely with nongovernmental entities in providing welfare-to-work services, community-based and faith-based social service programs are the very programs where government partnerships will need to expand. Government funding of for-profit and especially of large, professionalized nonprofit welfare-to-work programs is already widespread. It is among community-based and faith-based programs that there is a potential for expansion, and these are the very agencies, with their strong community ties, whose expansion and strengthening will do much to build civil society in their communities. But if government is to encourage the expansion of these programs and to strengthen them in their current efforts, public policy will often have to assume more the position of wooing the programs than of being wooed by them. Government agencies need to be the pursuers more than the pursued. There are three basic ways in which government can play this role of pursuer.

The first is *to apply legal principles such as those found in charitable choice provisions to all programs in which government funds faith-based organizations.* Charitable choice has three basic goals: to allow faith-based organizations to compete for government contracts and grants on the same basis as secular organizations, to protect the religious autonomy rights of faith-based groups that receive government funds, and to protect the religious freedom rights of recipients of services from faith-based organizations. I will consider all of these goals later, but here I need to emphasize only the second one: protecting the religious autonomy rights of faith-based groups that receive government funds. One factor discouraging faith-based organizations from seeking government funds and, sometimes, even from accepting such funds when offered is those organizations' fears that doing so will require them to compromise their religious message and character. Research indicates that those fears are probably exaggerated, but that makes them no less real. This is especially true of faith-based/integrated programs.

Charitable choice seeks to allay these fears in three ways: it specifies that faith-based organizations may maintain a religious atmosphere by displaying religious art, scripture verses, or other religious symbols in their facilities; it clarifies that a faith-based organization with government funds may keep control "over the definition, development, practice and expression of its religious beliefs"; and it spells out that faith-based organizations will keep their right, provided in Section 702 of the Civil Rights Act of 1964 to make hiring decisions based on religious criteria.[8] All these protections are reasonable and essential if faith-based groups are to be encouraged to play a greater role in meeting basic social service needs. If faith-based groups are to be encouraged to expand their programs with the help of government funding, they need to be reassured that the price will not be the loss of their religious distinctiveness. This distinctiveness comes out in certain religiously rooted practices, such as praying, displaying religious art, and referring to God's love, care, and expectations. This study and others document that religious references are often used to bolster clients' sense of self-worth and to provide a motivation to struggle to move ahead against seemingly overwhelming obstacles. The faith-based programs' distinctiveness also reveals itself in an emphasis in programming aimed at strengthening clients' life skills. For many of the faith-based groups, these practices are defining practices. Without them, the very essence of their programs would be lost. Thus, if they feel government funding would mean jettisoning these practices, they would believe this is too high a price to pay for "Caesar's coins." The major potential objection to allowing such practices as a part of programs receiving government funds relates to church-state issues and to dangers to the religious freedom rights of the clients. I will return to these matters later.

Here, I take a closer look at the issue of faith-based organizations being able to make hiring decisions based on religious criteria even though they receive government funding. Of the several charitable choice provisions, this has proven to be the most controversial. Americans United for Separation of Church and State has framed the issue as whether or not "religious groups will be legally permitted to discriminate in hiring despite receiving federal tax dollars."[9] Democratic congressman Bobby Scott of Virginia called this provision "an assault on our civil rights laws."[10] A national poll by the Pew Research Center for the People and the Press found upwards of three-fourths of the public stating that faith-based organizations receiving government funds should not be allowed "to only hire persons who share their religious beliefs."[11] As I reported earlier, 56 percent of the faith-based/integrated welfare-to-work programs studied here reported that they either give preference in hiring staff or only hire staff who agree with their religious orientation. In addition, our site visits suggest that this figure may actually be understated. Even in faith-based organizations that did not indicate in their questionnaire responses that they hired on the basis of religion, we found that all or almost all the persons we interviewed were in agreement with the organization's religious orientation.

In untangling and examining this highly controversial issue, I consider, first, two important facts that need to be kept in mind. Second, I consider two assumptions often made by those opposed to allowing faith-based organizations receiving government funds to make hiring decisions based on religion. Third, I explain why I believe the charitable choice provision concerning hiring decisions is appropriate and necessary.

One important fact to keep in mind is that charitable choice is not carving out some new exemption for faith-based organizations; civil rights laws already make clear that religious organizations are allowed to make hiring decisions based on religion even though secular organizations are not. As I showed earlier in chapter 4, this exemption for religious organizations has been upheld by a unanimous Supreme Court. The Court ruled that this exemption was crucial for a religious organization's ability to maintain its religious identity. Thus, the issue, properly framed, is whether or not a faith-based organization that receives full or even partial funding from the government for one of its programs loses the right to make hiring decisions based on religion.

Courts have usually answered no to this question. As Ira Lupu and Robert Tuttle point out, courts have generally ruled that faith-based organizations receiving government funds keep whatever exemptions from nondiscrimination requirements the law grants them: "All court decisions—save one—have rejected arguments that private entities that accept government funds waive whatever statutory exemption from nondiscrimination laws they otherwise possess. . . . [The Supreme] Court has on several occasions repudiated the contention that private actors must behave as if they were the state once they accept state funds."[12]

The second relevant fact is that, based on this study and other available evidence, the overwhelming majority of faith-based social service programs that hire on the basis of religion define "hiring on the basis of religion" very broadly. It is not a matter of churches or denominational groups wanting to hire persons from their own specific church or denomination—Baptists only hiring Baptists, Catholics only hiring Catholics, or the Salvation Army only hiring Salvationists. Instead, it is usually a matter of such groups wishing to hire persons whose religious values and commitments fit within their religious commitments, broadly conceived. For example, in one case that made the news several years ago, a Salvation Army program for victims of domestic abuse hired as a staff member someone who had said on her application that she was Catholic. That posed no problem for the program. But later, when it turned out that she had lied on her application and was not Catholic but a follower of the ancient, pagan religion of Wicca, she was let go.[13] In our site visits, we frequently came across Catholics working in Protestant agencies and vice versa, as well as persons from one Protestant tradition working in an agency of another Protestant tradition. In the real world the issue is not whether a particular religious tradition may only hire from within its own narrowly defined tradition. Rather, the issue is, for example, whether or not a Christian agency must hire a total nonbeliever, a Jewish agency must hire a Muslim, or a Catholic agency must hire a Satanist.[14]

Next, it is important to consider two assumptions seemingly made by those who argue that faith-based organizations receiving government funds should not be allowed to make hiring decisions based on religion. The first assumption is that religious beliefs are irrelevant to the social services provided by faith-based organizations and that taking religion into account in hiring decisions is therefore an exercise in prejudice. It is assumed that there is no rational connection between the religious beliefs of a faith-based organization's staff members and the social services being delivered. What, in fact, is the appropriate secular parallel to a faith-based organization desiring to take religion into account in making hiring decisions? Is it that of a white factory owner in the pre-1960s South who—literally or figuratively—had a sign out front saying, "No Blacks need apply"? Or is it that of an abortion rights group that has an unstated, but very real, policy of not hiring persons who are strong right-to-life advocates? We as a society have happily decided that the first case is a matter of prejudice pure and simple and thus cannot be tolerated. In the second case, almost all persons believe that if the abortion rights organization is to maintain its nature and integrity, it must be able to hire only those whose beliefs are in line with its own. I suspect that many of the political leaders and members of the general public who argue that faith-based groups receiving government funds should not be allowed to take religion into account in their hiring decisions have made the hidden assumption that the faith-based groups are asking to act on the basis of prejudice.

This study, however, has revealed that for many faith-based groups—and especially for the faith-based/integrated groups—this is definitely not the case. For them, the true parallel to their situation is that of the abortion rights group that wishes to take prospective staff members' views on abortion rights into account in its hiring. Seventy-nine percent or more of the faith-based/integrated welfare-to-work programs reported opening or closing meetings with prayer, using religious values to motivate their staffs, and using religious values to encourage clients to change attitudes (see table 4, in chapter 2). As I reported earlier, this study also found—through the site visits—frequent references in faith-based programs to religious concepts of work as a means of living out God's calling in one's life and of God as a source of support and help. For programs that believe prayer, religious motivations, and religious values are integral to the nature of their programs, the desire to hire persons who themselves accept such religious concepts is no exercise in blind prejudice. It is, in fact, as important to the nature and integrity of these programs as it is for a secular organization to hire persons in agreement with its goals and ideology.

I suspect that a second hidden assumption underlies much of the opposition to the taking account of religion in the hiring practices of faith-based organizations that receive government funds. This assumption is rooted in the mind-set that when a faith-based or any nonprofit organization receives government funds, it ceases to be a distinct, autonomous entity and instead becomes an arm or extension of the government. Its actions become governmental actions. As noted in chapter 1, Sheila Kennedy, Steven Rathgeb Smith, and Michael Lipsky have clearly articulated this assumption. If one makes this assumption, it reasonably follows that that organization should have no more right to make hiring decisions based on religion than would government itself.

This is where pluralist theory, discussed in chapter 1, is highly relevant. Government funding, I contend, does not turn a faith-based organization into a government agency or its actions into government actions. If one accepts that it does not, there is no reason why government funding should result in the loss of a right that has been given to faith-based organizations by legislation and confirmed by the Supreme Court. It is still a private, faith-based organization, and its right to hire based on religious criteria is just as important after receiving governmental funding as it was before. In both situations, its continued existence as a distinct religious entity is at stake.

The conclusion I reach—based on the current legally protected right of faith-based organizations to make hiring decisions based on religion mentioned earlier, on the faith-based organizations' broad definition of "hiring on the basis of religion," and on the rejection of the two frequently made assumptions just discussed—is that the charitable choice provision protecting faith-based organizations' right to take religion into account in their hiring decisions is appropriate and necessary. The first reason I have reached this conclusion is that for some faith-based organizations, it is understandably very important that their staffs be composed of persons who share their religious perspectives. For those faith-based organizations that believe that their religious perspective—whether displayed in subtle or in overt ways—is closely bound up with what they are and are seeking to be, it becomes imperative that their staffs share that religious perspective.

Religious beliefs are for them a bona fide employment qualification. For example, a Christian welfare-to-work program committed to reflecting a Christian view of human dignity, work, and responsibility would find its whole approach undercut if it largely had thoroughgoing secularists as staff members. To allow such an agency to take prospective staff members' religious beliefs and commitments into account is no more an exercise in prejudice than to allow an environmental group to take prospective staff members' views on environmental protection into account or to allow a spouse abuse shelter to take into account prospective staff members' views of women's rights. The desire of some faith-based programs to take religion into account in making hiring decisions is parallel to secular organizations' desire to take into account prospective staff members' views on issues and attitudes directly relevant to their goals and programs. The faith-based organizations are asking for no more and no less.

A more practical reason for protecting the right of faith-based groups to continue to be able to make hiring decisions based on religious criteria is that if this is not done, many faith-based groups will not accept government funding. If there are public policy gains to be made by including a wider number of social service programs in governmental partnerships, many of those gains will be lost if it is insisted that all faith-based groups partnering with government must give up the right to take religion into account in their hiring. Some faith-based groups would not find this problematic, but others would find this deeply troubling, and it would drive them away from governmental partnerships. Without this protection, many faith-based groups with much to contribute will remain small and with limited impact, whereas with government funding, they could grow and offer their services to a much wider number of persons in need. This may especially be true of the conservative Protestant programs, which, as I noted earlier, may be entering the social services field in large numbers, even as the mainline Protestant organizations are withdrawing. Forty percent of the conservative Protestant programs studied indicated in their questionnaires that they either only hire persons in agreement with their religious orientation or give preference in hiring to persons in agreement with their religious orientation. Many of these would no doubt be scared off from accepting government funding if their right to consider religion in their hiring would be the price they would have to pay.

The right of faith-based groups to use religious standards in hiring staff members does not in any way weaken their legal responsibility to serve all persons without regard to race, gender, sexual orientation, or religion; nor does it weaken their legal responsibility not to discriminate on the basis of race or gender in their hiring.[15] These considerations are distinguishable from hiring decisions based on religion, since the law only gives religious organizations the right to make hiring decisions based on religion; it does not give them the right to make decisions on whom to serve based on religion, nor does it give them the right to make hiring decisions based on race or gender. These considerations are also distinguishable from hiring decisions in that this study found hardly any faith-based programs that had any desire to make decisions concerning hiring or whom to serve based on these considerations. Such considerations are simply not an issue. For example, only 2 out of 120 faith-based programs indicated they gave preference to persons of their own faith in accepting clients.

Not only should charitable choice provisions be added to all programs in which government funds faith-based organizations, but those provisions are in need of additional clarification. As I showed in chapter 3, charitable choice stipulates that government funds provided directly to faith-based providers may not "be expended for sectarian worship, instruction, or proselytization." As I also stressed in chapter 3, the terms used in this stipulation are highly ambiguous. Uncertainty clouds their meaning. Both faith-based providers and enforcing governmental officials are left to figure out what activities government funds may and may not help finance. Any clarity that can be brought to these terms by defining them more precisely would help to allay the fears and suspicions that many faith-based organizations now harbor—assuming that the terms are defined in a sufficiently narrow manner that they will not inhibit faith-based providers from using broad religiously rooted values and perspectives in their programming. Shortly—when considering client dignity and rights—I will discuss some principles to be followed in making these clarifications.

In addition to applying clarified charitable choice provisions to all programs in which government funds social services provided by faith-based organizations, more community-based and faith-based organizations can be enticed to enter into financial partnerships with government by two other means. One is *to use local organizations that are known and trusted in their communities as intermediary funding agencies.* Currently, two problems, uncovered by this study, often exist when small community-based and faith-based organizations deal directly with government. One is what appears to be an overwhelmingly complex application process that is followed, when application is successful, by extensive reporting and record-keeping requirements. The other is an ingrained fear or distrust when dealing with government. If one's agency is small and inexperienced in dealing with government and if one has read or heard rumors about horror stories that others have experienced, one may very well opt not to bother with application for government funds. Yet almost all cities have well-established, locally respected agencies with many ties to small, community-based groups. These well-established agencies usually already receive government funds and have learned how to successfully navigate the waters of public-private partnerships. Government officials trust them; smaller faith-based and community-based organizations trust them. I am suggesting here that government agencies form direct partnerships with these larger, more sophisticated agencies, providing grants for certain designated purposes. These agencies would then solicit, work with, and pass on funds to the smaller faith-based and community-based organizations. They would translate governmental regulations and record-keeping requirements to these smaller providers and assist them in fulfilling these requirements. Government agencies would be freed from having to deal with a host of small, often inexperienced and suspicious providers; the small providers could deal more informally with persons they trust and understand; and by working with many smaller agencies, the larger, coordinating agencies would increase their influence and reach in their communities.

This proposal is similar to the one Congress enacted in 2002 in the $30 million Compassion Capital Fund.[16] Under this program, the Department of Health and Human Services granted money to 21 intermediary organizations in order for them to give technical assistance and make some small grants to community-based and faith-based organizations wishing to apply for governmental funds. Under my proposal, the program would be greatly expanded, and the emphasis would be on the intermediary organizations making grants and awarding contracts to small community groups (some faith-based, some not), rather than on giving technical assistance to help them in qualifying for funding under ongoing government programs.

A third concrete public policy proposal aimed at encouraging more community-based and faith-based organizations to enter into financial partnerships with government is *to create special state and community offices whose purpose is to work with faith-based and community-based organizations.* Many states and some localities have already done this, but more offices would be helpful. These offices would serve two roles. First, they would serve as liaisons between the faith-based and the small community-based groups and the state or city governments. They would explain funding opportunities and requirements and encourage especially worthy faith-based and community-based groups to enter into partnerships with government. Second, they would serve as ombudsmen for faith-based and community-based organizations in their relationships with state and municipal funding and regulatory agencies. In this role, they would work to resolve any disputes or differences in interpretations that may arise between funding agencies and the provider organizations. Currently, many of the smaller, less experienced providers feel they are at an overwhelming disadvantage should any disputes break out. With state or local liaison offices in existence, they could feel that there is at least someone who understands them and could serve as an advocate in case a dispute should arise.

All three of these proposals—to apply the legal provisions of charitable choice more widely, to use established local organizations as intermediary funding agencies, and to create state and local offices to work with faith-based and community-based agencies—are aimed at encouraging more small, faith-based and community-based organizations to enter into financial partnerships with government agencies in providing welfare-to-work or other social services. They are aimed at responding directly to fears I have often heard expressed by those providers who were slow or hesitant to work with government. Their basic aim is not, first of all, to help or aid these small providers but to enable them to play a larger role in meeting the needs of persons now in desperate need. Helping those needy persons by making a wider range of program options available to them is the goal of these policy proposals.

The second of four basic public policy goals on which this section is built is **to protect and increase the independence of for-profit and secular nonprofit organizations that are already in financial partnerships with government agencies.** One of the findings of this study is the apparent loss of autonomy often suffered by nonprofit and for-profit organizations that are now in close financial partnerships with government. As is documented by the questionnaire results reported in chapter 4, these two program types are largely funded by government. From the 17 site visits my associate and I made to nonprofit/secular and for-profit programs, it became clear that this financial support has come at a price—namely, a significant loss of autonomy by these organizations. As I noted in Chapter 4, the specific services they offer—and those they do not offer—are largely determined by what grants and contracts they are able to secure from government funding sources. To a large extent, they have become creatures of the state. There would be certain public policy advantages if their level of autonomy could be increased above where it is now. If one of the goals of public-private partnerships is to give persons in need more choices and to introduce greater flexibility and creativity into the provision of social services, it would seem wise to work to develop public policies that would enable and even encourage these two types of providers to exercise greater flexibility in the services they provide and in how they go about providing them. Doing so would increase their level of autonomy, thereby enabling them to act in a more independent manner, which, in turn, means they would more fully approximate the social role that pluralist theory envisages for them. They would be more fully marked by the "pluralist autonomy" called for by Peter Frumkin (as I noted in chapter 1). Although there is no easy way to achieve this autonomy, there are four specific ideas that would help move the large, professionalized, secular nonprofits toward greater independence.

The first two proposals are intended to work in tandem. One is *to increase the tax incentives for individuals, corporations, and foundations to contribute to nonprofit social service organizations.* This can be done several ways. For individuals, the proposal most often discussed recently is to allow persons who do not itemize their federal tax deductions to nevertheless take a tax deduction up to a certain amount—such as $100 or $200—for contributions made to nonprofit social service organizations.[17] One could even go beyond this and offer tax credits for up to a certain amount of dollars contributed to nonprofit social service organizations. Similar incentives could be crafted for corporations and foundations. These efforts are of course aimed at making private fundraising easier for nonprofit organizations who help the needy—and thus, at reducing such organizations' dependence on government funds.

A second proposal that would work in tandem with the first proposal requires government agencies *to make much greater use of contracts and grants that do not fully reimburse nonprofit programs for their expenses.* As I pointed out in chapter 4, when government funds a program at 100 percent, powerful forces are let loose that almost inevitably will result in those programs surrendering their independence. It may appear that when a nonprofit is providing a valuable service to needy persons, the best way to help those persons is to expand that program as quickly as possible through funding it entirely. But what may be most effective in the short run in meeting persons' needs may not be most effective in the long run. By completely meeting the costs of a nonprofit program, that program is made so dependent on government funding that it loses much of its independence. The creativity, flexibility, and community ties that originally fed its vision are jeopardized. By requiring matching funds, government will require nonprofit organizations to develop and maintain ties with independent funding sources, and with those independent funding sources will come an independence and flexibility that will increase the organizations' effectiveness in their communities. If the previous proposal is also adopted, it will become easier for these organizations to raise the needed matching funds. Of course, these first two proposals would also help community-based and faith-based organizations to maintain a strong measure of independence.

These first two proposals only apply to nonprofit organizations, but the next two can also apply to for-profit organizations. One of these requires the federal government—and possibly state and local governments as well—*to create a large fund administered by an independent government agency to which for-profit, nonprofit/secular, community-based, and faith-based organizations could apply for funds to support innovative programs designed to meet pressing needs.* Such a fund would be housed in a government foundation (similar to the National Science Foundation) and would operate somewhat like a private grant-making foundation. It is now too often the case that the only government funds for which a private social service organization can apply are governed by very strict RFPs (Requests for Proposals), in which the funding agency states what it wants done and how it wants it done and then solicits organizations to carry out this program. There is room for such an approach, but there is also a pressing need for a more open-ended process in order to encourage innovation and to bypass bureaucracies that sometimes are rigidly wedded to past programs and approaches.

A final policy innovation is *to allow for-profit firms to compete on an equal basis with nonprofit agencies for government contracts and grants.* Generally, it is hard to make a case for treating for-profit social service providers differently than nonprofit social service providers. Both are providing similar or the same services. Often, we found for-profit clients and sometimes even frontline workers who were unaware they were with a for-profit, not a nonprofit, organization. As I noted earlier in this book, it was impossible to distinguish between for-profit and nonprofit organizations based on worker motivation or sense of concern. For-profit firms have the potential advantage of bringing to the table fresher, more flexible and innovative ideas and approaches. This potential may or may not prove to be the case in practice. But there seems to be no a priori reason to believe that either for-profits or nonprofits provide welfare-to-work and other social services more effectively. If government contracts and grants fund the programs only partially, as I have recommended, the for-profit firms may be at a disadvantage as compared to the nonprofit agencies, since they have less potential to raise funds from private sources. Nevertheless, this does not seem to be a basis on which to exclude for-profit firms at the outset. Free and open competition for government contracts and grants would appear to be the best policy. This competition may not in itself lead to greater independence on the part of the competing providers, but a more open process will encourage innovation and creativity and discourage long-term, overly comfortable relationships. This, in turn, will motivate providers to dare new approaches and new techniques of helping those in need. Now, maintaining long-established patterns with government agencies is too often the safe, comfortable course; with increased competition for funds, there may be greater rewards for breaking the mold and thinking and acting outside the box.

The third underlying goal of my specific policy recommendations is **to protect and enhance the dignity and choice of clients who are receiving services from governmental and nongovernmental service providers.** This goal is a direct attempt to put wheels on my fifth assumption articulated earlier in this chapter—namely, the importance of respecting and strengthening the human worth and dignity of the program clients. Persons who are dependent on welfare assistance to survive are by definition needy persons and often are highly vulnerable. They have typically suffered more than their share of life's difficulties. Often, this has resulted in a lack of even basic educational skills, in weak support networks, or in an inner self that is emotionally damaged. The programs designed to help such persons to move ahead should not add to already present feelings of failure and inadequacy.

This means that welfare-to-work, as well as other social service programs, ought to put a strong emphasis on caring, personal, thoughtful assistance. Clients ought not to be made to feel they are once more pawns in a game that they barely understand and whose goals are far removed from their needs. Instead, they should receive help that meets actual needs and is given in a context of personal understanding and concern. This does not rule out tough demands and an insistence on accountability. In fact, one way to show concern and faith in persons' ability to move ahead is to hold them to high expectations. All this says something about the type of programs that government itself should create and with whom government should seek to build public-private partnerships. But it does not speak to the policies that ought to govern those partnerships. There are four specific public policy proposals that I believe lead to policies that treat clients of welfare-to-work and other social service programs with the respect and dignity they deserve.

The first policy proposal is that any program that accepts government funding must be willing *to accept clients without regard to race, ethnicity, gender, sexual orientation, or religion.* Moreover, they should not be allowed to treat clients differently based on any of these characteristics. Nondiscrimination and equal treatment must be the uncompromised guideline; a basic concern for the clients and a respect for them as persons demand no less. This policy is happily already being followed.

The second policy proposal requires that any program receiving government funds is *not to subject clients to mandatory sectarian worship, instruction, or proselytization.* In proposing this, I interpret the phrase "sectarian worship, instruction, or proselytization" both narrowly and broadly. I interpret it broadly to include attempts to pressure persons to join any particular movement or organization, whether these are religious or secular in nature. Similarly, I interpret the term *sectarian instruction* to include attempts to instruct persons in detailed ideas or doctrines of specific, narrowly conceived movements or groups, whether religious or secular in nature. Thus, in a conservative Protestant program, persons could not be required to attend sessions that teach, for example, the doctrine of biblical inerrancy. Similarly, in a secular program run by a feminist organization, persons could not be required to attend sessions that teach, for example, the details of Betty Frieden's approach to feminist issues. In the conservative Protestant program, persons could not be pressured—with positive or negative inducements or psychological pressures—to join the sponsoring church or to attend a Bible study. Neither could the program sponsored by a secular feminist group pressure persons to join a feminist organization. In either case, one could argue that the ties and relationships one might gain from the church or feminist involvements might be a help to the person, but a basic respect for the freedom and innate dignity of the client would rule against mandatory activities such as these. A neutral, evenhanded approach between religious and secular groups argues that both should be treated on the same basis.

This policy proposal should be taken narrowly, however, in the sense that mandatory parts of a program receiving government funds may include references to values, attitudes, and patterns of behavior. Many welfare-to-work workers interviewed by either my associate researcher or me deemed classes in such topics as self-esteem, the importance of work, and anger management to be very important. Yet these topics naturally and inherently involve underlying values and perspectives on life. Thus, a Christian organization, a Jewish organization, a secular feminist organization, and a secular organization with a community development perspective are all likely to stress different underlying values and perspectives on such topics. That is all right. To require a feminist organization to give up its feminist perspective, a community development organization to give up its economic and neighborhood perspective, a Christian organization to give up its Christian perspective, and a Jewish organization to give up its Jewish perspective would wreak havoc with what those groups are and might fatally weaken the strength of the messages they are seeking to use to help those in need. Narrow, partisan, sectarian instruction is inappropriate when mandatory or funded by government, while broad, value-expressive instruction that is relevant to the goals of a social service program is appropriate even when mandatory or government funded. Although there is no bright line separating the two types of instruction, policymakers—whether legislators on the state or national level or rule makers in administrative positions—should seek to define and implement this distinction. Experience, along with some trial and error, will serve as a guide.

A third policy proposal is *to give clients as much a choice of providers as is practicable.* This choice must be an informed choice, one based on accurate and timely information concerning the various programs and their nature. Ideally, in an effort to maximize choice, clients should be given vouchers and the needed information on the programs where they can redeem those vouchers for services. This method is empowering for the clients. It presents them with options and encourages them to make decisions based on their needs and inclinations. Charitable choice requires—and rightly so—that when clients are assigned to a faith-based program for services, a secular alternative be available. A requirement that clients be informed of this right to receive services from a secular provider should be a part of future charitable choice legislation. No one should be forced to receive services from a faith-based provider against his or her will. But if one's vision of client choice stops there, it is too limited. Ideally, if a client is assigned to a secular program and would prefer a faith-based program, he or she should have this as an available option. The beauty of vouchers is that they totally remove the element of being assigned and, thereby, most fully treat clients as people with the power to make their own decisions.

Vouchers have the additional benefit of taking government out of the business of deciding what grants and contracts, worth how much money, should go to what nongovernmental agencies. When determining who gets how much money, there is the constant danger that political connections and overly cozy, long-term relationships will play a larger role than competence and positive results. By the use of vouchers, those sorts of decisions are taken out of the hands of government officials and given to the recipients of the services. This also has positive implications for preserving the autonomy of organizations partnering with government. In addition, vouchers have some positive implications in terms of church-state issues, as I will discuss shortly.

Sometimes, however, it will not be practical to provide services by way of vouchers. Especially in small towns and rural areas, it may not be possible to have a full range of faith-based and secular service providers from which clients can choose. Under those circumstances, compromises from the ideal need to be made. As is often the case in implementing public policies, the ideal will often not be fully attainable. Yet the ideal can continue as a goal from which deviations are made when necessary. In large metropolitan areas, especially those with strong public transit systems, the ideal described here can usually be attained for most social service programs.

Even when it is practical to use vouchers, the implementation of voucher plans is not without potential problems. Any voucher plan requires that for each type of social service that has been voucherized, some government office must draw up a list of approved agencies where vouchers can be redeemed, along with a description of the agencies and their programs. This can present more of a challenge than one might first imagine. For example, an agency may be doing very good work but may not be providing the type of welfare-to-work services that a particular program envisages. Should it be an approved agency for receiving the program's vouchers? If one says yes, the welfare-to-work boundaries may be stretched to a very questionable extent; if one says no, innovation and creativity—which one hopes would be stimulated—may be lost. This, however, is a challenge, not an insurmountable obstacle.

Also, even a voucher system may favor already established programs over small, newly created programs. Under a voucher system, an ongoing program that can attract clients must already exist. It is hard to start up a new program based on vouchers, whereas a direct grant program can make money available to a new, start-up provider that the funding agency deems valuable to the community. This concern can in part be met by private foundations and corporations, which could provide seed money for a new program. Assuming the program is able to attract the requisite number of clients, government-provided vouchers could then become a source of income for the program. As I argued earlier, I am convinced it is much better if government does not fund programs at 100 percent of their costs in any case. Thus, nongovernmental social service programs should be able to exist and to provide certain services apart from government funds. Vouchers can then play the supplementing role that allows these programs to expand and improve on the services they are already offering.

Some potential problems with voucher programs could be met by way of a modified voucher approach, one that eliminates vouchers per se and reimburses participating providers on a per capita basis. Participating providers would receive funding directly from the funding government agencies and would get a certain set amount for each client that chooses their programs.

The fourth underlying goal of my specific policy recommendations is **to meet the fears of those who see legal-constitutional and practical dangers and problems in public-private partnerships.** Although little controversy accompanied the addition of charitable choice provisions to four pieces of legislation in the 1990s, political opposition has risen since President George W. Bush created the White House Office of Faith-Based and Community Initiatives and advocated more government partnerships with faith-based and community-based programs. Partisan considerations may be playing a role in this opposition. It may also be that those with doubts about the wisdom of such an approach did not make an effort to be heard or that the media may not have picked up on their concerns as long as it was not a highly visible issue. Whatever the reason, a once relatively noncontroversial policy initiative has now migrated into an initiative that is anything but noncontroversial. Concerns and fears abound. Thus, a final goal of my policy recommendations is to respond to some of these fears and to seek to make public-private partnerships less controversial. I believe that one policy change and one mind-set change would go a long way toward building broader consensus on this issue.

The policy change is *to require that government partnerships can only be established with for-profit or nonprofit groups*. This means that government could not fund the social service programs of churches or other religious congregations. Charitable choice and most versions of the current administration's faith-based initiative allow religious congregations with social service programs to receive government funds directly without having to create a separate nonprofit entity, such as a 501(c)(3) nonprofit organization. This seems unwise and too close to unnecessarily mixing church and state.

As my research reported in this book has demonstrated, welfare-to-work programs sponsored by faith-based nonprofit entities are not necessarily any less religious than those sponsored directly by religious congregations themselves. In making my policy recommendation, I do not assume that they are. My assumption is, rather, that whenever the government sends funds to an organized church—even if for the church's social service activities—the red flags of an overly close relationship between church and state arise. If a congregation does not segregate its governmental funds into a separate account, all the financial records of the congregation may be subject to audit. Even if it does segregate the government funds it has received, questions can still be raised about whether or not the congregation has properly segregated those funds. In addition, the symbolism of the government writing checks directly to churches is all wrong and runs the danger of creating the impression that traditional church-state boundaries are being violated even when they are not. If there is a slippery slope toward greater and inappropriate church-state collaborations, allowing government funds to go directly to churches tends to increase the incline and slipperiness of that slope more than does sending government funds to a nonprofit organization affiliated with a church.

In addition, direct funding of religious congregations is not necessary to having strong, healthy government partnerships with faith-based providers. The value added to services through such funding arrangements is minimal. In fact, this study found that less than 30 percent of the faith-based welfare-to-work programs were run directly by congregations. For a religious congregation to create a legally separate entity and then obtain nonprofit status for it is not an overly onerous process. For those congregations that are small and without the requisite finances or experienced members that make this a fairly easy process, special help should be provided by way of an intermediary agency that can provide technical assistance or perhaps through the state or local ombudsman-like office I proposed earlier.

A mind-set change is also important and relates to those who believe that government funding of programs sponsored by religious groups that are other than completely secular inevitably violates basic church-state norms. Persons taking this position emphasize that history has taught us the dangers of government using tax dollars to fund religion. If one's mind-set is that church-state separation and, thus, religious freedom are threatened whenever tax dollars support any activities of a religious organization or support the teaching of any values or habits of life that are rooted in religious beliefs, one is very likely to oppose government funding for the social service programs of faith-based organizations like those I studied in my research.

Persons who take this stance face big problems if they are to be consistent. How can they approve fire and police protection of houses of worship, tax exemptions for houses of worship, government-funded scholarships for low-income students attending religiously oriented colleges and universities, paid chaplains in the armed services, and so on? Besides, they make the implicit assumption that if all religion is carefully removed from a social service program, that program is genuinely neutral on matters of religion. But is it? If social service programs were to avoid any reference to religion when dealing with such issues as motivations to work, the worth of all human beings, responsibility toward one's family, and honesty in the workplace, would these programs not be implicitly communicating the message that religion is irrelevant or unimportant for these issues? Given the fact that these are all issues in which religion has frequently spoken, such thoroughly secularized social service programs would hardly be neutral on matters of religion. Instead, secular belief systems would be favored over religious ones. Thus, the mind-set that posits as a bedrock principle the idea that no government funding may ever flow to religious organizations and their activities suffers from some very tangible defects in the real world.

A different mind-set, one that is more attuned to the realities of the actual world, would be *to build on the concept of governmental neutrality as the bedrock principle of church-state concerns.* As I described earlier, governmental neutrality requires that government actions neither favor nor disfavor, advantage nor disadvantage, any particular religion or either religious or secular systems of belief. Genuine neutrality on matters of religion assures that government will not make it easier or harder for anyone to follow any particular religion or either religious or secular worldviews generally.[18]

Applying this concept of neutrality to government and its partnerships with nongovernmental social service entities means that government should neither favor nor disfavor any particular entity because it is or is not faith-based in nature. Government policies ought not to make it easier or harder for a client to obtain services from either a secular or a faith-based provider. However, government would be anything but neutral if it eagerly entered into partnerships with a wide range of secular programs deeply rooted in a variety of secular perspectives but rejected partnerships with similar, equally effective programs that are faith-based. Alternatively, if government would only agree to partner with faith-based programs on the condition that they give up large segments of their religious character, tax dollars would be being used to pressure faith-based groups to secularize. Again, this situation is far removed from governmental neutrality on matters of religion. Government could maintain its religious neutrality by agreeing not to fund any nongovernmental programs or by agreeing to fund them all, based on neutral criteria, such as effectiveness and client satisfaction. Government cannot maintain its religious neutrality if it funds secular programs but refuses to fund faith-based programs because they are faith-based. Nor can government maintain its neutrality if it only funds faith-based programs on the condition that they give up their religious character.

If the mind-set that emphasizes a genuine neutrality on the part of government toward social service providers would be the mind-set with which policymakers and policy implementers approach public-private partnerships, many of the concerns of those who now fear public-private partnerships with faith-based providers would disappear.

If the four policy goals and the twelve specific policy initiatives subsumed under them that I propose in this section would be fully implemented, what is already a common practice—that of government entering into financial partnerships with nonprofit and some for-profit organizations for the provision of welfare-to-work services—would be expanded to include many more community-based and faith-based providers. Equally important, the terms and conditions of these partnerships—now often shrouded in uncertainty and confusion—would be clarified and regularized.

Questions in Need of Further Research

Although the findings of the study reported in this book carry with them many implications that stretch beyond their immediate focus, the study itself deals with only a specific, limited phenomenon: programs seeking to assist persons of four major metropolitan areas in receiving some form of welfare assistance to improve their economic situation. The written questionnaire that was used to gather the basic data for the study, while useful for obtaining certain types of information, does not lend itself to obtaining other types of information. Also, this study did not have many comparable studies on which to draw. It thus has had an exploratory, issue-framing quality. It has mapped the lay of a largely unexplored terrain, many details of which are in need of further exploration. Most obviously, welfare-to-work programs in other cities and at other points in time need to be explored. I also believe that several findings of this study are particularly important for the future of public-private partnerships. It is essential that these findings be explored in other contexts and by other researchers. Whether or not these findings are confirmed by other studies, as well as the greater details that other studies would provide, will deeply affect the debates over creating a more inclusive range of public-private partnerships and over the nature of those partnerships. In this final section, I outline five findings that I believe future research needs to explore in greater depth and in additional settings.

The first—and perhaps the most important—of the five questions that this study poses for future research concerns *the potential loss of autonomy, flexibility, and creativity when a nongovernmental entity enters into a partnership with government.* It is especially crucial to relate the loss of autonomy, flexibility, and creativity to the proportion of a program's funding that comes from government. This is an important question, since almost all of the arguments being made for the devolution of the delivery of many social services to nongovernmental entities would disappear if the services offered by those entities and the way they provide those services would be squeezed into a common, government-determined mold. Violence would then be done to those entities and to the potential additional value they could bring to providing services to those in desperate need. They would be turned into vendors, "offer[ing] goods for sale especially habitually or as a means of livelihood" (*Merriam-Webster Unabridged Dictionary*). On the one hand, the questionnaire responses in my study showed that most of the nongovernmental entities that were receiving money from the government—whether for-profit, nonprofit, or faith-based—reported positive results from their financial relationships. They also generally reported many contacts with government and were satisfied with those contacts. The on-site visits, on the other hand, made clear that something had been lost as well as gained by the nongovernmental entities. This seemed especially true of those providers that were receiving government funding constituting at or near 100 percent of their total budgets.

These findings raise a number of crucial questions for future research, all related to the effects of government funding and, more importantly, to the level of government funding on entities' autonomy and freedom of action. If future research could develop measures of social service providers' freedom of action and then correlate them with the sources of their funding, much insight would be given into the effects of varying levels of government funding on the agencies and the services they provide. This is crucial information if one is to assess the nature of the optimal public-private partnership.

The second crucial question that this study indicates is in need of further exploration concerns *the nature of sectarian instruction and proselytization that is occurring in both secular and faith-based social service programs.* This study and others have demonstrated that both secular and faith-based welfare-to-work programs seek to change their clients' values, attitudes, and patterns of behavior. It also has demonstrated that although many faith-based organizations make religious references in these attempts, those religious references are to broad religious themes, not to doctrines specific to certain narrowly defined religious traditions. Also, these appeals seem to be made in an affirming, nonjudgmental manner. Although differing from secular appeals in terms of content, they are very similar to secular appeals in tone or spirit. These findings need to be tested by additional research in other contexts. They run counter to a culturally ingrained image of religious messages being delivered in a judgmental, high-pressure manner and of secular messages being delivered in a nonjudgmental, winsome, "neutral" manner. Popular images of faith-based social service programs may have been too much shaped by Hollywood's portrayal of Elmer Gantry–like characters. This information, in turn, will be vital in analyzing the differences and similarities between the faith-based and the secular agencies' methods of service delivery and in analyzing what implications those differences and similarities hold for government partnerships with them.

A third, more focused question in need of further research is *whether or not there currently is a bias against community-based and especially faith-based groups in government's grant-making and contracting processes.* This study has found circumstantial evidence that discrimination is indeed occurring. Faith-based welfare-to-work programs were less likely to receive government funds, and when they did receive government funds, they received less money than the secular providers of similar services. Also, they were more frequently turned down for government funds than were the secular providers. I found this to be true not only when faith-based programs were compared to the large, professionalized nonprofit programs but also when they were compared to the small, nonprofessionalized nonprofit programs. But when questioned about the lack of government funds, many of the faith-based programs cited issues other than, or at least in addition to, bias on the part of government officials or a fear of loss of religious freedoms. Thus, additional systematic studies are needed to probe more deeply for the causes behind the fact that faith-based programs often receive no or very limited government funding. Also, more detailed information is needed concerning the nature of the faith-based programs that were turned down for funding and of the similar secular, community-based programs that were granted funds. As this information is compiled, we will be in a much better position to conclude whether or not the circumstantial evidence of this study indeed represents real discrimination and barriers, or if other factors can explain this apparent bias against faith-based providers.

A fourth question in need of additional research concerns *the level of compassion, concern, and caring exhibited by the different types of welfare-to-work providers.* The preliminary conclusion of this study is that it is difficult, if not impossible, to distinguish between the levels of concern for clients among the staff members at the six different types of providers. However, this conclusion was based not on the systematic questionnaire portion of the study but on the qualitative interviews with program staff members during the 51 on-site observations and visits. Thus, a more systematic interview or questionnaire study of a representative sample of workers at different types of programs would either confirm or indicate a need to reevaluate what this study has concluded. A systematic study of the clients' perceptions of the extent to which they were treated respectfully and with a sense of care and concern would be even more helpful. Such research would either support or discredit what tends to be conventional wisdom—that the workers at government agencies, for-profit firms, and even large, professionalized nonprofit agencies are less caring and client-oriented than workers at small community-based and faith-based agencies. Depending on the outcome of such research, the case for government devolving to smaller community-based and faith-based agencies the delivery of social services that have high levels of client contact will either be weakened or strengthened.

A fifth question particularly in need of additional research concerns *the role and importance of conservative Protestants in providing social services.* The prevailing wisdom has been that conservative Protestants are largely inward looking and little concerned with the welfare of the needy outside of their own membership. Mainline Protestants, it has been thought, are the Protestant bearers of the long-standing Christian concern for the poor and needy in society. This study has demonstrated, however, that conservative Protestants dominate the faith-based welfare-to-work providers in the four cities studied.

The question to be researched is whether these findings are an aberration or one of the first demonstrations of a new, emerging pattern on the religious-social service scene. If this is an emerging trend, it is important also to ask how the evangelical social service groups are providing social services. These are important questions because conservative Protestants are growing in numbers and influence, while mainline Protestants are shrinking in numbers and losing influence. Some have seen this as evidence that Protestantism is going to have less of an impact in the social services field. But if the place of mainline Protestants is being taken over by conservative Protestants, the overall Protestant contribution may not decrease and may even increase. Protestant social services may also change in character, depending on the nature of the social services provided by the conservative Protestant programs.

The public image of conservative Protestantism is often dominated by pictures of television evangelists with promises of health and wealth if only the audience accepts Christ and mails in money. Rounding out the stereotype are in-your-face, high-pressure evangelism; a condemning, judgmental attitude; and conservative politics. This study indicates that in the welfare-to-work field, this stereotype is badly in need of revision. The conservative Protestant programs we visited tended to be caring, nonjudgmental, and more concerned with meeting human needs than with chalking up converts. In short, it is important to confirm whether or not conservative Protestants are in fact moving into the social services field in force and whether or not this study's findings in regard to the manner in which they are delivering social services holds true more broadly in their social service programs. The answers to these questions carry many implications for governmental partnerships with faith-based organizations.

In conclusion, as with all studies, this study has answered many questions but raised others. My hope is that by way of the questions it has been able to answer and the remaining questions it has framed, the study of public-private partnerships has been advanced. Through this advancement of knowledge, we as a society can learn to better meet the needs of those among us who are suffering a severity of deprivations that the rest of us can barely imagine. Thus, my deepest hope is that this book will in some small manner result in the improvement of the lives of the most needy among us.

Appendix A
The Questionnaire Survey

Identifying All of the Welfare-to-Work Programs in the Four Target Cities

A major part of this study is based on the results of a questionnaire mailed to comprehensive lists of welfare-to-work programs in four targeted cities: Chicago, Dallas, Los Angeles, and Philadelphia. Any program offering welfare recipients one or more of the services listed in question 1 of the questionnaire was considered a welfare-to-work program. (See app. C for a full copy of the questionnaire.) The initial goal was to identify all of the welfare-to-work programs operating in the four cities. Either my associate researcher or I spent approximately two weeks in each of the four cities, working on compiling these lists. Student assistants and my associate researcher made many follow-up telephone calls. A total of 1,438 welfare-to-work programs in these four cities were thereby identified. One means we used both to check on the completeness of the initial lists and to add any programs that may have been missed was to ask the questionnaire respondents to "give the names and addresses of three programs or organizations in your area that you know are providing similar services to those that your program provides or other programs that help persons on welfare to improve their economic circumstances" (see app. C, Q23).

The returned questionnaires named a total of 422 programs or organizations in response to this question. Of these 422 programs, 301 either were already on our lists of welfare-to-work programs in the four cities or had been eliminated earlier due to our determining that they do not offer the type of welfare-to-work services that were the focus of our study. Questionnaires were sent to the remaining 121 programs named, giving a total of 1,559 programs to which questionnaires were sent.

This means that 71 percent of the programs named in response to the question asking organizations to give the names of additional programs similar to their own either were already on our original lists of welfare-to-work programs or were programs we had previously determined did not offer welfare-to-work services of the type we were studying. Of the remaining 29 percent, an unknown number no doubt did not provide welfare-to-work services of the type we were researching. Based on this, I concluded that our original lists used for mailing out the questionnaires included the vast majority of all the welfare-to-work programs in the four target cities. Also, of the programs or agencies that were named by two or more respondents, 92 percent were already on our lists. This helps to confirm that our original mailing lists included nearly all of the programs that were at all significant players in the welfare-to-work field in the four cities. If there was any bias in the lists of welfare-to-work programs that we compiled, it was in the direction of missing relatively few very small, little-known programs. Since we mailed questionnaires to the 121 programs that were listed by our respondents and were not on our original lists, many of the apparently very small, little-known programs that were originally missed were also ultimately included in our study.

The Representativeness of the Responding Welfare-to-Work Programs

This leaves the question of whether the welfare-to-work programs that completed our questionnaire were representative of our entire list, or whether a bias was introduced by those who did or did not respond. As I noted earlier, we mailed out a total of 1,559 questionnaires. We received a total of 582 back, for a response rate of 37.3 percent (see table 40). Among the respondents, 73 (12.5 percent) stated they were not providing at that time any of the welfare-to-work services listed in the questionnaire. This left 509 completed, usable questionnaires. As table 40 shows, the best response rate was from Dallas at 41.5 percent, followed closely by Los Angeles at 41.3 percent, with Chicago at 36.1 percent and Philadelphia at 30.0 percent. We are not certain why the response rate varied somewhat from one city to another. That the study was based at Pepperdine University, which is located in the Los Angeles area, may have added to the credibility of the study in the eyes of the Los Angeles programs, encouraging a higher response rate there. The Philadelphia list included a fairly large number of religious congregations with welfare-to-work programs, and many of these were very small, perhaps making responding more difficult for them. Also, Philadelphia was the first city for which we assembled our mailing list of programs, and we may have become more skilled at compiling accurate lists as we acquired more experience. The fact that almost 25 percent of the Philadelphia programs that responded—the highest percentage of the four cities—said they did not provide any welfare-to-work services listed in our questionnaire indicates that our Philadelphia list may not have been as accurate as the ones we compiled for later cities.

Our general impression—based on two weeks spent in each city, becoming acquainted with its welfare-to-work structure and ferreting out welfare-to-work programs—is that the responding programs are at least roughly representative of all the welfare-to-work programs in the four cities. We tested this general impression by checking the zip codes of the responding questionnaires with those of all the programs

TABLE 40. Response Rates, by City

City	Number of Questionnaires Sent Out	Percentage of Questionnaires Returned	Percentage of Returned Questionnaires from Respondents Not Doing Welfare-to-Work	Total Number of Respondents Included in the Study[a]
Chicago	413	36.1	10.7	133
Dallas	272	41.5	16.8	94
Los Angeles	511	41.3	5.5	200
Philadelphia	363	30.0	24.8	82
Total	1,559	37.3	12.5	509

[a]Sixteen respondents did not provide sufficient information in their questionnaires for them to be classified into one of the six categories of program types, so for most of the study's analyses, $N = 493$.

on the lists. Since zip codes, or geographic locations, tend to correspond to such characteristics as racial and ethnic makeup and socioeconomic status, we felt that if the responding programs were representative geographically of all programs receiving the questionnaire, our confidence in the representativeness of the respondents would be significantly increased.

We divided each of the four cities into a number of neighborhoods based on similar ethnicity and socioeconomic characteristics. Thirteen such neighborhoods were identified in Los Angeles, 8 in Chicago, 8 in Dallas, and 6 in Philadelphia. Next, we determined the percentage of programs that were on the original lists of welfare-to-work programs that fell into each of these neighborhoods for each of the four cities, and we determined the percentage of the responding programs that fell into each of these neighborhoods. We then determined for each of the 35 neighborhoods the differences between the percentage each neighborhood contributed to the mailing lists for each city and the percentage each contributed to the total number of responding programs for each city. The average difference for each city is as follows: Chicago, 2.5 percentage points; Dallas, 1.6 percentage points; Los Angeles, 3.3 percentage points; and Philadelphia, 2.1 percentage points. The average for all 35 neighborhoods was only 2.5 percentage points, indicating that, based on neighborhood or geographic location, the programs that responded to the questionnaire were indeed closely reflective of the 1,559 programs on the mailing lists.

Following are the zip codes for each of the neighborhoods into which we divided the four cities.

Los Angeles

Neighborhood 1: 91311, 91344, 91306, 91303, 91335, 91406, 91367, 91371, 91411, 91326, 91330, 91324, 91325, 91307, 91364, 91356, 91316, 91436, 91304.
Neighborhood 2: 91340, 91345, 91331, 91352, 91402, 91405, 91605, 91401, 91606, 91040, 91042, 91505, 91506, 91607, 91423, 91604, 91602, 91601.
Neighborhood 3: 90042, 91504, 91502, 91208, 91204, 91205, 91101, 91103, 91104, 91105, 91106, 91107, 91780, 91010,

Appendixes

91011, 91214, 91020, 91001, 91501, 91201, 91207, 91202, 91203, 91206, 91024, 91006, 91007, 91775, 91108, 90041, 90065, 90031, 90039, 91016.

Neighborhood 4: 90045, 90066, 90272, 90049, 90073, 90402, 90403, 90404, 90094, 90293, 90292, 90291, 90025, 90401, 90405.

Neighborhood 5: 90027, 90064, 90035, 90077, 90210, 90046, 90019, 90068, 90024, 90212, 90211, 90069, 90067, 90036, 90028, 90048.

Neighborhood 6: 90029, 90038, 90012, 90004, 90026, 90071, 90021, 90010, 90026, 90057, 90006, 90017, 90015, 90020, 90005, 90014, 90013, 90031.

Neighborhood 7: 91770, 91732, 91733, 91755, 91803, 90063, 90023, 90022, 91030, 90032, 91801, 91776, 90033, 91754, 91755, 91731.

Neighborhood 8: 91702, 91741, 91711, 91768, 91773, 91750, 91722, 91791, 91723, 91724, 91740, 91767, 91790, 91706.

Neighborhood 9: 91746, 91748, 91744, 91789, 91792, 91792, 91765, 91766, 91745, 90601, 90602, 90603, 90604, 90605, 90606, 90608, 90638, 90670, 90650, 90701, 90703.

Neighborhood 10: 90034, 90016, 90018, 90007, 90089, 90008, 90230, 90232, 90056, 90043, 90062, 90037, 90301, 90305, 90047, 90044, 90302, 90304, 90303, 90250, 90247, 90248, 90249, 90504, 90506, 90260, 90003, 90061.

Neighborhood 11: 90011, 90040, 90058, 90640, 90660, 90001, 90255, 90201, 90270, 90240, 90280, 90002, 90241, 90242, 90262, 90059, 90278, 90222, 90220, 90221, 90503, 90710, 90254, 90717, 90732, 90274, 90275, 90732, 90723, 90706.

Neighborhood 12: 90245, 90266, 90277, 90501, 90502, 90505.

Neighborhood 13: 90713, 90715, 90716, 90747, 90745, 90810, 90744, 90731, 90804, 90805, 90806, 90807, 90808, 90822, 90814, 90712, 90803, 90813, 90815, 90802.

Chicago

Neighborhood 1: 60639, 60634, 60630, 60631, 60646, 60641, 60656, 60707.

Neighborhood 2: 60645, 60626, 60660, 60625, 60640, 60659.
Neighborhood 3: 60618, 60613, 60657, 60647, 60614.
Neighborhood 4: 60301, 60302, 60304, 60402, 60804, 60638.
Neighborhood 5: 60651, 60622, 60644, 60624, 60612, 60623, 60608.
Neighborhood 6: 60601, 60605, 60606, 60607, 60610, 60661, 60611, 60616, 60602, 60604, 60654, 60603.
Neighborhood 7: 60621, 60653, 60632, 60609, 60615, 60637, 60636, 60629.
Neighborhood 8: 60652, 60619, 60406, 60419, 60409, 60426, 60620, 60633, 60649, 60617, 60628, 60643, 60655, 60805, 60456, 60469, 60472, 60473, 60827.

Dallas

Neighborhood 1: 75001, 75006, 75019, 75038, 75039, 75060, 75061, 75062, 75063, 75234, 75240, 75244, 75247, 75248, 75254, 75261.
Neighborhood 2: 75040, 75041, 75048, 75089, 75042, 75043, 75080, 75081, 75082, 75088, 75243.
Neighborhood 3: 75205, 75206, 75209, 75214, 75214, 75220, 75225, 75228, 75229, 75230, 75231, 75235, 75238, 75251, 75275.
Neighborhood 4: 75050, 75051, 75052, 75104, 75115, 75137, 75212, 75249.
Neighborhood 5: 75226, 75201, 75202, 75204, 75207, 75219, 75246.
Neighborhood 6: 75116, 75208, 75211, 75224, 75232, 75233, 75236, 75237.
Neighborhood 7: 75217, 75149, 75150, 75203, 75215, 75216, 75223, 75210, 75227, 75241.
Neighborhood 8: 75134, 75141, 75146, 75159, 75172, 75180, 75181, 75182, 75253.

Philadelphia

Neighborhood 1: 19118, 19119, 19127, 19128, 19150, 19138, 19144, 19126, 19141, 19120, 19129.
Neighborhood 2: 19149, 19114, 19116, 19136, 19111, 19152, 19115, 19135, 19154.
Neighborhood 3: 19140, 19124, 19134, 19132, 19133, 19121, 19122, 19125, 19130, 19123, 19137.
Neighborhood 4: 19131, 19151, 19143, 19104, 19139.
Neighborhood 5: 19153, 19148, 19142, 19145, 19112.
Neighborhood 6: 19102, 19103, 19106, 19107, 19146, 19147.

Appendix B
Two Key Distinctions

The Faith-Based/Segmented versus Faith-Based/Integrated Distinction

The respondents that stated they had a continuing religious orientation were sorted into those with an integrated approach (in which religious elements tend to be explicit and woven into the delivery of services) and those with a segmented approach (in which religious elements tend to be implicit and kept separate from the delivery of services). This sorting was done according to a scale based on responses to question 11 of the questionnaire (see app. C).

We first assigned respondents 1 to 5 points for each religious practice in which they reported engaging. The practices that tended to be separate and distinct from the welfare-to-work services being provided were assigned fewer points, and those that tended to bring religious elements into the services provided were assigned more points. We then divided the programs into integrated and segmented based on the total number of points received. Following are the points that were assigned for each religious practice in which the respondents indicated they engaged.

Placing religious symbols or
  pictures in the facility where
  your program is held   2
Opening or closing sessions
  with prayer   3

Using religious values as a guiding motivation for staff in delivering services	1
Having voluntary religious exercises, such as worship or Bible studies	3
Having required religious exercises, such as worship or Bible studies	5
Using religious values or motivations to encourage clients to change attitudes or values	5
Encouraging clients to make personal religious commitments	5
Giving preference in hiring staff to persons in agreement with your religious orientation	3
Hiring only staff in agreement with your religious orientation	5
Giving preference in accepting clients to those in agreement with your religious orientation	4
Other practices your program engages in that are motivated by your religious orientation	1
Total possible points	**37**

The scores ranged from 0 to 33 points. The mean score was 10.3 points, and the median score was 9 points. Those programs scoring 12 points or higher were classified as faith-based/integrated, and those scoring 11 points or lower were classified as faith-based/segmented. We chose 12 points as the score a program had to attain to be classified as integrated, since if we had chosen either the mean or the median score, a program could have qualified for the integrated category simply by engaging in only two of the practices that we had valued at 5 points. Setting the cutoff point slightly higher assured that a program had to engage in at least three of the practices in order to be placed in the integrated category.

The Nonprofit/Secular versus Community-Based Distinction

As I discussed in chapter 2, the distinction between nonprofit/secular programs and community-based programs is frequently made in discussions of governmental partnerships with nonprofit organizations for the delivery of social or health services. To operationalize this distinction, we took into account three variables.

The first variable we took into account was the number of full-time employees. As I discussed in chapter 2, we concluded that the number of full-time employees was the best measure available to us of program size. We assigned 1 point to the responding programs that reported six or fewer full-time employees and 2 points to those reporting seven or more full-time employees. Our choice of six as the number of employees a program could have and still be considered community-based in terms of size was based on the fact that (as I noted in chap. 2, n. 63) six was the number of employees used in Senate Bill 272, Section 701(f) (the CARE Act of 2003) and in some other formal governmental actions to define community-based nonprofit organizations.

The second variable we took into account was the education of employees. We found the mean educational level of each program's full-time and part-time employees by assigning 1 point for each employee with less than a high school education, 2 points for each with a high school education, 3 points for each with some college, 4 points for each with a college degree, and five points for each with a graduate degree. We then multiplied the number of employees at each educational level with that level's point value and divided by the total number of employees. This gave the mean educational level of all employees (full-time and part-time) for each responding program. We next assigned 1 point to each program with a mean staff educational level of 3.0 or less (i.e., where the average education level was that of some college education or less), 2 points to each program with a mean staff educational level over 3.0 (i.e., where the average educational level was greater than that of a some college education).

The third variable we took into account was the ratio of volunteers and part-time employees to full-time employees. For each responding program, we took the total number of full-time employees and divided by the total number of full-time employees, part-time employees, and volunteers to get the percentage of full-time employees out of the total workforce of the program (i.e., full-time and part-time employees and volunteers). We assigned 1 point to those programs whose full-time employees constituted less than one-half of their total workforce, 2 points to those programs whose full-time employees constituted more than one-half of their total workforce.

Thus, those programs that were assigned single points were small programs, with less-educated staff and with a majority of staff members who were either volunteers or part-time workers. These would seem to fit the conceptualization of community-based programs as small programs, with a nonprofessionalized staff. Those programs assigned double points were large programs, with more highly educated staff and with a majority of staff members who were full-time employees. These would seem to fit the conceptualization of nonprofit programs that are large and professionalized.

Next, we added up each program's scores for all three variables, to give each program a total score of 3 to 6. Those programs with scores of 3 or 4 were placed in the community-based category (i.e., they had to fall into the community-based category on all three or two of the variables), and those with scores of 5 to 6 were placed in the nonprofit/secular category (i.e., they had to fall into the nonprofit/secular category on all three or two of the variables). If, due to some missing information, a program had only two scores, it was placed in the community-based category if both the scores were 1 (indicating two community-based characteristics) and in the nonprofit/secular category if both scores were 2 (indicating two nonprofit/secular characteristics) or if one score was 1 and the other score was 2. The latter judgment was made because we wanted to err on the side of more restrictive criteria—rather than on more liberal criteria—for categorizing a provider as community-based. If, due to missing information on two of the criteria, a program had only one score, it was dropped from the analysis. As I noted in chapter 2, this process yielded for this study a total of 139 nonprofit/secular programs and 83 community-based programs.

Finally, I should note that although, throughout this book, I have referred to the large, professionalized programs by the term *nonprofit/secular* and to the small, nonprofessionalized programs by the term *community-based,* both programs are in fact secular in nature. All faith-based programs were placed in one of the two faith-based categories.

Appendix C
The Questionnaire

Following is the questionnaire sent to the welfare-to-work programs in the four cities. To save space, some changes have been made in the layout of the questionnaire as it appears here.

Questionnaire on Programs to Assist Persons towards Economic Self-Sufficiency

Introduction: If the organization of which you are a part has more than one program, please answer the following questions in terms of your specific program, not in terms of the entire organization or agency.

Q1. Which of the following services are provided by your program? *Please circle as many as apply.*
   1. Job search
   2. Education/literary
   3. Education/English as a second language
   4. Education/GED preparation
   5. Education/vocational training, work skills
   6. Work preparedness (job interviewing skills, relating to co-workers, appropriate dress, etc.)
   7. Life skills (self-esteem, budgeting, etc.)
   8. Job placement
   9. Job internships/apprenticeships
   10. Client assessment

11. Mentoring
12. Other welfare-to-work type services. Please specify.

If your organization or agency does not offer any of the above services or other services that work to help persons move from welfare to economic self-sufficiency, please go to Q24.

Q2. Are the above services offered at only one site or at multiple sites?
  1. One site.
  2. Multiple sites. How many?

Q3. Do different groups of clients normally take part in the different services you offer, or do most clients take advantage of all of the above services?
  1. All/most clients receive the same services.
  2. Different groups of clients receive different services.

Q4. Approximately what percentage of the persons you serve are receiving assistance under TANF or other welfare assistance programs?

Q5. In what year did your program first start offering any of the above services?

Q6. What is the estimated total annual budget for the above services in the current fiscal year?

Q7. Do your current plans call for you to: *Circle only one.*
  1. Expand your services greatly in the next 5 years?
  2. Expand your services somewhat in the next 5 years?
  3. Keep your services at the same size they are now?
  4. Reduce the size of your program?

Q8. If you had the opportunity and resources to do so, would you prefer to: *Circle one.*
  1. Expand your services greatly? *Go to Q9.*

2. Expand your services somewhat from what they are now? *Go to Q9.*
3. Even if you could expand your services, you prefer to keep them the same size they are now. *Go to Q8a.*

Q8a. Why don't you wish to expand? *Circle as many as apply.*
1. We are afraid we would lose our effectiveness.
2. We are afraid we would lose touch with our community.
3. We have no physical space where we are now to expand.
4. All the needs in our community are already being met. No need to expand.
5. With increased size would come increased headaches and problems.
6. Other. Please specify.

Q9. Which statement best describes your program? *Circle one.*
1. A public, government program. *Go to Q13.*
2. A private, for-profit program. *Go to Q13.*
3. A private, nonprofit program with no religious base or history. *Go to Q13.*
4. A private, nonprofit program that at one time had a religious orientation, but today has evolved into a program that is largely secular in nature. *Go to Q12.*
5. A private, nonprofit program that continues to have a clear religious base and orientation. *Go to Q10.*

Q10. If your program has a continuing religious orientation, please indicate its relationship to its religious tradition.
1. It is sponsored and run by a religious congregation.
2. It is sponsored and run by a national denomination or a regional network of congregations.
3. It is sponsored by a religious congregation, but a separate entity has been created to run the program, such as a 501(c)(3).
4. It is sponsored by several local congregations, but is run by a separate entity.

5. It is sponsored by a national denomination or a regional network of congregations, but is run by a separate entity.
6. It is run by a separate entity that is largely supported by individuals, **not** sponsored by a religious congregation or network of congregations.
7. Other. Specify.

Q11. If your program has a continuing religious orientation, please indicate which of the following practices characterize your program. *Circle as many as apply.*
1. Placing religious symbols or pictures in the facility where your program is held.
2. Opening or closing sessions with prayer.
3. Using religious values as a guiding motivation for staff in delivering services.
4. Having voluntary religious exercises, such as worship or Bible studies
5. Having required religious exercises, such as worship or Bible studies.
6. Using religious values or motivations to encourage clients to change attitudes or values.
7. Encouraging clients to make personal religious commitments.
8. Giving preference in hiring staff to persons in agreement with your religious orientation.
9. Hiring only staff in agreement with your religious orientation.
10. Giving preference in accepting clients to those in agreement with your religious orientation.
11. Other practices your program engages in that are motivated by your religious orientation. Please specify other practice(s).

Q12. If your program at one time had or continues to have a religious orientation, would you describe that orientation as: *Circle one.*
1. Jewish
2. Roman Catholic

3. Orthodox
4. Protestant denominational. Which denomination?
5. Protestant interdenominational, evangelical
6. Protestant interdenominational, pentecostal
7. Protestant interdenominational, mainline or liberal
8. Muslim
9. Other. Please specify.

Q13. Which of the following types of government funds (national, state, or local) do you receive? *Circle as many as apply.*
   1. We receive no governmental funds of any kind. *Go to Q14.*
   2. We are a government agency, with all or almost all of our funds from the government. *Go to Q19.*
   3. Federal Department of Labor or HUD funds. *Go to Q15.*
   4. TANF funds. *Go to Q15.*
   5. State government funds. *Go to Q15.*
   6. Local government funds. *Go to Q15.*
   7. Funds for supportive services such as child care or transportation. *Go to Q15.*
   8. Grants of in-kind materials (food, supplies, etc.). *Go to Q15.*
   9. Other types of government funds. Please specify.

Q14. If your receive no government funds, is this due to: *Circle one, then go to Q17.*
   1. A self-conscious policy not to seek government funds?
   2. Your having applied for government funds, but not being awarded any?
   3. Your having made inquiries about government funds, but deciding not to apply?
   4. That is just the way things have worked out.

Q15. Approximately what percentage of your program's total annual budget comes from government funds?

Q16. Which of the following have occurred in your program because you receive government funds? *Circle as many as apply.*
   1. Expanded the number of clients we are able to serve.

2. Hired staff with higher levels of education.
3. Hired staff with stronger qualifications and more experience.
4. Put more time and effort into paperwork than should be necessary.
5. Improved our facilities to better serve our clients.
6. Cut down on our religious emphasis or practices.
7. Received fewer private gifts and volunteer hours than we otherwise would.
8. Became more "bureaucratic" and less flexible and creative.
9. Provided services more professionally and effectively.
10. Became less efficient.
11. Other. Please specify.

Q17. Have you had any of the following contacts with government? *Circle as many as apply.*
1. Government offices have referred clients to us.
2. We have referred clients who had problems with which we could not deal to government offices.
3. We are licensed by a government agency.
4. We have undergone health or safety inspections by the government.
5. We have placed clients in jobs in government offices.
6. We have had informal consultations or exchanges of information with government offices.
7. Other contacts with government agencies or officials. Please specify.
8. We have had no contacts with government offices. *Go to Q19.*

Q18. Generally would you say your contacts with government officials and agencies have been:
1. Very satisfactory.
2. Usually satisfactory.
3. Neither satisfactory nor unsatisfactory.
4. Usually unsatisfactory.
5. Very unsatisfactory.

Q19. Do you attempt to follow the progress of clients after they have completed a program of services?
1. Yes. *Go to Q19b.*
2. No. *Go to Q20.*
3. Yes, for some program of services; no, for other programs of services. *Go to Q19a.*

Q19a. For which programs of services you offer do you attempt to follow the progress of clients who have completed the program of services?

Q19b. How successful are you in keeping track of clients who have completed a program of services?
1. Very successful, we know where most are.
2. Somewhat successful, we know where some are.
3. Not very successful, we only know where a few are.
4. Not at all successful, we don't know where any are.

Q19c. Of those you have been able to follow, how many are: *Circle one number on each line.*
a. No better off. Most, Some, Few, None.
b. In an improved economic situation, but still receiving welfare assistance. Most, Some, Few, None.
c. No longer receiving welfare, but still under the poverty line. Most, Some, Few, None.
d. Off welfare and above the poverty line. Most, Some, Few, None.

Q20. Please give me some indication of the size of your program:
a. The approximate number of full-time, paid employees involved in providing services.
b. The approximate number of part-time, paid employees involved in providing services.
c. Of the paid employees (both full- and part-time), approximately how many have: *If none, write in* 0.
   1. Less than a high school education?
   2. A high school education?

3. Some college education?
4. A college degree?
5. A graduate degree such as a master's in social work?
d. Of the paid employees (both full- and part-time), approximately how many are former clients who are graduates of your program? *If none, please write 0.*
e. What is the approximate number of volunteers in any one month?
f. What was the approximate number of clients you served in the year 2000?
g. What was the approximate percent of the above clients who completed your program during 2000?
h. **In 1996,** were you offering the same services as you are today, or were you offering different services?
  1. Much the same services as today.
  2. Quite different services in 1996.
  3. We were not in existence in 1996. *Go to Q21.*
i. **In 1996,** approximately how many clients did you serve?

Q21. Approximately what percentage of your <u>paid staff</u> are: *If none, please write 0.*
  1. African American
  2. Caucasian
  3. Latino
  4. Asian American
  5. Native American
  6. Other. Please specify.

Q22. Approximately what percentage of your <u>clients</u> are: *If none, please write 0.*
  1. African American
  2. Caucasian
  3. Latino
  4. Asian American
  5. Native American
  6. Other. Please specify.

Q23. Please give the names and addresses of three programs or organizations in your area that you know are providing similar services to those that your program provides or other programs that help persons on welfare to improve their economic circumstances.

Q24. I will not use the name of you or your organization or program in any publications, but the following information will tell me you have completed the questionnaire so I can remove your name from the follow-up list and to get back to you for any further information, if I should need to do so.

Name of your program.
Name of the organization sponsoring the program.
Your name.
Phone number where I can reach you.

Q25. Would you like a summary report of the findings from this study?
1. Yes.
2. No.

THANK YOU FOR YOUR HELP IN FILLING OUT THIS QUESTIONNAIRE. If you need additional space to answer any questions or have any other comments about the topic of this questionnaire, please use the remaining pages.

Notes

Chapter 1

1. The Post-Modernity Project of the University of Virginia, *The State of Disunity,* vol. 2 (Ivy, VA: Medias Res Educational Foundation, 1996), tables 7, 10.J, 10.R.

2. Lester M. Salamon, "Partners in Public Service: The Scope and Theory of Government-Nonprofit Relations," in Walter W. Powell, ed., *The Nonprofit Sector: A Research Handbook* (New Haven: Yale University Press, 1987), 110.

3. Peter Berger and Richard John Neuhaus, *To Empower People: The Role of Mediating Structures in Public Policy* (Washington, DC: American Enterprise Institute, 1977), 1.

4. Ibid. (emphasis omitted).

5. I am less than happy to use the term *faith-based* to refer to organizations or programs that have a religious orientation or that are rooted in a religious tradition. I believe that many secular organizations or programs are rooted in a secular faith—that is, that they are based on certain treatment modalities or hold to certain goals that, while not religious, are rooted in certain worldviews that are not subject to empirical verification. In that sense, they are faith-based. Thus, I would prefer to use the term *religiously based* to refer to programs and organizations that are religious in nature. Nevertheless, the term *faith-based* has come to be used so frequently to refer to religiously based programs and organizations that I will bow to common usage and use the term *faith-based*.

6. David Osborne and Ted Gaebler, *Reinventing Government* (New York: Penguin Books, 1993), 47.

7. See, for example, the three books by E. S. Savas on privatization: *Privatizing the Public Sector: How to Shrink Government* (Chatham, NJ: Chatham House, 1980), *Privatization: The Key to Better Government* (Chatham, NJ: Chatham House, 1987), and *Privatization and Public-Private Partnerships* (New York: Chatham House, 2000).

8. Ram A. Cnaan, *The Newer Deal: Social Work and Religion in Partnership* (New York: Columbia University Press, 1999), 16.

9. See, for example, Joe Klein, "In God They Trust," *New Yorker,* June 18, 1997, 40–48; Robert Worth, "Amazing Grace: Can Churches Save the Inner City?" *Washington Monthly,* January/February 1998, 28–31; "Faith-Based Institutions as Anchors for Local Partnerships Serving High-Risk Youths: A New Demonstration," *Public/Private Ventures News* (fall 1998): 2–3; E. J. Dionne Jr., *Community Works: The Revival of Civil Society in America* (Washington, DC: Brookings, 1998); "What's God Got to Do with the American Experiment?" *Brookings Review* 17 (spring 1999); "Can Churches Save America?" *U.S. News and World Report,* September 9, 1996, 179–82; Albert R. Hunt, "Faith-Based Efforts: The Promise and Limitations," *Wall Street Journal,* August 12, 1999, p. A23; Monica Yant, "Houses of Worship Seek Role in New World of Welfare," *Philadelphia Inquirer,* December 9, 1998; Annette John-Hall, "Taking Advantage of Charitable Choice," *Philadelphia Inquirer,* August 8, 1999, p. G7; Adam Cohen, "Feeding the Flock," *Time Magazine,* August 25, 1997, 46–48; and Tobi Jennifer Printz, *Faith-Based Service Providers in the Nation's Capitol: Can They Do More?* (Washington, DC: Urban Institute, 1998).

10. E. J. Dionne Jr., "Take It on Faith" *Washington Post Magazine,* June 20, 1999, p. W07.

11. George W. Bush, "The Duty of Hope," speech given July 22, 1999.

12. Al Gore, "On the Role of Faith-Based Organizations," speech given May 24, 1999, quoted in Fred Glennon, "Blessed Be the Tie That Bind? The Challenge of Charitable Choice to Moral Obligation," *Journal of Church and State* 42 (2000): 825.

13. George W. Bush, foreword to "Rallying the Armies of Compassion," January 2001, http://www.whitehouse.gov/news/reports/text/faithbased.html.

14. On the Clinton endorsement see the cover of the 1993 Plume edition of the book. On the Gore initiative see Don Kettl, *Reinventing Government: A Fifth-Year Report Card* (Washington, DC: Brookings, 1998). On Stephen Goldsmith see his *The Twenty-First Century City: Resurrecting Urban America* (Lanham, MD: Rowman and Littlefield, 1999), 9, 25. Goldsmith has gone on to serve in the George W. Bush administration.

15. For a good account of the troubles and trials encountered by the Office of Faith-Based and Community Initiatives in its first year see Kathryn Dunn Tenpas, "Can an Office Change a Nation? The White House Office of Faith-Based and Community Initiatives: A Year in Review" (Pew Forum on Religion and Public Life, February 2002). Available at http://pewforum.org/publications.

16. The list I offer here of objections that have been raised to governmental partnerships with faith-based organizations has been culled from many sources.

See, for example, the essays by Julie Segal, Melissa Rogers, Alan Brownstein, and Derek Davis in Derek Davis and Barry Hankins, eds., *Welfare Reform and Faith-Based Organizations* (Waco, TX: J. M. Dawson Institute of Church-State Studies, 1999). Also helpful are the various issues of the periodical put out by Americans United for Separation of Church and State, *Church and State*.

17. See, for example, Dan Morain, "Davis to Close State's Privately Run Prisons," *Los Angeles Times*, March 15, 2002, pp. A1, A23. Morain reports that a corrections officers' union in California contributed $2.3 million to Governor Gray Davis's campaign fund and that Governor Davis later decided (perhaps coincidentally) to abandon California's program of having for-profit companies run some state prisons.

18. Stephen Goldsmith has summarized five arguments made against government contracting with for-profit companies and responds to them. See Goldsmith, *The Twenty-First Century City*, 70–73.

19. D. W. Miller, "Measuring the Role of 'the Faith Factor' in Social Change," *Chronicle of Higher Education*, November 26, 1999, p. A21.

20. *Finding Common Ground: Twenty-Nine Recommendations of the Working Group on Human Needs and Faith-Based and Community Initiatives* (Washington, DC: Search for Common Ground, 2002), 30.

21. Avis C. Vidal, "Many Are Called, but Few Are Chosen: Faith-Based Organizations and Community Development," in E. J. Dionne Jr. and Ming Hsu Chen, eds., *Sacred Places, Civic Purposes: Should Government Help Faith-Based Charity?* (Washington, DC: Brookings, 2001), 127.

22. Ana Greenberg, "Doing Whose Work? Faith-Based Organizations and Government Partnerships," in Mary Jo Bane, Brent Coffin, and Ronald Thiemann, eds., *Who Will Provide? The Changing Role of Religion in American Social Welfare* (Boulder: Westview, 2000), 178.

23. Luis E. Lugo, *Equal Partners: The Welfare Responsibility of Governments and Churches* (Washington, DC: Center for Public Justice, 1998), 19.

24. Ibid.

25. "Fairfield, Connecticut, Town Records," in Ralph E. Pumphrey and Muriel W. Pumphrey, eds., *The Heritage of American Social Work* (New York: Columbia University Press, 1961), 22 (modern spelling, capitalization, and punctuation added).

26. Walter I. Trattner, *From Poor Law to Welfare State: A History of Social Welfare in America*, 2d ed. (New York: Free Press, 1979), 17.

27. Ibid., 32–33.

28. See Marvin Olasky, *The Tragedy of American Compassion* (Washington, DC: Regnery, 1992), 14.

29. J. Bruce Nichols, *The Uneasy Alliance: Religion, Refugee Work, and U.S. Foreign Policy* (New York: Oxford University Press, 1988), 24–25.

30. See Lester M. Salamon, *Partners in Public Service: Government-Nonprofit Relations in the Modern Welfare State* (Baltimore: Johns Hopkins University Press, 1995), 85.

31. Ibid.

32. Frank A. Fetter, "Subsidizing of Private Charities," *American Journal of Sociology* 7 (1901): 360.

33. See Steven Rathgeb Smith, "Government Financing of Nonprofit Activity," in Elizabeth T. Boris and C. Eugene Steurle, eds., *Nonprofits and Government: Collaboration and Conflict* (Washington, DC: Urban Institute Press, 1999), 178.

34. Dennis R. Young, "Complementary, Supplementary, or Adversarial? A Theoretical and Historical Examination of Nonprofit-Government Relations in the United States," in Elizabeth T. Boris and C. Eugene Steurle, eds., *Nonprofits and Government: Collaboration and Conflict* (Washington, DC: Urban Institute Press, 1999), 48.

35. Steven Rathgeb Smith and Michael Lipsky, *Nonprofits for Hire: The Welfare State in the Age of Contracting* (Cambridge: Harvard University Press, 1993), 9.

36. Smith, "Government Financing of Nonprofit Activity," 179.

37. Mark Carl Rom, "From Welfare State to Opportunity, Inc.: Public-Private Partnerships in Welfare Reform," in Pauline Vaillancourt Rosenau, ed., *Public-Private Policy Partnerships* (Cambridge: MIT Press, 2000), 166.

38. See ibid., 171–72.

39. Lester M. Salamon, *America's Nonprofit Sector: A Primer*, 2d ed. (New York: Foundation Center, 1999), 49.

40. Ibid., 114.

41. Ibid., 112.

42. Stephen V. Monsma, *When Sacred and Secular Mix: Religious Nonprofit Organizations and Public Money* (Lanham, MD: Rowman and Littlefield, 1996), 65.

43. In the following discussion, I will not seek to document and footnote every contention that I cite for or against government partnerships with non-governmental entities. To do so is not necessary and would not add to the case being made here. To anyone acquainted with the arguments being made for and against these partnerships, the arguments I cite here will, I am sure, sound very familiar.

44. Greenberg, "Doing Whose Work?" 180.

45. Many studies documenting these and other similar patterns are found in

Cnaan, *The Newer Deal*, 133–56, and in Byron R. Johnson, *Objective Hope: Assessing the Effectiveness of Faith-Based Organizations: A Review of the Literature* (Philadelphia: Center for Research on Religion and Urban Civil Society, University of Pennsylvania, 2002), 10–15.

46. For news accounts of this struggle see Nicholas Riccardi, "Political Struggle Centers on Welfare-to-Work Contractor," *Los Angeles Times*, June 20, 2000, p. B1; "A News Summary: Action Delayed on Welfare-to-Work Pact," *Los Angeles Times*, June 21, 2000, 4; and Nicholas Riccardi, "Supervisors Privatize Job-Training Services," *Los Angeles Times*, July 12, 2000, p. B3.

47. Tanya Akel, quoted in Riccardi, "Political Struggle Centers on Welfare-to-Work Contractor," p. B1. Akel is an analyst with the Service Employees International Union, Local 660.

48. Annelle Grajeda, quoted in "A News Summary: Action Delayed on Welfare-to-Work Pact," 4. Grajeda is the general manager of the Service Employees International Union, Local 660.

49. E. J. Dionne Jr. and Ming Hsu Chen, "When the Sacred Meets the Civic: An Introduction," in E. J. Dionne Jr. and Ming Hsu Chen, eds., *Sacred Places, Civic Purposes: Should Government Help Faith-Based Charity?* (Washington, DC: Brookings, 2001), 15.

50. On libertarianism see David Boaz, ed., *The Libertarian Reader* (New York: Free Press, 1997).

51. Young, "Complementary, Supplementary, or Adversarial?" 33.

52. See Olasky, *The Tragedy of American Compassion*. In his later book, *Renewing American Compassion* (New York: Free Press, 1996), Olasky takes a less libertarian approach.

53. Sheila S. Kennedy, "When Is Private Public? State Action in the Era of Privatization and Public-Private Partnerships," *Civil Rights Law Journal*, 11 (2001): 223.

54. Smith and Lipsky, *Nonprofits for Hire*, 116.

55. J. Brent Walker, "Separating Church and State," *New York Times* (September 14, 1995), p. A17 (emphasis added).

56. Stephen Macedo, "The Constitution of Civil Society: School Vouchers, Religious Nonprofit Organizations, and Liberal Public Values," *Chicago-Kent Law Review* 75 (2000): 448.

57. Peter Frumkin, "After Partnership: Rethinking Public-Nonprofit Relations," in Mary Jo Bane, Brent Coffin, and Ronald Thiemann, eds., *Who Will Provide? The Changing Role of Religion in American Social Welfare* (Boulder: Westview, 2000), 206.

58. Glennon, "Blessed Be the Tie That Bind?" 835.

59. For a more complete presentation of the framework I am presenting here

see Stephen V. Monsma, *Positive Neutrality* (Westport, CT: Greenwood, 1993), chap. 4. Also very helpful are J. Bryan Hehir, "Religious Ideas and Social Policy: Subsidiarity and Catholic Style of Ministry," in Mary Jo Bane, Brent Coffin, and Ronald Thiemann, eds., *Who Will Provide? The Changing Role of Religion in American Social Welfare* (Boulder: Westview, 2000), 97–120; Lugo, *Equal Partners;* and Richard J. Mouw, "Some Reflections on Sphere Sovereignty," in Luis E. Lugo, ed., *Religion, Pluralism, and Public Life* (Grand Rapids, MI: Eerdmans, 2000), 87–109.

60. "The Responsive Communitarian Platform," *Responsive Community* 2 (winter 1991–92): 4.

61. R. E. M. Irving, *The Christian Democratic Parties of Western Europe* (London: Allen and Unwin, 1979), 42.

62. The subsidiarity principle was first clearly articulated by Pope Pius XI in his 1931 encyclical *Quadragesimo Anno*. For an excellent summary of the concept and its application to today's policy debates see Hehir, "Religious Ideas and Social Policy," 97–120.

63. Hehir, "Religious Ideas and Social Policy," 100.

64. Lugo, *Equal Partners,* 12.

65. Ibid., 14.

66. Quoted in Douglas Pike, "Churches and the Modern State," in Leicester C. Webb, *Legal Personality and Political Pluralism* (Melbourne, Australia: Melbourne University Press, 1958), 143. Pike cited the source of the quotation as the U.S. Supreme Court case *Poulos v. New Hampshire,* 345 U.S. 395 (1953), but I could not find it anywhere in this case. Apparently, the quotation is miscited and, since Pike is now deceased, must remain anonymous.

67. Hehir, "Religious Ideas and Social Policy," 118.

68. See Frumkin, "After Partnership," 198–203.

69. Ibid., 214.

70. *Everson v. Board of Education,* 330 U.S. 16, 18 (1947).

71. See, for example, Monsma, *When Sacred and Secular Mix,* especially 63–80; Bernard J. Coughlin, *Church and State in Social Welfare* (New York: Columbia University Press, 1965); Thomas H. Jeavons, *When the Bottom Line Is Faithfulness* (Bloomington: Indiana University Press, 1994); and Thomas Maier and Tom Curran, "Church Services: Public Funds Help O'Connor to Help Others," *Newsday,* May 17, 1993, 6, 26.

72. Justice Lewis Powell, writing for a 6–3 majority in *Hunt v. McNair,* 413 U.S. 735, 743 (1973).

73. Susanna Dokupil, "A Sunny Dome with Caves of Ice: The Illusion of Charitable Choice," *Texas Review of Law and Politics* 5 (2000): 189–90. The best-known Supreme Court decisions resting on neutrality principles are *Rosenberger*

v. Rector, 515 U.S. 819 (1995), *Mitchell v. Helms* 530 U.S. 793 (2000), and *Zelman v. Simmons-Harris*, 536 U.S. 639 (2002). For a volume that presents pro and con views on the neutrality principle as it was found in the *Mitchell v. Helms* case see Stephen V. Monsma, ed., *Church-State Relations in Crisis: Debating Neutrality* (Lanham, MD: Rowman and Littlefield, 2002).

74. Jeffrey Rosen, "Is Nothing Secular?" *New York Times Magazine*, January 30, 2000, 40, 42.

75. Justice Clarence Thomas, *Mitchell v. Helms*, 530 U.S. 810 (2000).

76. *Bradford v. Roberts*, 175 U.S. 291 (1899); *Bowen v. Kendrick*, 487 U.S. 589 (1988).

77. Don. A. Dillman, *Mail and Telephone Surveys: The Total Design Method* (New York: John Wiley, 1978).

78. Here and elsewhere throughout this book, I use the term *client* to refer to persons who are receiving services from welfare-to-work or other social service programs. Some people have objected to the use of this term, claiming that it implies a passivity on the part of those receiving the services or that it implies a bureaucratized approach by the service provider. The *Merriam-Webster Unabridged Dictionary* (online ed.), however, defines *client* as "a person who engages the professional advice or services of another." The older definition is "a person under the protection of another." Since *client* is more commonly used today in the neutral meaning I quoted first, I believe it is the most accurate term, as well as the easiest to use, to refer to persons who are receiving services from a welfare-to-work or other social service provider.

Chapter 2

1. Lester M. Salamon, *America's Nonprofit Sector: A Primer*, 2d ed. (New York: Foundation Center, 1999), 17.

2. Ibid., 164–65.

3. Elizabeth T. Boris, *Myths about the Nonprofit Sector,* Charting Civil Society, no. 4 (Washington, DC: Center on Nonprofits and Philanthropy, Urban Institute, 1998), 1.

4. Salamon, *America's Nonprofit Sector*, 165. Also see Robin Garr, *Reinvesting in America: The Grassroots Movements That Are Feeding the Hungry, Housing the Homeless, and Putting Americans Back to Work* (Reading, MA: Addison-Wesley, 1995).

5. See, for example, Joe Loconte, "The Seven Deadly Sins of Government Funding for Private Charities," *Policy Review*, no. 82 (March–April 1997): 28–36.

6. Both community-based and nonprofit/secular organizations are, of

course, nonprofit and secular in nature, but I here choose to use the term *nonprofit/secular* for the larger, more professionalized organizations, to avoid cumbersome wording. I use the term *community-based* for the smaller, less professionalized organizations, since this term has come into general usage to refer to small, grassroots, neighborhood-oriented social service organizations.

7. Ronald J. Sider and Heidi Rolland Unruh, "No Aid for Religion? Charitable Choice and the First Amendment," *Brookings Review* 17 (spring 1999), 48.

8. I distinguish between what have sometimes been called "faith-saturated" programs and what I term "faith-based/integrated" programs. The former terminology implies that religious elements pervade every aspect of an organization's programs, while the latter implies that religious elements are integrated into the organization's programs but do not necessarily pervade all aspects of them. For a study that uses the term *faith-saturated* as part of a categorization see *Finding Common Ground: Twenty-Nine Recommendations of the Working Group on Human Needs and Faith-Based and Community Initiatives* (Washington, D.C.: Search for Common Ground, 2002), 34–38.

9. Salamon, *America's Nonprofit Sector,* 111.

10. Ibid., 112.

11. Laudan Y. Aron and Patrick T. Sharkey, *The 1996 National Survey of Homeless Assistance Providers and Clients: A Comparison of Faith-Based and Secular Non-Profit Programs* (Washington, D.C.: Office of the Assistant Secretary for Planning and Evaluation, U.S. Department of Health and Human Services, 2002), available at http://aspe.hhs.gov/hsp/homelessness/NSHAPC02.

12. See Mark Carl Rom, "From Welfare State to Opportunity, Inc.: Public-Private Partnerships in Welfare Reform," in Pauline Vaillancourt Rosenau, ed., *Public-Private Policy Partnerships* (Cambridge: MIT Press, 2000), 170.

13. See ibid., 174.

14. Eric C. Twombly, *Human Service Nonprofits in Metropolitan Areas during Devolution and Welfare Reform* (Washington, D.C.: Urban Institute, 2001), 2.

15. Ibid., 3.

16. Ibid.

17. Peter Frumkin, "After Partnership: Rethinking Public-Nonprofit Relations," in Mary Jo Bane, Brent Coffin, and Ronald Thiemann, eds., *Who Will Provide? The Changing Role of Religion in American Social Welfare* (Boulder: Westview, 2000), 199.

18. Rom, "From Welfare State to Opportunity, Inc.," 161.

19. Ibid., 170.

20. Thomas H. Jeavons, *When the Bottom Line Is Faithfulness: Management of*

Christian Service Organizations (Bloomington: Indiana University Press, 1994), xiv.

21. Peter Dobkin Hall, "The History of Religious Philanthropy in America," in Robert Wuthnow and Virginia A. Hodgkinson, eds., *Faith and Philanthropy in America: Exploring the Role of Religion in America's Voluntary Sector* (San Francisco: Jossey-Bass, 1990), 38–39.

22. See Virginia A. Hodgkinson, Murray S. Weitzman, and Arthur D. Kirsch, *From Belief to Commitment: The Community Service Activities and Finances of Religious Congregations in the United States: Findings from a National Survey* (Washington, DC: Independent Sector, 1988).

23. Salamon, *America's Nonprofit Sector*, 153.

24. Aron and Sharkey, *The 1996 National Survey of Homeless Assistance Providers and Clients*, 4.

25. Ram A. Cnaan, *The Newer Deal: Social Work and Religion in Partnership* (New York: Columbia University Press, 1999), 184.

26. Ibid., 275–76.

27. Peter Dobkin Hall, "Philanthropy, Public Welfare, and the Politics of Knowledge: Acquiring Knowledge by Taking Risks," in Deborah S. Gardner, ed., *Vision and Values: Rethinking the Nonprofit Sector in America* (New York: Nathan Cummings Foundation, 1998), 17.

28. Salamon, *America's Nonprofit Sector*, 149.

29. On this distinction see Stanley Carlson-Thies, "Faith-Based Institutions Cooperating with Public Welfare: The Promise of the Charitable Choice Provision," in Derek Davis and Barry Hankins, eds., *Welfare Reform and Faith-Based Organizations* (Waco, TX: J. M. Dawson Institute of Church-State Studies, 1999), 50–51.

30. Carol J. De Vita and Sarah Wilson, *Faith-Based Initiatives: Sacred Deeds and Secular Dollars,* Emerging Issues in Philanthropy Seminar Series (Washington, D.C.: Urban Institute; Cambridge, MA: Hauser Center for Nonprofit Organizations, 2001), 4.

31. Avis C. Vidal, "Many Are Called, but Few Are Chosen: Faith-Based Organizations and Community Development," in E. J. Dionne Jr. and Ming Hsu Chen, eds., *Sacred Places, Civic Purposes: Should Government Help Faith-Based Charity?* (Washington, DC: Brookings, 2001), 133. On the prevalence of faith-based community development corporations see also Jeremy Nowak, "Community Development and Religious Institutions," in ibid., 111–26. Also see the Web site of the Christian Community Development Association (http://www.ccda.org); this national organization in the conservative, or evangelical, Protestant tradition has over 500 member organizations in 100 cities and 32 states.

32. Wesley K. Willmer, J. David Schmidt, and Martyn Smith, *The Prospering Parachurch* (San Francisco: Jossey-Bass, 1998), xi. Also see ibid., 10.

33. John C. Green and Amy L. Sherman, *Fruitful Collaborations: A Survey of Government-Funded Faith-Based Programs in 15 States* (Charlottesville, VA: Hudson Institute, 2002), 10.

34. Cnaan, *The Newer Deal,* 242–75.

35. Salamon, *America's Nonprofit Sector,* 158.

36. "Lieberman Renews Call for Larger, Lawful Space for Faith in American Public Life," March 1, 2001, http://www.senate.gov/~lieberman/speeches/01/03/2001821610.html. Also see Rabbi David Saperstein's comments—revealing the same assumption—in "Appropriate and Inappropriate Use of Religion," in E. J. Dionne Jr. and Ming Hsu Chen, eds., *Sacred Places, Civic Purposes: Should Government Help Faith-Based Charity?* (Washington, DC: Brookings, 2001), 301.

37. Stephen V. Monsma, *When Sacred and Secular Mix: Religious Nonprofit Organizations and Public Money* (Lanham, MD: Rowman and Littlefield, 1996), 78. On international aid agencies and colleges and universities see ibid.

38. Green and Sherman, *Fruitful Collaborations,* 18.

39. Carol J. De Vita, "Nonprofits and Devolution: What Do We Know?" in Elizabeth T. Boris and C. Eugene Steurle, eds., *Nonprofits and Government: Collaboration and Conflict* (Washington, DC: Urban Institute Press, 1999), 223.

40. Mark Chaves, "Religious Congregations and Welfare Reform: Assessing the Potential," in Andrew Walsh, ed., *Can Charitable Choice Work?* (Hartford, CT: Leonard E. Greenberg Center for the Study of Religion in Public Life, 2001), 125.

41. Vidal, "Many Are Called, but Few Are Chosen," 134.

42. De Vita, "Nonprofits and Devolution," 223.

43. De Vita and Wilson, *Faith-Based Initiatives,* 3–4.

44. Arthur E. Farnsley II, "Can Faith-Based Organizations Compete?" *Nonprofit and Voluntary Sector Quarterly* 30 (2001): 105. In his book-length study of congregations in Indianapolis, Farnsley questions the capacity of "most congregations to meet pressing social needs" (*Rising Expectations: Urban Congregations, Welfare Reform, and Civic Life* [Bloomington: Indiana University Press, 2003], 122).

45. For all of these figures see Green and Sherman, *Fruitful Collaborations,* 15, table 5.

46. Chaves, "Religious Congregations and Welfare Reform," 126.

47. This is Ram Cnaan's estimate for the number of religious congregations in the United States: see Cnaan, *The Newer Deal,* 28.

48. De Vita, "Nonprofits and Devolution," 224.

49. Cnaan, *The Newer Deal*, 233.
50. De Vita, "Nonprofits and Devolution," 223.
51. Rom, "From Welfare State to Opportunity, Inc.," 171.
52. Ibid.
53. Kirsten A. Gronbjerg, "The U.S. Nonprofit Human Service Sector: A Creeping Revolution," *Nonprofit and Voluntary Sector Quarterly* 30 (2001): 279.
54. Ibid., 283.
55. Salamon, *America's Nonprofit Sector*, 55.
56. Gronbjerg, "The U.S. Nonprofit Human Service Sector," 295.
57. David Horton Smith, "The Rest of the Nonprofit Sector: Grassroots Associations as the Dark Matter Ignored in Prevailing 'Flat Earth' Maps of the Sector," *Nonprofit and Voluntary Sector Quarterly* 26 (1997): 115. Also see Kirsten A. Gronbjerg and Sheila Nelson, "Mapping Small Religious Nonprofit Organizations: An Illinois Profile," *Nonprofit and Voluntary Sector Quarterly* 27 (1998): 13–31.
58. Smith, "The Rest of the Nonprofit Sector," 118–19.
59. Robert L. Woodson Sr., "Success Stories," in Michael Novak, ed., *To Empower People: From State to Civil Society* (Washington, DC: AEI Press, 1996), 115.
60. Ibid., 106.
61. Christian Smith, for example, has used self-identification successfully in categorizing Christian believers into fundamentalists, evangelicals, mainline Protestants, and liberal Protestants. See Christian Smith, *American Evangelicals: Embattled and Thriving* (Chicago: University of Chicago Press, 1998), 233–47. Self-identification has also been used for years by pollsters and scholarly voting studies to determine voters' partisan affiliation.
62. In selecting six employees as the dividing point, the bill introduced in the Senate in 2003 by Senators Rick Santorum of Pennsylvania and Joe Lieberman of Connecticut and entitled the CARE Act of 2003 offered some guidance. This bill's provision for a Compassion Capital Fund was in part aimed at making some special consideration and funding available for small, community-based providers. In doing so, it defined a community-based organization as "a nonprofit corporation or association that has (1) not more than 6 full-time equivalent employees who are engaged in the provision of social services, or (2) a current budget (current as of the date the entity seeks assistance under this section) for the provision of social services, compiled and adopted in good faith, of less than $450,000." In other words, a nonprofit agency would be considered community-based if it either had six or fewer full-time employees or had a budget of less than $450,000. See Senate Bill 272 (2003), Section 701(f).
63. Table 1 shows a total of 493 rather than 500 programs because, due to

missing information, four programs could not be classified as being either nonprofit/secular or community-based and three programs could not be classified as being either faith-based/segmented or faith-based/integrated.

64. I want to be careful not to claim more for my findings than the data strictly allow. Thus, here and elsewhere throughout this book, I refer to the programs that responded to the questionnaire. As I demonstrate in appendix A, however, there is reason to believe that the programs that completed the questionnaire are at least roughly representative of all the welfare-to-work programs in the four cities.

65. I realize, of course, that one would expect the differences found in table 2, since these are the criteria that were used in distinguishing community-based programs from nonprofit/secular programs.

66. As with the differences between nonprofit/secular and community-based programs, one would expect differences such as one sees in table 4, since the number and type of religiously based practices in which the faith-based programs reported engaging was the basis for the integrated and segmented distinction. I include this table, however, because it demonstrates that the measure I used to distinguish between faith-based/segmented and faith-based/integrated programs in fact resulted in distinguishing programs with clearly different approaches to relating their programs to their religious commitments.

67. See, for example, John J. DiIulio Jr., "Supporting Black Churches: Faith, Outreach, and the Inner-City Poor," *Brookings Review* 17 (1999): 42–45.

68. Green and Sherman, *Fruitful Collaborations,* 10.

69. Here and elsewhere throughout this book, I use the term *conservative Protestant,* rather than the often used term *evangelical Protestant,* to refer to the theologically conservative wing of Protestantism. I do so because, most appropriately, evangelicalism, fundamentalism, and Pentecostalism are all distinguishable subgroupings or traditions within conservative Protestantism. To use the term *evangelical* to refer to all three subgroupings, even though this is often done, is technically not correct. I include evangelicalism, fundamentalism, and Pentecostalism within conservative Protestantism. I am, of course, referring to theological conservatism, and I make no judgment here on whether or not theologically conservative Protestant organizations are also politically conservative—many are, but others clearly are not. On these distinctions see George Marsden, *Evangelicalism and Modern America* (Grand Rapids, MI: Eerdmans, 1984); and Randall Balmer, *Mine Eyes Have Seen the Glory: A Journey into the Evangelical Subculture in America* (New York: Oxford University Press, 1989).

70. Peter Dobkin Hall, "Historical Perspectives on Religion, Government, and Social Welfare in America," in Andrew Walsh, ed. *Can Charitable Choice*

Work? (Hartford, CT: Leonard E. Greenberg Center for the Study of Religion in Public Life, 2001), 82.

71. Theda Skocpol, "Religion, Civil Society, and Social Provision in the U.S.," in Mary Jo Bane, Brent Coffin, and Ronald Thiemann, eds., *Who Will Provide? The Changing Role of Religion in American Social Welfare* (Boulder: Westview, 2000), 47.

72. Robert D. Putnam, *Bowling Alone: The Collapse and Revival of American Community* (New York: Simon and Schuster, 2000), 76. On the mainline denominations' loss of membership and the growth of conservative Protestant churches see also Salamon, *America's Nonprofit Sector,* 156.

73. Christian Smith, *American Evangelicals,* 43.

74. Green and Smith, *Fruitful Collaborations,* 9.

75. Carl S. Dudley and David A. Roozen, *Faith Communities Today: A Report on Religion in the United States Today* (Hartford, CT: Hartford Institute for Religion Research, Hartford Seminary, 2001), 48.

76. On Governor Bush and Texas see the report of a task force he appointed to study means to encourage greater cooperation between Texas state government and faith-based social service agencies: Governor's Advisory Task Force on Faith-Based Community Service Groups, *Faith in Action: A New Vision for Church-State Cooperation in Texas* (1996). In an address delivered on June 30, 2001, Mayor Street stated: "I hope you share the pride I feel knowing Philadelphia is a national leader in the development and implementation of faith-based programs" (Mayor John Street, "Faith-Based Initiatives: An Old Idea Whose Time Has Come," http://www.phila.gov/radio/prelease.asp?id=30). Also see Judy Paternak, "Mayor Relies on Faith to Deliver Services," *Los Angeles Times,* April 9, 2001, p. A4.

77. Here and when reporting the budget size and number of clients, I use the median, rather than the mean, because some very large outliers tended to distort the means. I concluded that the median gave a more accurate picture of the relative size of the various types of programs.

78. Virginia Hodgkinson and Murray Weitzman, *Giving and Volunteering in the United States: 1992 Edition* (Washington, DC: Independent Sector, 1992), 25, cited in Smith, "The Rest of the Nonprofit Sector," 123–24.

Chapter 3

1. For a thoughtful survey of some of these arguments see Charles L. Glenn, *The Ambiguous Embrace: Government and Faith-Based Schools and Social Agencies* (Princeton: Princeton University Press, 2000), 6–7, 13–41. Also see Marvin Olasky, *The Tragedy of American Compassion* (Washington, DC: Regnery, 1992);

and Robert L. Woodson Sr., *The Triumphs of Joseph: How Today's Community Healers Are Reviving Our Streets and Neighborhoods* (New York: Free Press, 1998).

2. See, for example, Marvin Olasky, "The Corruption of Religious Charities," in Michael Novak, ed., *To Empower People: From State to Civil Society* (Washington, DC: AEI Press, 1996), 94–104; and Joe Loconte, *Seducing the Samaritan: How Government Contracts Are Reshaping Social Services* (Boston: Pioneer Institute, 1997).

3. See, for example, Stephen Goldsmith, *The Twenty-First Century City: Resurrecting Urban America* (Lanham, MD: Rowman and Littlefield, 1999); and David Osborne and Ted Gaebler, *Reinventing Government* (New York: Penguin Books, 1993).

4. For example, a 1998 resolution adopted by the American Federation of State, County, and Municipal Employees (available at http://www.afscme.org/about/resolute/1998/r33–041.htm) reads in part: "WHEREAS: Private companies are aggressively pursuing business opportunities created by the passage of the 1996 federal welfare reform law by seeking new contracts to administer, integrate and manage health and human services programs of state and local governments; and WHEREAS: These companies include Lockheed Martin IMS, Maximus, Inc., Electronic Data Systems, Unisys, Andersen Consulting, America Works, as well as numerous nonprofit organizations including Goodwill Industries and local nonprofit organizations; and WHEREAS: These companies have a poor track record administering health and human services programs, including lack of accountability, cost overruns, inefficiency, and failure to perform adequately; . . ."

5. Laudan Y. Aron and Patrick T. Sharkey, *The 1996 National Survey of Homeless Assistance Providers and Clients: A Comparison of Faith-Based and Secular Non-Profit Programs* (Washington, D.C.: Office of the Assistant Secretary for Planning and Evaluation, U.S. Department of Health and Human Services, 2002), available at http://aspe.hhs.gov/hsp/homelessness/NSHAPC02.

6. Aron and Sharkey do not give any details on their definition of the term *faith-based* or on how they operationalized that definition in analyzing their data. See ibid., 35 n. 3.

7. Ibid., 4.

8. Philip Moss and Chris Tilly, *Stories Employers Tell: Race, Skill, and Hiring in America* (New York: Russell Sage Foundation, 2001), 44 (italics omitted).

9. Malcolm L. Goggin and Deborah A. Orth, "How Faith-Based and Secular Organizations Tackle Housing for the Homeless" (report presented at the Roundtable on Religion and Social Welfare Policy, Rockefeller Institute of Government, October 2002), 45.

10. Wolfgang Bielefeld, Laura Littlepage, and Rachel Thelin, "Organi-

zational Analysis: The Influence of Faith on IMPACT Service Providers," in Sheila Suess Kennedy and Wolfgang Bielefeld, *Charitable Choice: First Results from Three States* (Indianapolis: Center for Urban Policy and the Environment, School of Public and Environmental Affairs, Indiana University—Purdue University, Indianapolis, 2003), 65–86.

11. Ibid., 76.

12. William H. Lockhart, "Getting Saved from Poverty: Religion in Poverty-to-Work Programs" (Ph.D. diss., Department of Sociology, University of Virginia, 2001).

13. See ibid., 216–17, table 6.2.

14. Ibid., 268.

15. Lawrence M. Mead, "The Rise of Paternalism," in Lawrence M. Mead, ed., *The New Paternalism* (Washington, DC: Brookings, 1997), 2.

16. Fredrica D. Kramer, Demetra Smith Nightingale, John Trutko, Shayne Spaulding, and Burt S. Barnow, *Faith-Based Organizations Providing Employment and Training Services: A Preliminary Exploration* (Washington, D.C.: Urban Institute, 2002), 3.

17. Ibid., 24.

18. Ibid., 25. Based on his study of faith-based welfare-related services in California, David Campbell has also argued the importance of distinguishing between religious congregations and "nonprofits that organize church-based networks and coalitions" (David Campbell, "Beyond Charitable Choice: The Diverse Service Delivery Approaches of Local Faith-Based Organizations," *Nonprofit and Voluntary Sector Quarterly* 31 [2002]: 223).

19. John C. Green and Amy L. Sherman, *Fruitful Collaborations: A Survey of Government-Funded Faith-Based Programs in 15 States* (Charlottesville, VA: Hudson Institute, 2002), 15–16.

20. Ibid.

21. Lockhart, "Getting Saved from Poverty," 223.

22. Ibid.

23. Ibid., 205.

24. Ibid.

25. Ibid., 260.

26. Lockhart especially makes this point at ibid., 259–63.

27. Aaron Bicknese, "Teen Challenge Drug Treatment Program" (Ph.D. diss., Department of Political Science, Northwestern University, 1999), 20–28.

28. Goggin and Orth, "How Faith Based and Secular Organizations Tackle Housing for the Homeless," 46.

29. Ibid.

30. In their study of homeless transitional programs in Grand Rapids,

Goggin and Orth also found that the one government program they studied had religious elements in it. See Goggin and Orth, "How Faith-Based and Secular Organizations Tackle Housing for the Homeless," 8–9.

31. Section 104(b)(j) of Public Law 104–193, the Personal Responsibility and Work Opportunity Reconciliation Act of 1996. Similar language is found in other acts to which charitable choice provisions have been added.

32. "Executive Order: Equal Protection of the Laws for Faith-Based and Community Organizations," December 12, 2002, http://www.whitehouse.gov/news/releases/2002/12/20021212-3.html.

33. John Orr, *Religion and Welfare Reform in Southern California: Is Charitable Choice Succeeding?* (Los Angeles: Center for Religion and Civic Culture, University of Southern California, 2001), 54.

34. *Grand Rapids School District v. Ball,* 473 U.S. 373, 384 (1984). The internal quotation is from an earlier concurring opinion by Justice William Brennan in *Lemon v. Kurtzman,* 403 U.S. 657 (1970).

35. *Mitchell v. Helms,* 530 U.S. 793, 829 (2000).

36. For more on this see Stephen K. Green, "The Blaine Amendment Reconsidered," *American Journal of Legal History* 36 (1992): 38–69.

37. This phrase is from the 1963 Higher Education Facilities Act, quoted in *Tilton v. Richardson,* 403 U.S. 672, 675 (1971).

38. The issue is even further complicated by the fact that in the charitable choice legislation, "sectarian" presumably also modifies "proselytization" and not only "instruction and worship." Thus, government funding of "sectarian proselytization" is forbidden. Does this mean that religious proselytization is forbidden but that proselytization for secular groups or movements is not? Or does it mean that proselytization for narrowly construed religious groups is forbidden but that proselytizing for broad, mainstream religious groups is all right?

39. On a personal note, as a fairly liberal, Democratic member of the Michigan Senate in the late 1970s and early 1980s, I chaired the Appropriation Committee's Subcommittee on Social Services. At that time, I largely dismissed as a conservative myth the alleged problem of intergenerational welfare families under the old AFDC system—the claim that there were many persons who had made welfare a way of life and that welfare dependency was being passed down from mothers to daughters. But while conducting site visits during the course of this study, I often encountered frontline workers who volunteered the existence of the problem of intergenerational welfare recipients and expressed the need to change attitudes in order to break this cycle.

40. Goggin and Orth, "How Faith-Based and Secular Organizations Tackle Housing for the Homeless," 7–8.

41. Lockhart, "Getting Saved from Poverty," 268.
42. Walter I. Trattner, *From Poor Law to Welfare State: A History of Social Welfare in America,* 2d ed. (New York: Free Press, 1979), 82.
43. Goggins and Orth, "How Faith-Based and Secular Organizations Tackle Housing for the Homeless," 27.
44. Ibid., 46.
45. Lockhart, "Getting Saved from Poverty," 276.

Chapter 4

1. Carol J. De Vita, "Nonprofits and Devolution: What Do We Know?" in Elizabeth T. Boris and C. Eugene Steurle, eds., *Nonprofits and Government: Collaboration and Conflict* (Washington, DC: Urban Institute Press, 1999), 216–17.
2. Mark Carl Rom, "From Welfare State to Opportunity, Inc.: Public-Private Partnerships in Welfare Reform," in Pauline Vaillancourt Rosenau, ed., *Public-Private Policy Partnerships* (Cambridge: MIT Press, 2000), 170.
3. Lester M. Salamon, *America's Nonprofit Sector: A Primer,* 2d ed. (New York: Foundation Center, 1999), 37.
4. Ibid., 114.
5. Ana Greenberg, "Doing Whose Work? Faith-Based Organizations and Government Partnerships," in Mary Jo Bane, Brent Coffin, and Ronald Thiemann, eds., *Who Will Provide? The Changing Role of Religion in American Social Welfare* (Boulder: Westview, 2000), 180.
6. Stephen V. Monsma, *When Sacred and Secular Mix: Religious Nonprofit Organizations and Government Money* (Lanham, MD: Rowman and Littlefield, 1996), 68.
7. Explanatory preamble to the Final Rule (Sec. 98.30(c)) for the Child Care and Development Block Grant of the Department of Health and Human Services, quoted in Charles L. Glenn, *The Ambiguous Embrace: Government and Faith-Based Schools and Social Agencies* (Princeton: Princeton University Press, 2000), 113.
8. Monsma, *When Sacred and Secular Mix,* 78.
9. Greenberg, "Doing Whose Work?" 188.
10. John C. Green and Amy L. Sherman, *Fruitful Collaborations: A Survey of Government-Funded Faith-Based Programs in 15 States* (Charlottesville, VA: Hudson Institute, 2002). The four programs with charitable choice provisions are the Temporary Assistance to Needy Families program (1996), the Department of Labor's Welfare-to-Work program (1997), the Community

Service Block Grant program (1998), and the Substance Abuse and Mental Health Services Administration's drug treatment program (2000).

11. Fredrica D. Kramer, Demetra Smith Nightingale, John Trutko, Shayne Spaulding, and Burt S. Barnow, *Faith-Based Organizations Providing Employment and Training Services: A Preliminary Exploration* (Washington, D.C.: Urban Institute, 2002), 22.

12. Stanley Carlson-Thies, "Faith-Based Institutions Cooperating with Public Welfare: The Promise of the Charitable Choice Provision," in Derek Davis and Barry Hankins, eds., *Welfare Reform and Faith-Based Organizations* (Waco, TX: J. M. Dawson Institute of Church-State Studies, 1999), 36.

13. Steven Rathgeb Smith and Michael Lipsky, *Nonprofits for Hire: The Welfare State in the Age of Contracting* (Cambridge: Harvard University Press, 1993), 204.

14. See Monsma, *When Sacred and Secular Mix,* 81–99.

15. See, for example, *Unlevel Playing Field: Barriers to Participation by Faith-Based and Community Organizations in Federal Social Service Programs* (Washington, DC: White House Office of Faith-Based and Community Initiatives, 2001), available at http://www.whitehouse.gov/news/releases/2001/08/unlevelfield.html.

16. Glenn, *The Ambiguous Embrace,* 43–44.

17. Ibid., 51–52.

18. For example, a controversy broke out in 2002 in Claremont, California, when the county fire department insisted that a senior center build wider driveways to the back of the building to improve access for fire-fighting equipment. See Tipton Blish, "City: Fire Officials' Approval a Tough Sell," *Los Angeles Times,* December 18, 2002.

19. Salamon (*America's Nonprofit Sector,* 22) reports that 11 million people work as employees of nonprofit organizations, constituting about 7 percent of the entire workforce in the United States.

20. 78 Stat. 255 (1964), as amended by Stat. 103 (1972), 42 U.S.C. 2000e-1(a).

21. For more information on Title VII see Glenn, *The Ambiguous Embrace,* 196–98; and Ira C. Lupu and Robert W. Tuttle, "Government Partnerships with Faith-Based Service Providers: State of the Law" (report presented at the Roundtable on Religion and Social Welfare Policy, Rockefeller Institute of Government, December 2002), 53–55, available at http://www.religionandsocialpolicy.org/docs/legal/reports/12-4-2002_state_of_the_law.pdf.

22. *Congressional Record,* 92nd Cong., 2d sess., 1972, 118, pt. 4: 4503 (Feb. 17).

23. *Corporation of Presiding Bishop v. Amos,* 483 U.S. 327, 339 (1986).

24. Ibid., 342.

25. Testimony of John L. Avery before the Senate Judiciary Committee, quoted in Sheila S. Kennedy and Wolfgang Bielefeld, "Government Shekels without Government Shackles? The Administrative Challenges of Charitable Choice," *Public Administration Review* 62 (2002): 7.

26. See http://www.naadac.org/documents/index.php?CategoryID=1 and http://www.naadac.org/documents/index.php?Category ID=5.

27. Ram Cnaan, *The Newer Deal: Social Work and Religion in Partnership* (New York: Columbia University Press, 1999).

28. See Glenn's account of this controversy, in *The Ambiguous Embrace*, 62–73.

29. See Governor's Advisory Task Force on Faith-Based Community Service Groups, *Faith in Action: A New Vision for Church-State Cooperation in Texas* (1996). For a report arguing that these alternative credentialing and certifying processes have failed see the Texas Freedom Network Education Fund, "The Texas Faith-Based Initiative at Five Years," October 10, 2002, http://www.tfn.org.

30. Greenberg, "Doing Whose Work?" 189.

31. See chap. 2, n. 76.

32. The one exception was a for-profit community and youth center in Chicago that seemed to be rather poorly run, whose staff was not particularly helpful, and where we had a hard time determining its exact sources of funds.

33. The comparable figure for the faith-based/segmented programs was much lower. Only 1 out of the 16 programs that reported they either had a policy against accepting government funds or had inquired about government funds and decided not to apply also stated they desired to expand greatly. However, another 13 programs (81 percent) stated they desired to expand somewhat.

34. Glenn, *The Ambiguous Embrace*, 255.

35. For example, the following cases were in the lower courts as of 2003: *Americans United for Separation of Church and State et al. v. Warden Terry Mapes, Prison Fellowship Ministries, InnerChange Freedom Initiative, et al.*, which is a suit filed on February 12, 2003, in the federal district court of the southern district of Iowa that challenges a faith-intensive program for prisoners in a Iowa state prison; *Freedom from Religion Foundation v. McCallum*, 2003 U.S. LEXIS 6301 (7th Circuit, April 2, 2003), in which the federal Seventh Circuit Court affirmed a district court ruling that held indirect funding for an integrally faith-based drug treatment program was constitutional, *Freedom from Religion Foundation v. McCallum*, 179 F. Supp. 2d 950 (W.D. Wis. 2002), in which a federal district court held that direct funding of the same faith-based drug treatment program was unconstitutional; and *ACLU of Louisiana v. Foster*, 2002 U.S. Dist. LEXIS

13778 (ED Louisiana), in which a federal district court held that direct support to an integrally religious teen abstinence program was unconstitutional. For background information and analysis of these and other legal cases see http://www.religionandsocialpolicy.org/legal/index/cfm.

36. For example, a 2001 survey by the Pew Forum on Religion and Public Life found that among white evangelicals, 44 percent identified with the Republican party, and another 8 percent identified themselves as conservative independents; only 23 percent identified with the Democratic party. See "Faith-Based Funding Backed, but Church-State Doubts Abound." (Pew Forum on Religion and Public Life and Pew Research Center for the People and the Press, April 2001), sec. 3. Available at http://pewforum.org/publications.

Chapter 5

1. George W. Bush, "Executive Order: Establishment of White House Office of Faith-Based and Community Initiatives," January 29, 2001, http://www.whitehouse.gov/news/releases/2001/01/print/20010129-2.html (emphasis added).

2. On this distinction see Robert D. Putnam, *Bowling Alone: The Collapse and Revival of American Community* (New York: Simon and Schuster, 2000), 22–24.

3. Ibid., 22.

4. Douglas Laycock, "Formal, Substantive, and Disaggregated Neutrality toward Religion," *DePaul Law Review* 39 (1990): 1002.

5. Putnam, *Bowling Alone*, 76.

6. Ibid.

7. Support for this conclusion is also found in the recent political activism of conservative, evangelical Protestants in the ongoing effort to bend American foreign policy to take a more active stance in protecting the religious freedom rights of persons suffering persecution for their religious beliefs around the world. See Nicholas D. Kristof, "Following God Abroad," *New York Times,* May 21, 2002, A2. Allen D. Hertzke also chronicles this involvement in his forthcoming book *Freeing God's Children: The Faith-Based Movement for International Human Rights* (Lanham, MD: Rowman and Littlefield).

8. See Section 104 of the Personal Responsibility and Work Opportunity Act of 1996. The exact language of this section, as well as an excellent factual commentary of its provisions from the perspective of supporters of charitable choice, can be found at http://downloads.weblogger.com/gems/cpj/CCGuide.pdf. Also very helpful is Ira C. Lupu and Robert W. Tuttle, "Government Partnerships with Faith-Based Service Providers: State of the Law"

(report presented at the Roundtable on Religion and Social Welfare Policy, Rockefeller Institute of Government, 2002), available at http://www.religionandsocialpolicy.org/docs/legal/reports/12-4-2002_state_of_the_law.pdf.

9. Steve Benen, "On a Wing and a Prayer," *Church and State,* May 2001, http://www.au.org/churchstate/cs5011.htm.

10. Quoted in DeWayne Wickham, "Charity Plan Assaults Rights," *USA Today,* July 17, 2001, available at http://www.usatoday.com/news/comment/columnists/wickham/2001-07-17-wickham.htm.

11. "Faith-Based Funding Backed, but Church-State Doubts Abound" (Pew Forum on Religion and Public Life and the Press, April 2001), sec. 1. Available at http://pewforum.org/publications.

12. Lupu and Tuttle, "Government Partnerships with Faith-Based Service Providers," 44–45.

13. See my description of this incident in Stephen V. Monsma, *When Sacred and Secular Mix: Religious Nonprofit Organizations and Public Money* (Lanham, MD: Rowman and Littlefield, 1996), 155–58.

14. Section 702 and the position I am defending here would allow an organization to hire only from its own specific, narrowly defined religious tradition. Such situations are more hypothetical than actual. Any agency so narrowly conceived would have a hard time relating to the broader community to which it is offering services. Thus, it would have difficulty demonstrating the level of program competence and effectiveness necessary to win government grants or contracts.

15. This leaves the question of the right of faith-based organizations to make hiring decisions based on sexual orientation. This is a complex issue and is not one into which this study went. In brief, I believe faith-based organizations should not be able to take sexual orientation into account in making hiring decisions, but since homosexual practices are proscribed by most religions, faith-based organizations should be able take homosexual lifestyles or practices into account in making their hiring decisions. I would apply the same principle to heterosexual activities outside of marriage and to other such behavior or lifestyle practices clearly proscribed by the faith commitments of a faith-based organization.

16. On the Compassion Capital Fund see Lupu and Tuttle, "Government Partnerships with Faith-Based Service Providers," 64–66, and Anne Ferris, "A Look at Compassion Capital Funding One Year Later" (Roundtable on Religion and Social Welfare Policy, October 21, 2003). Available at http://www.religionandsocialpolicy.org/news/article.cfm?id=989. Senate Bill 272, the CARE Act of 2003, also contained in its Title VII (Section 701) a provision for a Compassion Capital Fund. But the emphasis is on technical assistance to small,

community-based and faith-based programs. I believe that the emphasis should be on nongovernmental intermediary agencies that could make actual grants to community-based and faith-based programs. John Orr, working from the University of Southern California, has also made a similar proposal based on a study of three southern California counties: see John Orr, *Religion and Welfare Reform in Southern California: Is Charitable Choice Succeeding?* (Los Angeles: Center for Religion and Civil Culture, University of Southern California, 2001), 53.

17. Senate Bill 272, introduced in the 108th Congress (2003) by Republican senator Rick Santorum of Pennsylvania and Democratic senator Joe Lieberman of Connecticut, provided that individual tax filers who do not itemize their tax deductions may take up to a $250 tax deduction for donations to nonprofit charities and that joint tax filers who do not itemize may take up to a $500 tax deduction for such donations.

18. I develop this concept of neutrality much more fully in Stephen V. Monsma, *Positive Neutrality* (Westport, CT: Greenwood, 1993); and Monsma, *When Sacred and Secular Mix,* especially chap. 6. Also see Laycock, "Formal, Substantive, and Disaggregated Neutrality toward Religion."

Bibliography

Books and Dissertations

Bane, Mary Jo, Brent Coffin, and Ronald Thiemann, eds. *Who Will Provide? The Changing Role of Religion in American Social Welfare.* Boulder: Westview, 2000.

Berger, Peter, and Richard John Neuhaus. *To Empower People: The Role of Mediating Structures in Public Policy.* Washington, DC: American Enterprise Institute, 1977.

Boris, Elizabeth T., and C. Eugene Steurle, eds. *Nonprofits and Government: Collaboration and Conflict.* Washington, DC: Urban Institute Press, 1999.

Cnaan, Ram. *The Newer Deal: Social Work and Religion in Partnership.* New York: Columbia University Press, 1999.

———. *The Invisible Caring Hand: American Congregations and the Provision of Welfare.* New York: New York University Press, 2002.

Coughlin, Bernard J. *Church and State in Social Welfare.* New York: Columbia University Press, 1965.

Davis, Derek, and Barry Hankins, eds. *Welfare Reform and Faith-Based Organizations.* Waco, TX: J. M. Dawson Institute of Church-State Studies, 1999.

Dionne, E. J., Jr. *Community Works: The Revival of Civil Society in America.* Washington, DC: Brookings, 1998.

Dionne, E. J., Jr., and Ming Hsu Chen, eds. *Sacred Places, Civic Purposes: Should Government Help Faith-Based Charity?* Washington, DC: Brookings, 2001.

Dionne, E. J., Jr., and John J. DiIulio Jr., eds. *What's God Got to Do with the American Experiment?* Washington, DC: Brookings Institution Press, 2000.

Farnsley, Arthur E., II. *Rising Expectations: Urban Congregations, Welfare Reform, and Civic Life.* Bloomington: Indiana University Press, 2003.

Garr, Robin. *Reinvesting in America: The Grassroots Movements That Are Feeding the Hungry, Housing the Homeless, and Putting Americans Back to Work.* Reading, MA: Addison-Wesley, 1995.

Glenn, Charles L. *The Ambiguous Embrace: Government and Faith-Based Schools and Social Agencies.* Princeton: Princeton University Press, 2000.

Goldsmith, Stephen. *The Twenty-First Century City: Resurrecting Urban America.* Lanham, MD: Rowman and Littlefield, 1999.

Hodgkinson, Virginia A., Murray S. Weitzman, and Arthur D. Kirsch. *From Belief to Commitment: The Community Service Activities and Finances of Religious Congregations in the United States: Findings from a National Survey.* Washington, DC: Independent Sector, 1988.

Jeavons, Thomas H. *When the Bottom Line Is Faithfulness.* Bloomington: Indiana University Press, 1994.

Kettl, Don. *Reinventing Government: A Fifth-Year Report Card.* Washington, DC: Brookings, 1998.

Lockhart, William H. "Getting Saved from Poverty: Religion in Poverty-to-Work Programs." Ph.D. diss., University of Virginia, 2001.

Lugo, Luis, ed. *Religion, Pluralism, and Public Life.* Grand Rapids, MI: Eerdmans, 2000.

Minow, Martha. *Partners, Not Rivals: Privatization and the Public Good.* Boston: Beacon, 2002.

Monsma, Stephen V. *Positive Neutrality.* Westport, CT: Greenwood, 1993.

———. *When Sacred and Secular Mix: Religious Nonprofit Organizations and Public Money.* Lanham, MD: Rowman and Littlefield, 1996.

Nichols, J. Bruce. *The Uneasy Alliance: Religion, Refugee Work, and U.S. Foreign Policy.* New York: Oxford University Press, 1988.

Novak, Michael, ed. *To Empower People: From State to Civil Society.* Washington, DC: AEI Press, 1996.

Olasky, Marvin. *The Tragedy of American Compassion.* Washington, DC: Regnery, 1992.

———. *Renewing American Compassion.* New York: Free Press, 1996.

Osborne, David, and Ted Gaebler. *Reinventing Government.* New York: Penguin Books, 1993.

Putnam, Robert D. *Bowling Alone: The Collapse and Revival of American Community.* New York: Simon and Schuster, 2000.

Rosenau, Pauline Vaillancourt, ed. *Public-Private Policy Partnerships.* Cambridge: MIT Press, 2000.

Salamon, Lester M. *Partners in Public Service: Government-Nonprofit Relations in the Modern Welfare State.* Baltimore: Johns Hopkins University Press, 1995.

———. *America's Nonprofit Sector: A Primer.* 2d ed. New York: Foundation Center, 1999.

Savas, E. E. *Privatizing the Public Sector: How to Shrink Government.* Chatham, NJ: Chatham House, 1980.

———. *Privatization: The Key to Better Government.* Chatham, NJ: Chatham House, 1987.
———. *Privatization and the Public-Private Partnerships.* New York: Chatham House, 2000.
Skocpol, Theda, and Morris P. Fiorina, eds. *Civic Engagement in American Democracy.* Washington, DC: Brookings; New York: Russell Sage Foundation, 1999.
Smith, Christian. *American Evangelicals: Embattled and Thriving.* Chicago: University of Chicago Press, 1998.
Smith, Steven Rathgeb, and Michael Lipsky. *Nonprofits for Hire: The Welfare State in the Age of Contracting.* Cambridge: Harvard University Press, 1993.
Trattner, Walter I. *From Poor Law to Welfare State: A History of Social Welfare in America.* 2d ed. New York: Free Press, 1979.
Walsh, Andrew, ed. *Can Charitable Choice Work?* Hartford, CT: Leonard E. Greenberg Center for the Study of Religion in Public Life, 2001.
Willmer, Wesley K., J. David Schmidt, and Martyn Smith. *The Prospering Parachurch.* San Francisco: Jossey-Bass, 1998.
Woodson, Robert L., Sr. *The Triumphs of Joseph: How Today's Community Healers Are Reviving Our Streets and Neighborhoods.* New York: Free Press, 1998.
Wuthnow, Robert, and Virginia A. Hodgkinson, eds. *Faith and Philanthropy in America: Exploring the Role of Religion in America's Voluntary Sector.* San Francisco: Jossey-Bass, 1990.

Articles and Reports

Aron, Laudan Y., and Patrick T. Sharkey. *The 1996 National Survey of Homeless Assistance Providers and Clients: A Comparison of Faith-Based and Secular Non-Profit Programs.* Washington, DC: Office of the Assistant Secretary for Planning and Evaluation, U.S. Department of Health and Human Services, 2002.
Boris, Elizabeth T. *Myths about the Nonprofit Sector.* Charting Civil Society, no. 4. Washington, DC: Urban Institute, 1998.
Campbell, David. "Beyond Charitable Choice: The Diverse Service Delivery Approaches of Local Faith-Based Organizations." *Nonprofit and Voluntary Sector Quarterly* 31 (2002): 207–30.
Chaves, Mark. "Religious Congregations and Welfare Reform: Who Will Take Advantage of Charitable Choice?" *American Sociological Review* 64 (1999): 836–46.
Dokupil, Susanna. "A Sunny Dome with Caves of Ice: The Illusion of Charitable Choice." *Texas Review of Law and Politics* 2 (2000): 150–208.

Farnsley, Arthur E., II. "Can Faith-Based Organizations Compete?" *Nonprofit and Voluntary Sector Quarterly* 30 (2001): 99–111.

Finding Common Ground: Twenty-Nine Recommendations of the Working Group on Human Needs and Faith-Based and Community Initiatives. Washington, DC: Search for Common Ground, 2002.

Gardner, Deborah S., ed. *Vision and Values: Rethinking the Nonprofit Sector in America.* New York: Nathan Cummings Foundation, 1998.

Goggin, Malcolm L., and Deborah A. Orth. "How Faith-Based and Secular Organizations Tackle Housing for the Homeless." Report presented at the Roundtable on Religion and Social Welfare Policy, Rockefeller Institute of Government, October 2002.

Green, John C., and Amy L. Sherman. *Fruitful Collaborations: A Survey of Government-Funded Faith-Based Programs in 15 States.* Charlottesville, VA: Hudson Institute, 2002.

Grønbjerg, Kirsten. "The U.S. Nonprofit Human Service Sector: A Creeping Revolution." *Nonprofit and Voluntary Sector Quarterly* 30 (2001): 276–97.

Grønbjerg, Kirsten, and Sheila Nelson. "Mapping Small Religious Nonprofit Organizations: An Illinois Profile." *Nonprofit and Voluntary Sector Quarterly* 27 (1998): 13–31.

Johnson, Byron R. *Objective Hope: Assessing the Effectiveness of Faith-Based Organizations: A Review of the Literature.* Philadelphia: Center for Research on Religion and Urban Civil Society, University of Pennsylvania, 2002.

Kennedy, Sheila S. "When Is Private Public? State Action in the Era of Privatization and Public-Private Partnerships." *Civil Rights Law Journal* 11 (2001): 203–23.

Kennedy, Sheila S., and Wolfgang Bielefeld, eds. *Charitable Choice: First Results from Three States.* Indianapolis: Center for Urban Policy and the Environment, School of Public and Environmental Affairs, Indiana University—Purdue University, Indianapolis, 2003.

Kennedy, Sheila S., and Wolfgang Bielefeld. "Government Shekels without Government Shackles? The Administrative Challenge of Charitable Choice." *Public Administrative Review* 62 (2002): 4–11.

Kramer, Fredrica D., Demetra Smith Nightingale, John Trutko, Shayne Spaulding, and Burt S. Barnow. *Faith-Based Organizations Providing Employment and Training Services: A Preliminary Exploration.* Washington, DC: Urban Institute, 2002.

Laycock, Douglas. "Formal, Substantive, and Disaggregated Neutrality toward Religion." *DePaul Law Review* 39 (1990): 993–1018.

Loconte, Joe. "The Bully and the Pulpit: A New Model for Church-State Partnerships." *Policy Review*, no. 92 (November–December 1998): 28–37.

———. "The Seven Deadly Sins of Government Funding for Private Charities." *Policy Review*, no. 82 (March–April 1997): 28–36.

Lugo, Luis. *Equal Partners: The Welfare Responsibility of Government and Churches*. Washington, DC: Center for Public Justice, 1998.

Lupu, Ira C., and Robert W. Tuttle. "Government Partnerships with Faith-Based Service Providers: State of the Law." Report presented at the Roundtable on Religion and Social Welfare Policy, Rockefeller Institute of Government, December 2002.

———. "Developments in the Faith-Based and Community Initiatives: Comments on Notices of Proposed Rulemaking and Guidance Document." Report presented at the Roundtable on Religion and Social Welfare Policy, Rockefeller Institute of Government, January 2003.

Macedo, Stephen. "The Constitution of Civil Society: School Vouchers, Religious Nonprofit Organizations, and Liberal Public Values." *Chicago-Kent Law Review* 75 (2000): 417–52.

Monsma, Stephen V. *Working Faith: How Religious Organizations Provide Welfare-to-Work Services*. Philadelphia: Center for Research on Religion and Urban Civil Society, University of Pennsylvania, 2002.

Orr, John. *Religion and Welfare Reform in Southern California: Is Charitable Choice Succeeding?* Los Angeles: Center for Religion and Civic Culture, University of Southern California, 2001.

Printz, Tobi Jennifer. *Faith-Based Service Providers in the Nation's Capital: Can They Do More?* Washington, DC: Urban Institute, 1998.

Sider, Ronald J., and Heidi Rolland Unruh. "No Aid for Religion? Charitable Choice and the First Amendment." *Brookings Review* 17 (spring 1999): 46–49.

———. "Evangelism and Church-State Partnerships." *Journal of Church and State* 43 (2001): 267–95.

Smith, David Horton. "The Rest of the Nonprofit Sector: Grassroots Associations as the Dark Matter Ignored in Prevailing 'Flat Earth' Maps of the Sector." *Nonprofit and Voluntary Sector Quarterly* 26 (1997): 114–31.

Smith, Steven Rathgeb, and Michael R. Sosin. "The Varieties of Faith-Related Agencies." *Public Administration Review* 61 (2001): 651–70.

Twombly, Eric C. *Human Service Nonprofits in Metropolitan Areas during Devolution and Welfare Reform*. Washington, DC: Urban Institute, 2001.

Unlevel Playing Field: Barriers to Participation by Faith-Based and Community Organizations in Federal Social Service Programs. Washington, DC: White House Office of Faith-Based and Community Initiatives, 2001.

Vanderwoerd, Jim R. "Is the Newer Deal a Better Deal: Government Funding of Faith-Based Social Services." *Christian Scholar's Review* 31 (2002): 301–18.

Index

Accreditation standards and private social service organizations, 135–36

Americans United for Separation of Church and State, 188–89

Aron, Laudan, 48, 85–86, 89–90, 128, 142

Autonomy of private providers in partnership with government, 35–36, 129–30, 136, 153–66, 169–70, 177–78, 180–81, 197–200, 209

Barriers to community-based partnerships with government, 143–45, 147, 167–68, 210–11

Barriers to faith-based partnerships with government, 141–47, 167–68, 210–11

Berger, Peter, 1–2

Bethel True Life, 50

Bonding social capital, 182

Boris, Elizabeth, 43

Brennan, Justice William, 134

Bridging social capital, 182

Bush, President George W., 3, 43, 81, 110, 113, 136, 139, 179, 204

Capacity of welfare-to-work and other social service programs, 33–34, 51–54, 71–78, 173–74

Carlson-Thies, Stanley, 129

Categorization of welfare-to-work programs, 57–65

Catholic faith-based programs, 66, 68, 81

Central Dallas Ministries, 50

Charitable choice, 4, 110–13, 187–94, 205

Charity Organization Society, 117

Chaves, Mark, 51, 53–54, 90

Chen, Ming Hsu, 19

Chronicle of Higher Education, 4

Church-state issues, 29–32, 36, 182–83, 206–8. *See also* First Amendment

Civil society, 185–86

Clinton, President Bill, 3

Cnaan, Ram, 2, 48, 50, 53

Community-based welfare-to-work programs, definition, 43–44

Concern for clients, by program type, 106–9, 211

Conservative Protestant faith-based programs, 66–68, 81, 110, 162, 183–84, 193–94, 211–12

265

De Vita, Carol, 51, 52, 54, 126
DiIulio, John, Jr., 4–5
Dilman, Don, 38
Dionne, E. J., 2, 19

Effectiveness of private social service programs, compared with government, 36
Equal treatment standard. *See* Neutrality standard
Ervin, Senator Sam, 134
Evangelical Protestant faith-based programs. *See* Conservative Protestant faith-based programs
Expansion plans and desires of welfare-to-work programs, by program type, 76–78

Faith-based, integrated programs, definition, 44–45
Faith-based, segmented programs, definition, 44–45
Faith traditions and welfare-to-work programs, 66–68
Farnsley, Arthur, 52
First Amendment, 16–17, 45. *See also* Church-state issues
Frumkin, Peter, 23, 27, 46, 197
Funding of welfare-to-work and other social services by government
and community-based organizations, 131, 138–47
and faith-based organizations, 126–29, 138, 138–47
and for-profit firms, 131, 138, 138–40
and nonprofit organizations, 8–12, 126, 138–40
Gaebler, Ted, 2, 3

Glenn, Charles, 132, 161
Glennon, Fred, 23
Goggin, Malcolm L., 87, 93, 94, 106, 116, 119
Goldsmith, Stephen, 3–4
Gore, Al, 3
Green, John, 50, 51, 53, 66, 81, 91–92, 94, 128–29, 130, 142–43, 157
Greenberg, Ana, 4, 126–28, 137
Grønbjerg, Kirsten, 55

Hall, Peter Dobkin, 47, 48–49
Hehir, J. Bryan, 27–28
Hiring by faith-based organizations in partnership with government, 133–34, 188–94
Hodgkinson, Virginia, 48

Informal networks of government and social service providers. *See* Networks of welfare-to-work and other social service providers
Intermediate structures, 2. *See also* Civil society
Irving, R. E. M., 25

Jeavons, Thomas, 47
Job-oriented services, 102–5
Johnson, President Lyndon, 10

Kennedy, Sheila, 21, 192
Kramer, Fredrica, 90–92

Libertarian approach, 20–22, 29, 178–79
Lieberman, Senator Joe, 50, 80
Life-oriented services, 102–5
Lipsky, Michael, 10, 21, 129–30, 192

Lockhart, William, 88, 92–93, 94, 116, 119
Lugo, Luis, 7, 27–28
Lupu, Ira, 189–90

Macedo, Stephen, 21
Mainline Protestant faith-based programs, 66–67, 81
Minority character of welfare-to-work programs, 65–66
Moss, Philip, 87

Networks of welfare-to-work and other social service providers, 137, 147–52, 170
Neuhaus, Richard John, 1–2
Neutrality standard, 31–32, 182–83, 207–8
Nichols, J. Bruce, 9
Nonprofit, secular programs, definition, 42–43
Nueva Esperanza, 50

Office of Faith-Based and Community Initiatives. *See* White House Office of Faith-Based and Community Initiatives
Olasky, Marvin, 20
Orth, Deborah, 87, 93, 94, 106, 116, 119
Osborne, David, 2, 3

Personalized concern for clients. *See* Concern for clients
Pervasively sectarian standard, 30–31
Pluralist approach, 23–29, 192
Positive neutrality. *See* Neutrality standard
Presiding Bishop v. Amos, 134

Proselytization, 110–12, 119–21, 124, 161, 194, 201–2, 210
Public policy implications of research findings, 79–83, 121–24, 166–71, 172–213
Public-private partnerships
 barriers to, 34–35, 175–77
 expansion of, 186–97
 extent of, 34–35, 175–77
 rationale for, 12–18, 180–81, 184–86

Reagan, President Ronald, 10–11
Regulation of social service providers by government, 132–36, 152–53, 170–71
Reinventing Government (Osborne and Gaebler), 2, 3
Responsive Community, The (journal), 24
Results of receiving government funds, by program type, 154–57
Rom, Mark Carl, 11, 46–47, 55, 126
Rosen, Jeffrey, 31–32

Salamon, Lester M., 1, 11, 28, 42, 43, 45, 47, 50, 55, 126
Santorum, Senator Rick, 80
Scott, Representative Bobby, 189
Sectarian worship and instruction, 110–13, 119–21, 124, 161, 194, 201–2, 210
Sharkey, Patrick, 48, 85–86, 89–90, 128, 142
Sherman, Amy, 50, 51, 53, 66, 81, 91–92, 94, 128–29, 130, 142–43, 157
Sider, Ron, 44
Size of welfare-to-work programs, by program type, 71–76

Smith, Christian, 67
Smith, David Horton, 55–56
Smith, Steven Rathgeb, 10–11, 21, 129–30, 192
Statist approach, 20–22, 29
Street, Mayor John, 139
Structural pluralism. *See* Pluralist approach
Subsidiarity, 26–27
Supreme Court, 29–30, 134, 161, 189–90

Thomas, Justice Clarence, 31
Tilly, Chris, 87
To Empower People (Berger and Neuhaus), 1–2
Tragedy of American Compassion, The (Olasky), 20
Trattner, Walter, 8–9, 117
Tuttle, Robert, 189–90
Twombly, Eric, 46
Types of services provided, by program type, 85–89, 94–105, 174–75

Types of welfare-to-work programs. *See* Categorization of welfare-to-work programs

Unruh, Heidi, 44
Urban Institute, 46, 85
Vendorism, 129, 170, 209
Vidal, Avis, 4, 49
Volunteers, by program type, 73–75
Vouchers for welfare-to-work services, 202–4

Welfare-to-work programs, definition, 37
West Angeles Community Development Corporation, 50
White House Office of Faith-Based and Community Initiatives, 3, 4, 42, 43–44, 80, 179, 204
Wofford, Senator Harris, 4
Woodson, Robert, 56

Young, Dennis, 10, 20

HIEBERT LIBRARY
3 6877 00194 2779

HV
95
.M65
2004

DATE DUE

Demco, Inc. 38-293